Sociology and the Real World

SOCIOLOGY and the REAL WORLD

◨ ◨ ◨

STEPHEN LYNG and DAVID D. FRANKS

ROWMAN & LITTLEFIELD PUBLISHERS, INC.
Lanham • Boulder • New York • Oxford

ROWMAN & LITTLEFIELD PUBLISHERS, INC.

Published in the United States of America
by Rowman & Littlefield Publishers, Inc.
4720 Boston Way, Lanham, Maryland 20706
www.rowmanlittlefield.com

12 Hid's Copse Road, Cumnor Hill, Oxford OX2 9JJ, England

British Library Cataloguing in Publication Information Available

Library of Congress Cataloging-in-Publication Data

Lyng, Stephen, 1950–
 Sociology and the real world / by Stephen Lyng and David D. Franks.
  p. cm.
 Includes bibliographical references and index.
 ISBN 0-7425-0175-2 (alk. paper) — ISBN 0-7425-0176-0 (pbk. : alk. paper)
  1. Sociology. I. Franks, David D. II. Title.

HM585 .L94 2001
301—dc21

                                                    2001041687

Printed in the United States of America

♾™ The paper used in this publication meets the minimum requirements of
American National Standard for Information Sciences—Permanence of Paper
for Printed Library Materials, ANSI/NISO Z39.48-1992.

this book is dedicated to the loving memory of

THERESA FRANKS

1962–2001

Contents

◙   ◙   ◙

Acknowledgments

This book is the product of a long collaboration between the two authors that began over a decade ago. Our effort to bring some analytical clarity to the nature of the "real world" has been profoundly influenced by real world events in both of our lives that have intertwined with our work on this problem. Because of the challenging character of some of these events, it is certain that the present volume would have never been completed without the important contributions of several individuals.

We owe a special debt of gratitude to Joseph Marolla, who as department chair provided administrative support for this project beyond what would ordinarily be expected. Individuals who helped at various stages with the typing and editing of the manuscript were Carol Wells, Kendra Cover, and Cynthia Starkey. We received crucial help from Dimitri Shalin, David Maines, and Doyle McCarthy, each of whom read selected chapters and gave helpful comments. Robert Perinbanayagam's time and straightforwardness are also greatly appreciated. Gideon Sjoberg and Viktor Gecas both played key roles in helping us get our ideas into print and providing critical evaluations of our early drafts. We would be remiss however if any of the above were held responsible for any failings in our final product. Thanks should also go to our colleague David Croteau for sound advise about copyediting and making changes in the manuscript after submission. Finally, we want to thank Robert Kowkabany for his patience, support, and great skill in improving the quality of the manuscript and expediting the final product.

◙ ◙ ◙

CHAPTER ONE

Introduction

This book addresses issues that relate to the conceptual underpinnings of sociological practice. It speaks to the fable of the little boy who was so unsocialized into his society's blinders that he alone saw that the emperor had no clothes. We deal herein with how sociology intersects with, or more importantly, *fails* to intersect with, what is commonly understood as the "real world." We say this with full knowledge of how it will be received. Many sociologists have blinders that the fable's boy would not have. The majority of sociologists are trained to look down on the phrase "real world" and thus do not miss connecting with it. Without our knowledge, the very terms needed to conceptualize the problem are not readily available to us. Too much of sociology has become an extreme case of Lorenz's (1977, 15) observation on Western thought: "Reflection, man's greatest discovery in the history of the human mind, was immediately followed by the greatest and gravest mistake—that of doubting the reality of the real world."

In order to make the case that sociological theory needs, and does not have, a link to the real world, we offer a way of reclaiming three words that in many sociological circles have fallen into disrepute—often for good reason, but often not. They are *objectivity, reality,* and *truth.*[1] As one of these falls or rises so too do the others. To reflect on one is to evoke the others; the devaluation of one diminishes the others. For example, the objective world is often used synonymously with the real, tangible world. Allegedly truth is implicated in this meaning of the real because it traditionally describes a correspondence, however vague, between our mind-formed knowledge and inanimate, objective reality. There are certainly problems here, but people who take the categorical position that there is no truth, no doubt believe in the truth of what they are saying. This hints at the possibility of forging some notion of truth, however different, from what is usually conceived.

Make no mistake: we have had long teaching careers laying bare the tautological and incoherent meanings of these words as commonly used. We have stressed, as well, the self-serving and deceptive ways they are used in scientific practice. In these pages we continue to deconstruct this triad, showing the multiple meanings of each term and contradictions in their everyday usage; but we do so in order to rebuild them more coherently. With all their contradictions, elements of these terms are too important to lose and we are seriously thwarted in our professional and even personal efforts without them. Often, sociologists seem blissfully unaware that without these concepts there are vast reverberations on the whole of our thinking. In this volume we will identify important aspects of experience that are closed off to us by our warranted ambivalence about using these important three terms.

We approach this task as sociologists. For us, one sense of objectivity is associated with the social processes creating intersubjectivity—that is, how human beings with different actual experiences of the same things convince themselves that they nevertheless live in a common world. In the social context, objectivity's cousin, "truth," is contrasted to the lie. As long as there are lies—and surely they abound—there are truths from which these lies diverge, or so is the assumption when these terms are used in face-to-face interactions (Franks and Keller 1997; Gergen 1991). Unfortunately, when the same reasoning is applied to the inanimate world of physical or social systems, problems arise. Here truth diverges from *error*, a term devoid of the moralistic implications of a lie. The truth from which error diverges is ultimately more evasive than that of a lie even considering the difficulties with the latter (Franks and Keller 1997). If we concede the existence of error—and like lies, error certainly abounds—we must also concede the existence of some kind of truth from which error diverges. Although on the interactional level lies may be interesting in themselves, a social world comprised solely of lies would lack the prerequisites for its continuance. Likewise, it is impossible to conceive of an inanimate world of complete error or a human being psychologically able to survive it. We conclude that error and truth are not to be so glibly discarded by those entrusted with thinking things through. Those who disregard truth on either level simply push the concepts below awareness. Here they thrive even more effectively being freed from the discipline of reflection. Our emotions testify to this. We become outraged when lied to and when others have the audacity to think we are lying to them.

Naïve notions of objectivity, reality, and truth have been greatly qualified by the sweep of twentieth-century thought, including critical sociology, postmodern critiques, and, more recently, the powerful findings of neuroscience. The traditional version of truth as a mental mirror of the real world independent of, and uncontaminated by, the projections of our peculiar mentalities and senses is simply dead in the water. In light of current neuroscience, any aspirations that human beings can transcend their seriously limited senses and minds to perceive a world "as it is" independent of them is no longer a "position" but dangerous ignorance. This is no cause to turn away from the notion of reality or truth, however. Current definitions of objectivity, reality, and truth do not belong to our predecessors—they belong to us. They are not fixed in some eternal sphere of perfect forms immune to change. As in any developmental process, we can and should revise them to better meet our ends. In these pages we shall see that the concept of truth is the most challenging of the terms and must undergo the greatest reconstruction in order to be useful to sociologists.

Nevertheless, as long as there are death and taxes, we live in a world that is surely, to an important extent, independent of our individual and collective wills. In nature as well as social life, events occur that we—whether as individuals or as collectivities—neither initiate nor desire. So, a type of independence that carries with it the character of objectivity and reality must be accepted. Along with this, a type of fidelity is still available. However, we must include in this fidelity the part played by our particularly *human* brains in our formulation of our three terms, and tie them in to how the world responds to our very limited actions and methodological initiatives upon it. The meaning of truth, like that of its two cousins, is bounded by the peculiarities of our primate bodies as we act on our environment, and on the inherently changeable discursive frameworks of our thought-communities. To see that as unacceptable because it is *limited* is to refuse to let go of expectations that are pathetically unrealistic to begin with. In the final chapter of this volume we will have more to say on this score.

With new and hopefully clearer meanings of these terms, we argue that compared to its sister fields of specialty, sociological theory fails to confront the real world. Hopefully, this book will encourage a remedy. As implied above, if the real is seen as a meaningless vestige, we will not seriously consider how sociological theory and method links or fails to link with such a world. Yet, the old contention of American pragmatism and the newer view of neuroscience are that mind developed as a tool to do just that, to enable us to act objectively on our environments (McCarthy 1996). Now that so much of social life and human meanings are seen as comprised of symbols that apply only to other symbols, this notion of mind as a device for acting on the environment has paled, only to be resurrected by students of the human brain.

SOCIOLOGY AND THE NARROWING OF ITS CONTACT WITH REALITY

With all our talk about empiricism, sociology's contact with the world outside of its own activities is alarmingly limited and we seem to be the last to know or care. For example, in a common scenario, sociological theories are reduced to testable hypotheses and data relevant to this task are collected. These data will presumably reflect something going on in what we call the empirical world. "Empirical" is often used as a code word for the real. Sometimes this reality is limited to real *words* as in self-reports. Presumably, these words reflect social phenomena that exist external to us as individuals. Then these data are organized, often put to statistical tests, and the resulting findings delivered at meetings, sent to a publisher, and duly recorded in our academic *vitae*, where the process, such as it is, stops. The "testing" stops with the statistical findings on paper. Actual feedback from application is not even considered. This so-called testing seldom leaves the written page to be tested in the real world of application referred to as "praxis." The only time we step out of the safe cocoon of sociological routine is in collecting our data. Frequently, even here, we selectively author the questions.

Because our notion of reality is so fuzzy, it totally escapes us that the real test has to be, like the rest of thinking behavior, in *how it enables us to act on our environments*. It is extremely hard for practical reasons to routinely apply sociological theory to actual problems in the world, and to have the feedback from this application further refine and redirect our theory. The powers that be are hardly interested in others' changing social structures that provide the vehicles for their privileged identities. The fact that such application is not routinely practical, however, should not block us from reflecting on these consequences and exploring options. True enough, there is a formal subfield of "sociological practice," and another of "applied sociology." But these are seen as offshoots, often looked down on by the pure theorists. They are hardly seen as routine and necessary tools of our trade, and the importance they hold for theory construction is generally overlooked completely. For those who do not draw firm and valued distinctions between fantasy and reality, this may not seem much of a loss, but this book will argue that it is.

Weinstein (2000) agrees. He characterizes academic sociology as a "literary pursuit" beginning and most often ending on paper. He warns against the assumption that such literary renderings of research have special powers to cut through the workings of think tanks and tenacious popular ideologies. One writes and only hopes that someone outside of sociology might apply it—that is, to the extent that one thinks outside of his or her specialty at all. The writing style demanded by journal editors usually assures that readers outside of the field will find it incomprehensible.

Weinstein reports the belittlement of students who want to be applied researchers and deal with the real world. These sociologists, he says, make up 50 percent of the profession but have comparatively little voice in academic settings. Overall, his warnings attest to the fact that the whole structure of the profession and its reward system has little to do with, and actually opposes, writings that exit the written page to enter the world of application.

THE ENLIGHTENMENT DUALISMS: WHAT TO KEEP; WHAT TO REJECT

Much of the most exciting and penetrating thinking of this century has been the poststructuralist, frontal attack on the hallowed terms above that were bequeathed by the Enlightenment thinkers.

As a part of our deconstruction, many of the chapters that follow question what has become known as the "Enlightenment dualisms." Objectivity/subjectivity, theory/fact, cognition/emotion, nature/nurture, mind/body, and applied/theoretical research are just a few cases in point. These dualities are pairings that have been viewed as irreconcilable contrasts to be purified of the other.[2] Dualistic thinking tends to be categorical in nature. For example, in order to be objective and thus reasonable, one must purge oneself of all contrastingly subjective tendencies—that is, all emotion—and rely totally on cognition seen as abstract logic, mathematics, and other impersonal symbolic systems. Because of the intangible nature of our cognitive productions, mind was placed in a disembodied realm detached from sensation, emotion, and intuition. Only because mind and nature were both propelled by principles of reason could we overcome the void between them. Nature was reasonable, and the reasoning mind could thus know it directly. Even now, in American analytic philosophy, the cognitive process—the essential vehicle of reason—is conceived as independent of, and unaffected by, the peculiarities of our bodies and human thought-communities. As we shall see in chapter 5, this is contrary to the findings of neuroscience (Damasio 1994), artificial intelligence (Dennett 1996), and an empirically responsible philosophy (Lakoff and Johnson 1999).

The term "dualism," then, reflects the misguided notion that body and mind, cognition and emotion, are irreconcilable and develop out of separate realms. The possibility that they are both phases of one common system and are equally necessary for the functioning of the other is not considered. Dualistic thinking, however appealing, has been found to block analytic thought and perpetuate serious fallacies. Even today, parts of business communities and some technocrats see emotion, in general, as the enemy of valid thought, a misconception that can produce psychopathic behaviors in "normal" people who are socialized into such frameworks (Damasio 1994). While emotions can thwart thought, contemporary science has shown them to be interconnected phases of a common neural system and absolutely essential to the effective functioning of each other.

In this volume we will demonstrate how dualities relevant to our argument overlap and are inseparably involved in each other, producing a more realistic and tenable understanding of these terms. The Enlightenment error that still influences the direction of Western society is the assumption that one has to *choose* which is the really important and consequential one. Thus an untenable notion of reality, objectivity, truth, and reason was promulgated that many reflective persons had to reject. At the same time that we demonstrate how the dualities overlap, we must develop a view that allows for the inevitable tension that can arise between them. The formula we suggest is: *Cancel the total opposition of the dualities but retain the possibility of tension.* In our view, postmoderns did a thorough job of canceling the opposition but forgot to retain the tension, especially between the verbal and the real world that the verbal enables us to know (see chapter 2). Consistent with this general rule, special attention will be given to a dialectic formulation of knowings and the known, subjective and objective, and mind and body.

THE RHETORICAL USE OF THE TERM "OBJECTIVITY"

One may well wonder why these dichotomies are so tenacious if they are so wrongheaded? One reason is because they comprise the discursive practices of our times and one is drawn into them in order to communicate. Thinkers like Kenneth Burke (in Gusfield 1998) and Hugh Duncan (1968) would suggest additional reasons. Their framework is helpful in our critique because they remind us of the need to be sensitive to the *rhetorical* function of words—that is, the use of words to convey far more than the ostensive subject at hand. They simultaneously announce the speaker as a member of a particular community and portray a kind of identification with that group. Eugene Halton (1995) facetiously describes how certain words become "dirties" and some become "cleans" as a matter of the changing climates of groups. A "clean" is contemporary and cool sounding, while a "dirty" is old fashioned and "out of step." People portray themselves as members of particular circles by using "cleans" and avoiding "dirties" as defined by that group. In intellectual circles the same thing happens. For example, Halton observes how the word "reality" has become a "dirty," while "fiction," "text," and "narrative" have become "cleans." Very recently "*self*-narrative" has become such a "clean" that its use can immediately propel a person into the highest regions of ethnographic sophistication.

In short, words can function to do three things: *identify* who the speaker is, *appeal* to and attract others, and *move* audiences to do one's bidding. Often this bidding is to capture their cooperation in supporting one's desired identity. The actors, of course, convince themselves of their identities as they convince others. People are often conscious of this and intentionally use it for their own purposes. But whether intended or not, words carry this identity-oriented, rhetorical, and potentially Machiavellian function.

The rhetorical functions of the words "truth" and "objectivity" for scientists in general are as powerful and popular as "patriotism" and "tax relief" are to politicians. Professors still pronounce to students that an object or event is not real unless it can be objectively measured. In so doing, they align themselves with objectivity and reality without being overtly ostentatious. As scientific as this might sound, it is alarmingly wrong headed—so much so that it is worth a closer look.

Anyone familiar with measurement theory knows that we can never measure objects in their totality, much less measure them directly. We measure observable indicators *of* objects. Not only are such indicators inherently selective, but we most frequently use little but prevailing common sense to choose them (see Feyerabend 1978). As numerous classics in the literature of methodology have pointed out, measurement begins and ends with indicants, not the objects themselves. Very seldom is hard evidence presented that an indicant actually belongs to the object or event.

According to well-accepted principles of sociology, it is quite possible that the objects are not there at all—and this applies equally to science in general (Brothers 1997). Many would argue this to be the case for concepts such as race. We create objects routinely in our everyday lives when we see sure "indications" of the devil, the inherent inferiority of minority members, or some medical syndromes, not to mention the very necessary process of construing others' behavior as being consistent with social roles (Turner 1962). In the riotous movie *Being There*, starring Peter Sellers, this process was presented in the extreme when everything an air-headed stumble-bum did was interpreted as being a sure sign of genius. The process of perceiving "indicants" of nonexistent objects, attributes, or events is so pervasive in the social process that Harold Garfinkel chose to make it *the* essential subject matter of his *Studies in Ethnomethodology* (1967). He refers to this process as the "documentary method." At its heart is the same circular logic of using measurement as a criteria for the real: The factualness of the object is presumed while at the same time selected events (indicants) are brought to bear as evidence for their existence (Brothers 1997). In science, this can render moot questions of the validity of some indicants. All the measurement in the world cannot decide whether what you measure has anything to do with the construct that motivated the process in the first place. Ironically, the ubiquitous statement "if it cannot be measured, it is not real" is neither logical nor scientific, but a sign of woeful ignorance of ontology, epistemology, ethnomethodology, and, last but not least, methodology!

Nonetheless, performed with the proper supercilious affect, this statement will sound impressive and present the speaker as authoritative to naïve audiences regardless of its lack of any substantive content. If professors, furthermore, with the proper affect show disdain for "mere philosophy" as being irresponsibly speculative in contrast to their own practices, we can wonder how they justify their own blatantly philosophical declarations about what is real. When this is part of a discursive style wherein the professors imply that anything subjective is trite and everything they do is objective, we can be assured that such declarations are obviously identity work—impression management and little else.

In sum, words are often used without reflection as to their coherence but as presentations of self. Ironically, in cases like the one above, which have hardly been uncommon in American universities of this century, the communication is: "I am the truth speaker and all others are false."

In spite of the deviousness of our measurement example, our point is not to rid our discursive practices of rhetoric. As used here, the rhetorical use of words is a vital and necessary part of communication. Our audience needs to know relevant aspects of our identity to place our words in the context necessary for their intended meanings, and we must speak a language that is both familiar enough and acceptable enough for them to give it a fair hearing. An element of unnoticed emotional appeal is a part of everyday discourse, as is keeping the attention of one's audience. However, like anything else, a balance must be stuck between *identity*-oriented and *task*-oriented interactions and their rhetorics. If the task is to make people reflective about their methods in order to make effective use of them, we need to also attend to the rhetorical use of words to engage persons in such a task. It is not unusual in human affairs that we do a number of things at once and that the secret to effectiveness is in the balance.

Our key point is that the word "objectivity" should not be left for the sole possession of those who use it unreflectively in a mindless kind of "rhetorical positivism." The misuse of the term has no doubt made it unappealing to others. Our purpose is to bring it back into the fold of transactional social constructionists and the broad range of sociological discourse, or at least to make it intellectually possible to do so.

THE TRANSACTIONAL FRAMEWORK AS A MEANS OF AVOIDING DUALISM

The recently rediscovered notion of "transaction" is presented as a way of avoiding dualistic, either/or thinking. Transactional analysis is a view of causation and interdependence. It assumes a world of actuality and the notion that thought did not originate for its own sake detached from everyday activities, but derived from, and subserved, action in a world of real consequences. Obviously, humans can think in a number of ways, but as future chapters will argue, thought for thought's sake is significantly different from thought refined by application. These differences are largely ignored by our "over-cognized" society. Consistent with the findings from current neuroscience, transaction does not allow for the "hypothetization" of thought detached from the practical activity of the body acting on the environment. It has nothing to do with the therapeutic approach using that name in the 1970s, and it is not a synonym for a social interactive framework. While it was sometimes referred to in sociological works, including those by us, it was not put on center stage in sociology until Emirbayer's writings in the latter half of the 1990s. "Transaction" refers to an epistemological framework that avoids looking at objects of analysis as having essentialistic characters in and of themselves, or as being understandable independent of other things. As a matter of fact, it chooses to view things not in and of themselves, but as components of action that are never self-sufficient (see also Ollman 1971). To Emirbayer (1997), units involved in a transaction take on their identity from the fluctuating roles they play within transaction. These roles, seen as dynamic unfolding process, become the primary unit of analysis rather than the constituent elements themselves. Things "are not assumed as independent existences present anterior to any relation, but gain their whole being first in and with the relations that are predicted of them" (Emirbayer quoting Cassirer 1953, 36).

For example, transaction provides us with a view that sees the micro and macro levels of analysis as different phases of common activity. Though assuming emergent processes, it avoids reifying structure into something *sui generis* independent from the everyday processes of the thinking and feeling of actual persons engaged in the process of communication. When, for another example, we give emotions names and view them as being separate unto themselves or as materially distinct systems in the brain, we are perfecting the art of reification and our documentary methods.

A transactional theory of relational activity is tailored precisely for avoiding dualistic thinking, but there are other reasons for following a transactional focus in this book. We attempt to get above the nominalism of our age. Ours is a time where, on many fronts, only words and definitions seem real. Words and definitions *are* real and absolutely critical to social life anywhere. But this important point cannot be used to minimize the crucial differences between "talking the talk and walking the walk," or fantasizing about something and actually *doing* that something. Playing basketball is something different from wearing the right shoes, despite our advertisement and purchasing culture. Goffman's depiction of such a society in his famous *Presentation of Self in Everyday Life* (1959) notwithstanding, appearance and its ubiquitous import do not destroy the difference between *appearing* to be something and *being* it, though both may overlap. A transactional approach in "asserting the right to see together what is talked about as separates" avoids the mistake made in much of postmodernist conversation, of throwing aside one-half of the dichotomies it attacks. This leaves one side as nonexistent, when in actuality they are both parts of one frame. In the example above, you do not have social structure without microprocesses and engaged selves—and you do not have microprocesses and engaged selves without structures (Giddens 1984).

In sum, to overcome the mistakes of the Enlightenment, so much of which is incorporated in its dualistic thinking, we must see things in combination. Overcoming dualism does not entail choosing one side over the other: subjectivity over objectivity, environment over organism, or a groundless social construction over some form of realism. It is not a matter of choice; it is not a matter of dismissing one in favor of the other. It *is* a matter of seeing each of them as part of one frame. What needs to be understood is how they are nonexistent without each other and nonetheless how tension between them will always appear. A critical tension that we must retain is that between symbolic action in a world we collectively create, and a much broader world that transcends present human knowledge. This latter world has the important function of tutoring and schooling our symbolic renditions. Once again, we are brought back to the pragmatic and neuroscientific understanding of the brain and mind as developed and maintained by subserving action on our environments. We will have much more to say on this score, much of it from the findings of neuroscience.

PRELIMINARY NOTES ON CONCEIVING REALITY

In preparation for what follows, we may be reminded that social behaviorism has already revised our conception of reality instead of dispensing with it. This revision was part of the larger twentieth-century confirmation that process rather than enduring structure characterizes the microscopic level. The first hint we have of reality as change comes with the recognition, as Heraclitus ([c. 500 B.C.] in Wheelwright 1960, 70–71) argued, that we "never step into the same stream twice." He was also aware that the humanly created *name* of the river remains the same regardless of the change that exists on the material microlevel. The water temperature and chemical content, the debris, and different temperatures go down the stream, metamorphosing as they go, never to return again. One would be tempted to think that the material path through the earth cut by the river remains the same, but even this is deceiving when looked at over the eons. The experience of sameness is not inherent in the river but in us—in the time frame we use to think about it and in the nature of linguistic categories.

If reality can be seen as flux and change, so must the microreality of the body. The self-process and its extrasensory constitution emerges only from a corporal prereflective foundation and never fully leaves it (Damasio 1999). According to Harth (1993), a single cubic millimeter of brain tissue contains over a million neurons. Conservative estimates relate that the brain contains approximately 200 billion neurons, along with a trillion or so supportive cells. Herein, indeterminacy *must* apply. The brain—which is to say the mind—is a creative, contingent process. This is critical to the argument in chapter 6.

In the case of the changing path of the river, our common-sense time frame makes us unaware of the slow but inexorable changes in the river's path, as well as the fact that we are using one particular macroscopic viewpoint. Likewise, it takes a highly technical extension of our eyes and the perspective of quantum physics to understand that a desk is really molecules in motion, with some individual molecules breaking away from the movement of the whole mass in an arbitrary chaotic fashion.

Yet human experience is, and must be, characterized by stability. We cannot build up human meanings without it. In the following chapters we elaborate on three reasons for this apparent stability: First, linguistic categories are projected onto this flux, imposing their own order on the kaleidoscopic world of possible stimuli. Chapter 5 expands on this. Such categories give the experience of stability within a particular language group, but because stable classifications are not given by nature, they exhibit vast differences in such groupings among societies. These differences only hint at the flux of the world that is language's task to hide. True, the world lends itself to this ordering, but it lends itself to a vast number of equally plausible orderings (Whorf 1964). One culture's likeness is another culture's outrage. These inevitable differences hint at the chaos we hide from ourselves.

Next, writers associated with postmodernism have looked at the human construction of stability as an insidious technique of power-as-domination. Such power distrusts change and encourages the status quo. Spontaneity and disorder are threats that must be controlled. Domination usually speaks of one enduring truth that only it possesses. Whatever truth there may be in this insight—and we think there is a great deal, viewing our linguistic stabilizing of the world as being exclusively an insidious power play is extreme and ignores the other crucial explanations.

Such a position is severely questioned by the third explanation of why we forge stability: namely, one rooted in the findings of neuroscience. The human brain itself is constructed to minimize flux and to seek out patterns. The eye, for instance, does not respond to each microscopic flash, but from the outset it seeks a gestalt in what it sees, and the pattern it looks for is the shape of things (Bronowski 1958). Our so-called left brain—Gazzaniga (1985) calls it the "interpreter"—will actually create the experience of patterns where there is none.

Suffice it for now to suggest that the twentieth century has gone decidedly beyond the common-sense, traditional notions of reality that create logical difficulties, encouraging thoughtful persons to turn away from the term. Our purpose is to make it more palatable by bringing some of these relatively unattended advances to the reader's attention.

◻   ◻   ◻

Throughout the twentieth century, social theory has challenged the dualities. It has shown how subjectivity is inseparable from objectivity, how the perceived environment is inseparable from the perceiving animal's senses and its particular brains. But, as we just described, in numerous cases these theorists have done their work only too well. In breaking down the contrasts they have lost the emphasis on the tension that derives from the healthy existence of both.[3] In this mind frame, a grossly obvious fact escapes us: That sociological theory is very limited—significantly limited—by lack of contact and subsequent refinement by the world external to it—a world that is in some important sense real and exists on a fundamentally different level than theory and words. The axiom coming out of postmodern and poststructuralist thought is "to keep the inquiry focused on discourse." For example, we are urged to study how people talk, feel, and think about emotions and to forget the impossible task of jumping out of our language to study the actual emotion as it is in itself. This has tremendous plausibility and seems at first-hand to be impervious to challenge. Under this dictum, excellent work has been done. But once again, with all its virtues, this strategy ignores the tension between words and deeds, between thinking of doing something and the experience of actually doing it, between our current symbolically enabled understandings and the admittedly humanized world that we are trying to understand.

In order to make our case against keeping analysis exclusively within the symbolic, many paths must be traveled and then brought together. In part I of this book we start with previous work on using words to get at the nonverbal and/or using the language of fixed *being* to deal with the world of *becoming* (Shalin 1993). We are not going to save the old notions of objectivity, reality, and truth. We are going to save *enough* of them to depict the tensions that they engender and to rid our sociology of the groundless relativity that bespeaks so much of the age in which we live.

In sum, the first part of this book deals with thought patterns in sociology that inhibit our interest in sociological application. We do not pretend to have the kind of hands-on knowledge of members of sociological practice and/or applied sociology. Our interest comes out of our understandings of academic sociology: namely, concerns about our field in terms of verification of theory and other consequences of our general detachment from the rest of society. Ironically, part I is a very abstract argument against the exclusive belief in thought for thought's sake that is pervading the field. But to us, irony is a part of life.

Chapter 2 discusses two important positions that flow throughout this book. First, we show the complications involved in distinguishing between word and deed and suggest resolutions (see Deutscher, Pestello, and Pestello 1993). Then we argue against the dictum of "all within discourse" that traps us in a nominalistic cage wherein the only real things are words. Strains in sociological theory that reflect this position, for example, "textualism," are identified and critiqued. We discuss how warranted concerns about avoiding "foundationalism" and "essentialism" can nonetheless be used to inhibit thought about sociological practice and the world beyond words. In this chapter we present Kenneth Burke's previous work on the irony of using words to attend to nonverbal actuality. In conclusion, some current writers that share our concerns are identified.

Pursuant to the goals articulated above, chapter 3 will elaborate on the transactional "meta-method" and end with a typology of action implied in this elaboration. The typology ranges from fantasy-action to deed and to a sociological view of collective praxis. In our discussion of deeds, we deal with words as mere words and words as full deeds, recognizing that they can be both. It should go without saying that in discussing humans as social symbolic animals, we can hardly over-emphasize the very real impacts and real consequences of words. Nevertheless, words alone do not encompass all human life. The typology is arranged on a continuum comprised of the kinds of resistance and constraints imposed by the consequences of our actions on the real world. It also attends to what this world more positively enables. Our interest in writing this book started when respected colleagues argued that there is no important distinction between merely *saying* something and actually *doing* it. For them, this followed from the realization that talk *is* human action. The typology allows us to get out of this subjective box.[4] Without a way of clearly conceiving the importance of nonverbal motor activity to human experience we miss the impact of Gerth and Mill's (1958, 75) transactional words that are so important to our thesis: "The realities of the world and the capacities of our own bodies are learned together. Both come to us in terms of resistance and mastery, limitation and capacity." The presentation of our typology leads into our arguments for a revision of what can be coherently meant by reality.

Chapter 4 deals with subjectivity and objectivity. It discusses the markedly varied usages or meanings of both terms and details how they are implicated in each other inside a transactional framework. This also means that we cannot talk meaningfully about the generic subjective and objective. We must specify *the senses* in which both are being taken in a particular context. This paves the way for their more coherent reconstruction and, once again, helps clarify what we can mean by reality. Emotion is discussed here in the context of subjectivity and the body and its important relationship to the rational.

We follow with a critique in chapter 5 of the purely cognitive notion that our society has of human thought, and we stress the superficial and imperceptive character that cognition can take on when it is divorced from real-world application. This amounts to another way of questioning the wisdom of textualism critiqued in chapter 2. A major argument in this context is that abstract cognition detached from real-life experience is not quite the perfect achievement of homo sapiens that the rationalists of the past centuries have taken it to be. As Kant summarized it, concepts without percepts are empty, and percepts without concepts are blind. True, he assumed a dualistic notion of both, but he correctly saw pure thought untutored by direct contact as weak and inadequate to human experience. We describe what happens when concepts are separated from bodily felt emotion and developed without application in the world of actuality. Noninvolved cognition leads not to a detached form of objective reason lifting us above human bias. The startling lesson from neuroscience is that logic, observation, and intellectual intelligence alone do not suffice for healthy survival in the everyday world of pragmatic decision making.

Damasio's (1994) clinical research on patients with prefrontal lesions is used to demonstrate how the practicalities of acting in the real world demand more than abstract intelligence and force choices that can only be sagaciously made with proper inputs from the emotional body. The empirically discovered inadequacy of mere intelligence to cope with actual problems of living, where felt values must guide choices and judgments, makes it necessary to reformulate our exclusively cognitive assumptions as to the nature of reason. This redefinition must be accomplished in the spirit of Lakoff and Johnson's "empirically responsible philosophy." Our formulation includes Damasio's "somatic marker" hypoth-

esis with its empirically based appreciation of the tight relationship
between emotion and cognition, wherein both processes support the
workings of each other. Without some acceptance of a real world "outside of human discourse," such findings could not have been possible.

◙   ◙   ◙

Part II of this volume explores the implications of our embodied transactional framework for a future sociology more capable of application to
real-life problems. Insights from part I are utilized to connect the sociology of the body with Jürgen Habermas's theoretical project to formulate
a transactional approach to social problems. One may well ask why we
need such a theory, and how "embodied" theory can help bring about
such application? Our answer is that embodiment defines a life-world on
the level of actuality that exists over against a disembodied system level.
These emergent structures form our "objectivized" world that we are
born into and die out of (Berger and Luckmann 1967). The system
includes our blend of capitalism and rational-efficient values, wherein we
find disembodied transactions in the realms of production, consumption,
and interaction. These institutional practices emerge from historical contexts and turn back to colonize the embodied transactions and consciousness of the life-world. Here, people draw on the body, in manipulative acts, and solve actual life problems. We expand on an embodied
semiotic where emotional nonverbal gestures operate much too fast to
be understood by our theories of deliberate consciousness (Katz 1999).

We join other contemporary pragmatists in criticizing Habermas for
pulling away from the life-world to the abstracted ideal-speech community. Indeed, we see sociology itself as a product of the social system and
existing on a systems level constituted by disembodied thought for
thought's sake. The chapters in part II suggest avenues of returning our
theories to incorporate the life-world where people are confronting
important social problems and where sociology can help them do so.[5]

In chapter 6 we present sociological thinking on the human body as
a way of materially grounding the symbolic self and rooting it in transactional activity. As we have said, the corporeal reality of the body is
constant flux and change. This chapter shows how the arbitrary contingency of human physiology is the key problem for selves and bodies. We
are ironically compelled to terminate the body's ultimately uncontrol-
lable tendencies. But some persons do so at a ghastly cost to others and
themselves. From a transactional viewpoint it becomes clear that this
key dilemma is an action problem rather than a systems problem.

Chapter 7 attempts to make the work of Habermas more compatible with a sociology that can help solve human problems. His work on the ideal-speech situation is critiqued from our transactional viewpoint, with the conclusion that he needs a theory of action that is not so exclusively wedded to words, shared symbols, and linguistically formed consensus. As mentioned above, we present a way of defining the life-world as emphasizing an actuality existing against a societal level that shapes thought by disembodied means. Chapter 7 comes full circle to suggest some ways by which sociological theory can test itself in the real world. It also presents an analysis of why sociology has failed—to the extent that it has—to impact the national public discussions of social problems. A bottom-up, countersystem analysis is suggested as a way of dislodging ourselves from our assumptive orders and gaining insight from engaged life-world groups at the local level. In this system, the sociologist becomes engaged but nevertheless deals with the important requirements of objectivity. Countersystem analysis offers a transactional and thoroughly pragmatic strategy for the field of social problems. It suggests how inputs from the real world of grass-roots problem-solving enter into theory construction. Theory is thus created, tested, and refined by participation and application in local arenas.

The book concludes with chapter 8—a summary of the conceptual links throughout the book, its contribution to sociological theory, and our attempts to make reality, objectivity, and truth more palatable to generations after us. Here we argue for the relationship between interpersonal truth and the generation of scientific truth. We conclude with a reminder of the turn to a one-sided, self-absorbed subjectivism that has pervaded our whole culture, and a caution against having it pervading our sociological practices as well.

CONCLUSION

The discursive practices identified as "foundationalism" and "essentialism" are, in this case, correctly seen as two other so-called "dirties," but we have some reservations (indicated below) about elements of the conversation. We are in sympathy with many of the reasons that these two "isms" are held in disrepute. In so far as essentialism is attacked for seeking the final nature of self-contained things and events, we fully concur with the rejection. The transactional framework is our answer to avoiding this and to clearing the way for connecting with the world outside of sociology. Foundationalism seeks a primary, abstract ground from which sociology can proceed to fully explain "the" social process in terms that ignore context, complexity, and variety. We also concur with this rejection. One primary reason is that this does not consider contemporary conflicts and interests that necessarily influenced the theory so constructed. We see no reason why a transactional viewpoint would lead to this.

An important dimension of the discussion concerning these two terms has to do with what one uses as an authority for making claims. This discussion contains discursive practices that can well mitigate against giving reality factors their due. A prevailing argument from within the formal Society for the Study of Symbolic Interaction and other voices (Seidman 1991) has to do with the issue of privileging. The argument is that every position should be seen as a separate narrative and that no "text" can be privileged over any others—a story, being all words, is a story, and the idea of a criterion for the true one is not to the point. For example, Durkheim was foundational in seeing everything conceivable, including God in his case, as emerging from the social process. He privileged the social process, and the last thing he had in mind was telling an earthly story. To Seidman, sociological theories are foundational when they attempt to uncover a unitary logic of society or a one true vocabulary that mirrors the social process and makes claims to final truth. We would agree with being highly suspicious of such theories. However, thinking of everything in terms of words to the exclusion of any sense of nonverbal action on the world involves its own type of privileging. This holds even if it cannot be accused of foundationalism.

In our case, we do see much of sociology as privileging the cognitive, and especially as privileging the word over such things as nonverbal actuality and emotion, the prereflective realities of the body, and experience. For our part, we privilege these over words, as critical as words may be. The reasons for such privileging form the content of this book.

In only apparent disregard to current warnings, we refer often to the writings of George Herbert Mead who, we agree, may be accused of being a foundational thinker in spite of his disclaimers for speaking final truths. But this is not the real point. Fine and Kleinman (1986) insist correctly that there can be no true (essentialistic) knowledge of what Mead "really meant." For some, this may be reason not to bother with him at all. Most of our references to Mead, however, are used to clarify the notion of transaction that went unnoticed by his postwar readers, because he was more involved in using it than explicating it. Especially, we make no attempt to capture "the" one correct interpretation of Mead. We unabashedly use him to clarify what we cannot say as clearly. Students of intersubjectivity know that only on the most abstract level do we manage full agreements, and this also applies to interpreting the past.[6] Insofar as our main goal is to offer a plausible argument for sociological application and renewed interest in "middle-ranged" theories, we offer no such totalizing practices. Our conversation with Mead is riddled with our own reading and must stand on its own merits.

For these authors, the meanings of reality, objectivity, and truth are human constructions and take on meaning by their coherence to us and, we hope, to you the reader. These meanings will change as our interests and knowledge change. Used in redefined ways, they are critical terms that keep us from a self-absorption that dims the world outside of us. Their disregard can well foster a mentality wherein theories of use to the rest of the world will not even cross our mind.

We do, indeed, see a neuroscience approach as complimenting a fully embodied pragmatism in an argument against thought for its own sake. It seems reasonable to us that thinkers should think about how we think. Neuroscience, "totalized" or not, has a great deal to say of interest, not only to pragmatists but also to all educators. To reject this field under any guise is to reject the knowledge of our times about how we know (Franks 1999). To know about it does not mean that we have to see it as a final story. This is a very new field; we can privilege positions to our own degrees and in many different ways.

NOTES

1. A fourth term is *reason*, which has suffered telling blows at the hands of postmodernists, among others, who have looked straight into the eyes of the tumultuous brutalities of the twentieth century—"the age of reason's" wayward child. From this historical viewpoint, "reason" can be seen as a construal of the right way to think, operating overtly through our discursive practices to ensure that society members can only think in ways that are controlled by the status quo. While much of reason surely can be so judged, it is decidedly less malevolent as used in this volume. Following the neuroscientist Antonio Damasio, the ability to reason is limited to decision making that makes normal life possible. It is not to be confused with what postmodernists and poststructuralists are discussing or the reason of "rational decision-making theorists."

2. To the confusion of some, dualism does not mean accepting both sides of the dichotomies, as the name implies. Dualism, in making both sides antithetical to each other, forces us to accept only *one* side as valid. For a balanced and logically coherent view we must accept the validity of *both* sides.

3. One does not have to be a postmodern theorist to be affected by its implications and style of thought. We will have more to say about how previous discourses still effect our current thinking in subtle ways.

4. This basic distinction between idea and actuality is a recognized prerequisite for childhood cognitive development and is an important distinction to the layperson. However, it has often escaped recognition and utilization by academics. Such is the power of the extreme constructionist's mind frame.

5. James A. Forte's *Theories of Practice: Symbolic Interactionist Translations* (2001) could be seen as a companion book to this volume. While his main emphasis is hardly on specifics of the refinement of social theory, his work should still be of interest to sociologists and especially symbolic interactionists who share concerns about application.

6. None of us can escape the existential dimension of life wherein only we ourselves must struggle and suffer regardless of the support of others. Thus, much of life is ours alone and cannot be fully shared or conveyed in words. (See the discussion of qualia in chapter 4.) So, of course, no one can offer a fully accurate interpretation of Mead. We strongly suspect that he himself would often not know what he originally meant if he would be so brash as to visit us now. William Saroyan was asked what he had meant by a line in his play, *Time of Your Life*. His response was to the effect: "I have no idea, but I can tell you what it means to me now."

◙   ◙   ◙

PART ONE

Breaking Down Dualities but Keeping the Tension: Sociology and Reality

◉   ◉   ◉

CHAPTER TWO

The Collapse of Word and Deed

In this chapter we will question two overlapping positions that involve the very conception of what action, and different kinds of action, may be. The heart of social behaviorism and a transactional framework rests on a conception of nonverbal sensorimotor activity that has important, but ignored, differences from that of symbolic communication. This will prepare us for the next chapter, which concludes with a typology starting with verbal actions and leading up to praxis. Some pertinent parts of this issue will be addressed in later chapters that bring neurological evidence to bear on the temporal and functional priority of manipulative activity to the development of symbolic processes.

Hidden—or perhaps to some quite evident—in the above is the second overlapping issue. The notion of communication as "simulacrums" aside, can we ever jump out of our symbolic, reflective skins to talk in terms of the objects to which our words refer? In some of the post-structuralist framework the answer is, "No, there is nothing to talk about outside of discourse." Again, we contend with this seemingly seductive position. We do so on the grounds that this collapses deed into word. It ignores the many arguments for the "preobjective" foundation of reflective thought. Ignoring this makes pragmatism and praxis "old hat," and transaction as well. This is because "all within discourse" renders impossible the tension that needs to be retained between knowings and the known, or symbolic thought and any conception of reality beyond our own words.

DISSOLVING THE DISTINCTION BETWEEN
WORD AND DEED: WHAT WE LOSE

Problems Related to "All Within Discourse" as a Strategic Frame among Others

One charmed night a colleague was critiquing an early draft of a paper on word and deed as we sat late in a restaurant, replete with wine after dinner and scribbles on napkins—the stuff of our dreams when we first imagined pursuing this vocation. My friend, an accomplished scholar, recommended dropping the attempt at differentiating types of action and to accept that everything—I mean every meaningful thing— must be viewed as within discourse. Yes, birth and death, emotion and everything considerable, for these only take intelligible form and/or become objectified through human language. Not only does this leave no possibility for reality testing but it deflects from the fact that emotions, for example, are comprised of much more than talk and are the very experiences underlying meaningful lives (see chapters 4 and 5). How many of us would find it an attractive offer to drive with a person who had read volumes about driving cars, but had never done so?[1] Nonetheless, further reading confirmed that this was an apt description of what was going on in much of the then-current literature. As we write, some of these positions have become dated. However, in our opinion the residues of the past conversations surrounding these positions have kept their momentum and are still with us in our discursive practices. They still set the tone to our thinking and subtly inhibit pushing beyond the subjectivism of our times into more balanced statements. We now turn to illustrations of such positions. Our primary purpose is not a complete exposition and critique; it is to illustrate the discourse that "over-relativizes" our field and creates the need for a transactional antidote.

According to Callinicos (1985), the "all within discourse" strain was first distinguished by Richard Rorty, who felicitously labeled it "textualism." While it is a part of the larger "linguistic turn," it is certainly not characteristic of all of it. Textualism to Rorty is a version of German idealism applied to language that reduces everything to discourse. Callinicos sees textualism as a part of poststructuralism characterized in particular by the work of Saussure and Derrida. Its reduction is not inherent in a more worldly poststructuralism that, in Callinicos's terms, allows room for relating the said and the unsaid, the discursive and nondiscursive, and, in our terminology, word and deed (Best and Kellner 1991, 33). This does not mean that poststructuralism cannot come close to discursive reduction.

The reduction takes the following form for Saussure and Derrida: The relationship between language and what it is about is not a consideration. The critical distinction is between the linguistic signifier and the signified. The object that is signified, however, is still placed within the mind. The signified is only a concept. It follows that the only issues to be discussed are within language itself (McCarthy 1996). From a transactional viewpoint this is a markedly nonrelational position. Characteristic of other theorizing, textualism escapes the charge of dualism by obliterating the relevance of the other side, that is, the real world. Thus the tension between the discursive and the world beyond is ignored. In so far as elements of textualism may appear in many works and voices, it invades the discursive practices of the sociological-thought community, where talking about refining thought and theory through real-world application is rhetorically out of vogue. Again, colleagues may wonder "what planet you've been on."

Words carry significance for Saussure only because their phonic differences allow distinction of each word from others. Signification lies only in these verbal distinctions. Neither the signifier nor the signified have any relation to what existed before or outside of the symbol. This contrasts strongly with our use in this volume of embodied semiotics. As we shall contend (following Lakoff and Johnson [1999]), this semiotic is dependent on metaphors taken from sensorimotor experience in a world that can justly be referred to as objective. But for Saussure, there was no critical distinction between mere verbal meanings and that dimension of more firmly felt meanings derived from one's own objective experiences with a physically resisting world. Meaning was only a matter of the relations of words to other words. For Katz (1999), who rejects the "linguistic turn" in his study of emotions, this would mean that we would be incapable of learning how to do anything but talk.

Derrida (1970, 249) built on the extremely relativized elements in Saussurian linguistics. As he so starkly put it, "There is no outside-text." Even if some doubt that he meant exactly what he wrote, we can hardly over-emphasize the influence of the words. In contrast, Lyotard (1971, 9), certainly a postmodern thinker, asserts that "the given is not a text, . . . there is within it a density, or rather a constitutive difference that is not to be read. . . ." He observes that this is continually forgotten in the process of signification. According to Best and Kellner (1991, 149) Lyotard rejects textualism that places texts and discourses over experiences and the senses. At the same time, in postmodern fashion, Lyotard rejects the possibility of a theory-endorsing praxis. This conclusion, shared by many, is based on the conviction that any attempt at overturning the system would "end up resembling the system it was designed to replace."[2] To Callinicos (1985), this leaves the cultural avant-garde with merely a radical rhetoric—a way of talking radically, but no way of forming and testing collective programs of application.

To return to the dinner conversation, our hunch was that placing everything within discourse was not avoiding dualisms, it was avoiding issues. The pragmatist position was firm: we must see things in relation or not at all. For us, words must be seen in possible tension with some nonverbal dimension of deed even if a person's words are often deeds. To say "all is within discourse" makes it difficult to keep the relational tension that grants ontological equality to both sides and avoids one-sided subjectivism.[3]

We follow Ostrow (1990), Shalin (1993), and Halton (1995) among others, who insist on a transactional tension between word and deed in personal life, or what these authors refer to after Dewey and Mcrleau-Ponty as the "qualitative immediacy" of experience. This term is important to what we mean by deed and is so critical to keeping the tension between the verbal and the nonverbal in lived experience that we must pause to unpack it.

Immediacy Beyond Discourse: An Illustration

To describe immediacy, actuality, or deed, we will tell another personal story. At the beginning of the summer, a friend of the second author of this book made an unexpected departure from his motorcycle at miles per hour in the three digits. (He happens to be the senior author so the second author will write in the first person.) Needless to say, my friend was lucky to be alive, but it took three four-hour operations to keep him that way. I had gone to the hospital in the morning during the first operation and waited, talking with his wife, until we found out the operation would take even longer than we thought. I decided to go home for a while and on the way I found the signs of where he left the road. As I got out and looked, there were broken small trees and mashed bushes beyond which was a hole that could have been the result of an exploding hand grenade. They told a horrific story of destruction, pain, and death. On the way back to the hospital room, going up the elevator, I rehearsed what I would say: "Well, you had a little experience with deed, huh? Was it more than discourse? Well," I continued to myself, "that's so unbelievably trivializing, how could I even think of it? Maybe I'd better say . . ." you get the picture, my mind was whirling with anticipations. Off the elevator I decided, "Whatever you do, be solid. That's all that really matters, let them lean on you and go with the flow." I entered the room as I intended, solid and in command. His wife was at the door, the time had come: actuality! It came with my glimpse of my actual friend in the bed, casts and bandages, looking straight ahead.

At that immediate moment of actual contact, all conscious thought, all deliberated rehearsals left me as useless as dust. I was overcome by the moment—a dumb, absolute realization of human pathos. All I could say was, "Steve!" His wife put her arms around me; I was overcome with a wave of tears, my rehearsals so inadequate to their task of preparing me for the moment. Even now I am without words adequate to describe why I was so overcome, and yet as I remember the emotion I "know" why, I know exactly: words can come so close, but it is beyond words to convey.

Does the fact that the ineffable feeling was mine alone mean that we are to disregard this moment—and a billion other magnified moments, all of which are virtual epiphanies of meaning? Do we gloss over them because they can only happen to one person, born as it is from our shared intelligence and unshared sensate reactivity? All of you have had such moments, some sexual, some hitting the bottom of despair, some of ecstasy of all sorts. Such moments may be born of human discourse, of interpretative intelligence, but though we can communicate it image-wise, there is a crucial immediate character that can never be recaptured or conveyed. This character is the point of actuality and runs unceasingly through every human endeavor. As Seneca said of human rage, "Wild beasts and all animals, except man, are not subject to anger, for while it is the foe of reason, it is nevertheless born only where reason dwells" (quoted in Tavris 1989). Reason and emotion are seen here transactionally not as opposites whose existence challenges the being and validity of the other, but as processes that depend on each other for their existence and yet can come into serious tension and oppose each other. The same is true for reflection and actuality, word and deed.

Hopefully this example, "writ large" so to speak by its personal drama, describes what we mean by the indeterminate immediacy inherent in everyday deed, and identifies the sense in which deed and the actuality it incorporates is so much more than our mere words. This is why it is characteristically surprising.

As mentioned above, Katz (1999, 4) has put significant emphasis on the nonverbal in his study of lived emotions. To repeat, this does not mean that we do not consciously understand them through the medium of language. Nor does it mean that we are not constantly defining and interpreting our worlds. But we cannot be so taken by the "linguistic turn" that it *distracts us from the vast proportion of human meanings that are conveyed sensually in manners that words cannot in fact describe.* The idea of the ineffably sensed "feel" of emotion that is only open to lived experience will make this clearer (see chapter 4).

In spite of Katz's (1999) observation that emotion is clearly "more than talk," our studies frequently end up analyzing mere talk about emotions as if this was the only way to avoid essentialism:

> If there is anything distinctive about emotions, it is that, even if they . . . occur in the course of speaking, they are not talk, not even just forms of expression. Indeed, to the extent that emotions are forms of expression, they are ways of expression that something is going on that talk cannot grasp. (Katz 1999, 4)

Let us look at a different example while granting the truism that all pages in this book are mere words, and we are using words to describe the nonverbal experience of immediacy. While engaged in their event, most good athletes are too busy performing to be conscious of themselves in that vital moment. Watching films of their performances, they are often surprised at what they did. Such reflection is a distraction to an athlete. When Sugar Ray Robinson, the great boxer in the 1950s, caught himself being *aware* of his opponent's opening, he knew he was no longer fast enough to stay on top—he should have already hit. Once more, we see that actuality and immediacy are inherently entwined as concepts; and both are, in some important, experiential sense, outside of the reflectiveness of symbolic interpretation. The actual and immediate—that direct, ineffable line to life that we mean by lived experience—carries a prereflective, preobjective dimension. If this comes as a truism it is no matter, the point being that we do not incorporate it strongly and firmly into our overly nominalistic semiotics and social psychology.[4]

The inadequacy of inner rehearsal is only an instance of a more general character of the tension between language in relation to the actual that moves beyond discourse. Consistent with the preliminary notes on the pragmatic view of reality discussed in the previous chapter, actuality asserts its independence from our word-formed expectations and categories.

The "I" and Immediacy

The "I" of Mead's "I" and the "me" lies exclusively in its relation to immediacy—this emergent present that is more than the "I" and more than the linguistic "me." This allows immediacy to be so replete with the unexpected. The "I" and the "me" are inseparable phases of the same moment of action. But, analytically, the "I" is not encompassed by the "me." Note that the "me" is reflective and discursive through and through—not so the "I." As Rochberg-Halton (1986) quotes Mead:

> That movement into the future is the step . . . of the "I." . . . However carefully we plan for the future it always is different from that which we can previse, and this something that we are continually bringing in and adding to is what we identify with the self that comes into the level of our experience only in the completion of the act. . . . *Now it is this living act that never gets directly into reflective experience.* It is only after the act has taken place that we catch it in our memory and place it in terms of that which we have done. (Rochberg-Halton 1986, 36)

This quote points to the dumb immediacy beyond discourse and the unpredictability of actuality. This was the point of seeing the friend in the hospital room. There is another challenge given below to what we see as the self-contained strategy to place all within discourse. It not only impedes our ability to articulate the tension between the real and the image of the real, but it discourages the appreciation of a tension that undergirds true discovery and the value of refining our knowledge by application in this wider world.

Immediacy: The Prereflective and Deed

Ostrow (1990, 29) has successfully argued for prereflective sociality that is antecedent to self-consciousness and thus language. He points to the fact that the seeing eye at the moment of seeing cannot be conscious of itself, not at that moment (1990, 28). This living part of the act never gets into reflection, because it is always making reflection possible. As the prime mover, the "I" and the immediacy of which it partakes are the epitome of the subjective, not in the Enlightenment sense of error or personal distortion, but in the subjective term's more original sense of "foundational" and being personally vital.

In fine transactional style, Ostrow argues that it is an error to formulate experience according to the logic of reflection. Immediacy is a different order from discourse, we repeat, even if it can only be known through discourse. Not only is immediacy of a different order than discourse, but no discourse will do it justice. Actuality will always be deeper, richer, stronger. John Wild, as quoted in Becker (1964, 57), drives this point home on a personal level:

> Only the real object surpasses us, leads us on, delights us, confuses, and withholds even as it reveals. In the fantasy world our powers grow to extreme proportions: there is nothing we cannot do or understand. But in the real world of objects our powers are tested, opposed, our under-

standings challenged, led on. The real object is the source of the only truth we know, even though we dress it in somewhat different garb. The fantasy object permits us to live in falsehood; it supports our paranoia, our sense of injustice, our perception of evil where we want to see ugliness and evil. Real external objects purify us; they let out the foul gas of our murky images.

This correction can only come about if we let it. We need to understand those many conditions when the novelty in actuality is sacrificed to our nonchanging "totalitarian" egos (Greenwald 1980) and when it is not. A body of knowledge that does not systematically test its theory in the world of praxis—that thinks validation stops with statistical tests—is simply duped by the nominalistic biases of our age.

Words as Actions

One can agree that talk is vital to what it is to be human and must not be categorically separated from some all-important nonverbal action that makes talk into epiphenomenon. One can agree that talking about doing something can be as much of a human act as what will actually be done about it at a later time, even if these acts are contradictory, which we know can be quite likely (Perinbanayagam 1985). But there are still times when "talk is cheap"— when it is reliably unrealistic—when it cannot, in its formulation, take into account the necessary exigencies of actuality. In using the phrase "word and deed" to emphasize the importance between the verbal and the aspect of lived experience that is beyond words, we need to grant that some words such as, "I will marry you" commits the person to an actual change in life that is more than words. Austin (1975) points out that such words "do things more than mere talk." In this sense they are deeds and attest to a continuum from *mere* words to actual deed. To ignore this, as textualism and other discourses often do, is to imply a radical subjectivism that cannot help but turn the mind away from any important semblance of the objective and the real. Shalin (1993, 23) insists that there are failed projects in self-identity:

> If you preach environmentalism, but refuse to recycle your garbage, declare support for trade unions but decline to donate your time, or pronominalize the word "individual" in a gender-inclusive fashion but let your spouse spend the night with a sick child—your identity is bogus, a failed project. If you have practiced what you preach and followed through on your promises on the other hand, you have a demonstrated identity.

Shalin later discusses the repair work needed to sometimes patch the differences between our words and deed, as does Perinbanayagam (1985).

Kenneth Burke (in Gusfield 1998, 79), a father of dramaturgy, explicitly encourages the distinction between word and deed and implicitly rejects the axiom of "all within discourse":

> Still there is a difference, and a radical difference, between building a house and writing a poem about building a house—and a poem about having children by marriage is not the same thing as having children by marriage. There are practical acts and symbolic acts.

Once again, this does not mean that practical acts are not constantly infused with symbolic processes by those enacting them. Burke then grants that the two very often overlap, wherein "practical acts take on a symbolic content." The visceral process of playing a football game may be intoned by the very different symbolic acts of being losers or winners, but this integration hardly negates their important difference. The symbolic act of losing may be worse than physical pain, but it does not, in itself, break legs. Elsewhere Burke warns that we like to forget the kind of relation that really prevails between the verbal and the nonverbal: "In being a link between us and the nonverbal, words are by the same token a screen separating us from the nonverbal" (Burke in Gusfield 1998, 58).

This overlap must be dealt with conceptually. He grants, as do we, that the part of us that gets separated from the nonverbal by the verbal would not exist in the first place without the verbal. An example would be when we say that reality is infinitely bigger than our thoughts could ever encompass. We are implying here that we can never find unity with this incomprehensible "extra-verbal" reality, and at the same time the whole notion of this reality is inconceivable without such verbalization. Nevertheless, Burke finds the distinction too important to ignore even if it has complications. He insists on keeping it and continues with the observation that our most precise terms are sheer emptiness as compared to the things they name: "*Language referring to the realm of the nonverbal is necessarily talk about things in terms of what they are not*" (Burke in Gusfield, 1998, 59, emphasis added). He sees the verbal as analogous to a road map that owes its great utility to its exceptional existential poverty, since it leaves out all detail about the actual trip except for abstract lines. All classes have this selective poverty that is at the same time essential to the conceptual organization of experience.

While words can certainly be deeds, our motivation to go beyond this position is supplied, as we have said, by the transactional approach and its warning to maintain the tension in such dichotomies.

Dramaturgy, and its warranted insistence that symbolic discourse is action vital to the generation of human meaning, does not preclude consideration of actuality, reality, and a world beyond discourse (Perinbanayagam 1985; 2000). Burke, unwittingly or not, illustrates our transactional axiom of breaking down the total opposition between the verbal and nonverbal while keeping their important tension that allows us to learn for ourselves. The symbolic process goes unabated simultaneously with our dealings with a larger actuality. Verbalizations make possible the very general idea of reality, but it is more than plausible from an evolutionary point of view that our ideas originally subserved our actions on this reality. Poststructuralism misses this altogether. This reality (Blumer's obdurate world), which we verbalize in such an abstract and "impoverished" manner, is, however, concretely known only by how it responds to our intentional and effective nonverbal actions on it. This reliable "answering back" on part of the world may be interpreted any number of ways. We have granted this—and indeed, stress its absolute importance as an empirically observable fact. But overall, the symbolic, interpretive process is jolted into action by this impartial "answering back" that is, in itself, nonverbal. In this world of objective consequence, our interpretations can be very wrong, however completely we may deny it. We do not move nature by mere verbalization.

Shalin's Critique of "All Within Discourse" in the Postmodern Literature

In a chapter comparing social behaviorism and classic postmodern literature, Shalin (1993) offers a critique of "all within discourse" that is more true to their own terminology and context than the above. He observes that Derrida sees Charles Saunders Peirce as a precursor for his own grammatology, but Derrida reads him selectively, ignoring the key role that Peirce assigned to action in the signification process. As we have seen, Derrida adapts the Saussurian linguistics that presents meaning as formed by the relation of one word to another word. But Peirce himself decidedly stepped out of discourse to state that the ultimate meaning of any sign consisted of an idea predominantly of feeling or of action and being acted on. This is highly consistent with our stress on deed. Shalin rejects Saussurian textualism, because it cannot incorporate the way objects respond to our sensorimotor actions toward them that is assumed by Ostrow (1990), Halton (1995), and Merleau-Ponty (1962) as well as by the more current work of Lakoff and Johnson (1999). Shalin replies to Saussure with his interpretation of the meaning of red lights to motorists. This meaning is not just to other colored lights;

it is interpreted, and thereby constituted, by motorist's behavior. The signifying process is directed outward, and is constituted by drivers actually stopping at red lights and actually going when they change; otherwise it is in grave danger of losing its full meaning. Shalin, as does Ernest Becker (1964), sees symbols as directives and gadflies, goading us into action. But, as our final chapters will emphasize, it is bodies that act whether this be verbal or nonverbal. Seen from this angle, Shalin summarizes that, "reality is a lot more than a text: it is composed of things and events bound together into a semi-ordered whole by our emotions, beliefs, and deeds." It is contingent on that transformative action that starts with an impulse to act that then selects objects for perceptual attention that are seen as answering to that impulse. This impulse-provoked manipulation is concluded in consummations (Mead 1938). The perceptual thing as an object does not precede action. The physical thing arises in manipulation. As we will discuss further, it may well be the case that we perceive most sagaciously that to which we can act.

CONCLUSION

In conclusion, we need to acknowledge the similarities between our work and that of other current pragmatists who are concerned with the lack of sociological interest in application. Compatibilities with Dmitri Shalin have already been indicated above. Eugene Halton (Rochberg-Halton [1986]; [1995]) also decries the structuralists' location of meaning in a verbal "netherworld" out of reach of human practice. In the pre-Rorty pragmatism he sees a "theory of meaning that has human praxis built into it, a theory that includes embodiment, as well as the bodying forth, of meaning" (Rochberg-Halton 1986). He points to varieties of poststructuralists who "turn world into word" and forget practice in the process. Our volume continues much of his agenda despite drawing on different perspectives.

Farberman (1991), more than a decade ago, voiced serious concern about the "linguistic turn" becoming a U-turn, leading symbolic interaction into a cul-de-sac. This concern was for the same reasons discussed above. He points to the blurring of the line between "reality" and fantasy and the lack of interest in practical or critical concepts. Many ethnographers were, as they still are, arguing against the need for explication of concepts relevant to sociology, because they were embedded in the description for the audience to discover for themselves. These are only some of the commonalties between Farberman and ourselves.

David Maines (1995) has also voiced doubts about not privileging texts. According to Maines, this results in a "believe us, don't believe us" message. In keeping with the pragmatic theme throughout this book, he points to what we see as the extremes of the linguistic turn. "New readings," writes Denzin (1992, 513), ". . . are justified, not because they yield more truth, but because they are new." Maines wonders ". . . if the new is good because it's new and if the old is bad because it is boring, then what do we do if we come up with something old that works?" Denzin's position deflects us from the existence of a world beyond texts that needs a brand of sociological knowledge that is intelligible to those outside the field.

The reader should be reminded that our primary purpose is not to offer a final critique of extant withdrawals into the land of words for word's sake. It suffices for us to point to their wide existence and to suggest that they are symptomatic of a larger world of discursive practices that draws attention away from sociology's relationship with the real world. The still-current inhibition on the use of words such as "reality" affect sociology as a whole and mitigate against practice generally. Our main purpose is to offer a way out of this netherworld, and to plea for a revival of the old pragmatism on two major grounds. First, the transactional foundation of the pragmatism of Mead and Dewey has been largely unread and ignored. Knowledge of this subtext in Mead may render much of the "old" into the "new." Second, our most current knowledge from neuroscience offers a new way of conceiving the theory of mentality in old pragmatism. Like Dewey in particular, neuroscience warns us against the shallowness of a Kantian pure reason and thought for thought's sake. When we admittedly favor these perspectives, we do so in the interest of a more healthy mentality. If this is just another story, such is not our purpose.

NOTES

1. The fact that reading and driving are both actions should not detract from the fact that they are very different kinds of actions (see chapter 3).

2. Many writers would argue that such knowledge is weak in the face of today's powerful social forces. Such futility renders "praxis" into a naïve "dirty" in Halton's terms. This issue notwithstanding, the purpose of this volume is to point out the qualitative difference in cognition that forsakes application and the "tyranny of abstraction" (O'Brien 1989) to which it leads. The purpose is over and beyond our argument that we do not empirically test our theories and benefit from the refinement thereof. However, the two are significantly related. Both avenues form important themes in this book.

3. For another critique of postmodernism concentrating on its disregard for an embodied theory of conception and the embeddedness of thought in the realities demanded by action, see Lakoff and Johnson (1999, 463–68).

4. Social psychology is becoming more and more aware of the importance of the preobjective, nonverbal aspects of lived experience and social interaction. Original arguments for attention to the nonverbal were made by Merleau-Ponty (1962), Polonyi (1962), Sudnow (1979), and Ostrow (1990). Scheff's emphasis (1990) on the speed of social interaction meant that deliberate inner or outer dialogue was too slow to explain what was happening. This set the stage for J. H. Turner's (1999) analysis of the faster-acting brain chemicals involved in lightning-fast gestures that assure that the speaker is the last to know his or her own nonverbal communications.

◙   ◙   ◙

CHAPTER THREE

Thought, Word, and Deed: Toward a Transactional Typology of Action

War nicht das Auge sonnchaft Die Sonne Konnt es nie erblicken.
("If the eye were not sunlike, it could never see the sun.")
—Goethe, as quoted by Konrad Lorenz (1977)

The purpose of this chapter is to systematically explicate what we mean by transaction and how it assumes the primacy of nonverbal motor action. Textualists and others notwithstanding, language is developed out of, and remains in tension with, our sensorimotor, manipulative actions on the world. Drawing from Mead's four-staged theory of the act, the "moment" of manipulation means acting on the world in such a way that desired changes are created; for example, the manipulation of a piece of flint to make a stone tool. As will become clear in other chapters, Lakoff and Johnson (1999) complement and further specify this practical rooting of language in nonverbal behavior, using current developments from neuroscience. This allows us to bring language and even our theory of concepts back down to the realities of our earthly existence where, as we contend, a refined but quite recognizable sense of objectivity is most relevant.

By ending the chapter with a typology of action ranging from the most unconstrained, purely symbolic covert activities to those overt activities most constrained by the dictates of obdurate realities, we offer a way to transcend dualistic problems. The typology of action offered herein allows for a more balanced analysis of knowing and the known, organism and environment, and the subjective/objective relationship. This transactional option for treating hither-to-fore conceived "opposites" as mutually sustaining sides to identical coins is not a fall into Hegelian mysticism. We shall see that transactions and purely symbolic interactions are not the synonyms that some of us take them to be (Dewey and Bentley 1949, 121–24). Some symbolic interactions are transactional and some are not, with important consequences.

One of our goals, especially in part II of this volume, is to indicate how the transactional framework helps to resolve difficult problems arising from several branches of critically oriented social theory—in particular, the Frankfurt School theorists and Jürgen Habermas—as well as various forms of "postmodern" social theory. All of these traditions struggle with the dualisms of the rationalist paradigm, but none provide completely satisfactory answers to the dilemmas that rationalism has bequeathed. The transactional perspective embraces many of the criticisms of rationalism offered by these "emancipatory" approaches, but avoids the troubling implications of their proposed solutions to rationalist dilemmas.

In sum, this chapter builds up to a typology of action that allows one to distinguish between mere words and actual deeds in a way that is nonetheless consistent with the assertions above that words are actions. We would only add that words are actions of a *type* among other types. As the early critical sociologists realized, praxis is an important concept for referencing the world of deed and the reality-testing that symbolically guided deed makes possible. As mentioned above, current professional rhetoric that discourages consideration of objectivity, truth, and reality has also meant that the concept of praxis has fallen into relative disuse in the last 20 years.

THE CONCEPT OF "TRANSACTION"

Transaction was originally coined by Dewey and discussed at length by Dewey and Bentley in *Knowing and the Known* (1949). It is a broad epistemological approach to nature in general, and is one of three models of action and causation. The three models are *self-action, interaction,* and *transaction.* In the history of science, the models represent a type of evolution in sophistication.

Self-Action

Dewey and Bentley describe this model as a prescientific and archaic view that regards things as possessing powers of their own. As Bronowski (1958) puts it: "The medieval mind did not ask why the ripe apple fell to the ground, it was in its nature to do so." This may strike us as an obvious tautology, but it fits a theistic age wherein different facets of nature were created in complete self-sufficiency with their own God-given natures. What did not act through its own power in ways fixed into it was looked upon as being defective. Rather than an object's behavior being dependent on, and qualified by, other elements, it acted as their Creator wound it up to behave. This view is a major obstacle to understanding the social nature of mind, self, and an intentional notion of emotion and rational choice. (See Emirbayer [1997, 283–85] for more examples.) In the felicitous words of Dewey and Bentley (1949, 131), when the animistic self-actional treatments were knocked out of physics, "all the spooks, fairies, essences, and entities that once inhabited portions of matter now took flight to new homes, mostly in or at the human body, and particularly the human brain." Within a Cartesian-like atomism, the mind is often presented as the "old self-acting 'soul' with its immortality stripped off, grown desiccated and crotchety." When mind is seen as directing a specific behavior, one must assume a model of causation that substitutes a name for an explanation in the tautological model of the Middle Ages (see Dewey and Bentley 1949, 131–32). Positing a resident "psyche" or mind within the organism that initiates and thus explains behavior is now seen as ancient custom in the history of social psychology, but its converse is still popular, which is: "according to which the organism is wholly passive, and is generally molded into shape . . . by independent environmental conditions" (Dewey and Bentley 1949). Both views are equally nonproductive. Certainly, leading writers in neuroscience agree that the object seen is as much the result of what our brains do, as it is the result of what objects do.

Neither should we be deluded that the self-actional imagery has been dismissed from contemporary theorizing, as implied above. Elias (1978) and more recently Sampson (1981), Baumeister (1986), Sarbin (in Harré 1986), Scheff (1990), and Geertz (1979) have mounted rear-guard attacks on our ideologically tinged concept of the self-contained, autonomous person.[1] Though they all have been influential, it can hardly be said that they have won the day. Elias has suggested that our notion of the autonomous individual with independently formed will, motivations, and interests is intuitively recognized as valid only because of the alien-

ated, anomic conditions of present Western society. The concept reso-
nates with our emotional state and feeling of isolation, where so many
insist that freedom means an across-the-board right to do as they please.

Interaction

Interactional views of nature won attention through Newton, who
allegedly saw the descent of the ripened apple as a phenomenon that
acted relative to effects of other particles outside of it and in turn
affected them. Not only does the moon pull the earth's waters into tides,
but also the gravitational pull of the earth keeps the moon in orbit.
Whereas the image of mutual effects upon discretely existing elements
marks an advance in scientific models, units are still unequivocally independent in terms of origin and existence. In the final analysis, interaction
as a model of nature still views the world as being comprised of individual things balanced against other independent things in causal intercon-
nection. According to Emirbayer (1997, 285–86), "Entities remain fixed
and unchanging throughout such interaction, each independent of the
existence of others, much like billiard balls. . . ." The interpenetration of
elements is limited to mutual causal influence. Variable analysis assumes
an interactional position (Emirbayer 1997, 286). The variables or elements are not viewed as inherently implicated in the existence of the
other. Here, accurate correlations depend on independence.

Transaction

It is important to understand the atomism that is implied in Dewey
and Bentley's critique, because this deficiency poses the problem that
made a fully transactional view necessary and provided its raison d'être.
The inadequacy of the concept interaction led Stone and Farberman
(1970, 149) to prefer the term "social behaviorism" over "symbolic interaction" as stated above. Considering the wide currency of the latter,
however, they settled for using it with explicit recognition of its inadequacies. The transactional viewpoint marks the level of sophistication
represented by the transactional relativity of Einstein, Eddington, and
Heisenberg in physics as well as Wittgenstein in social science. This
level of inquiry avoids attributing action to independent self-actors or
even to independently interacting elements.

RELATIONALISM IN TRANSACTION. The transactional viewpoint rests on
the assumption of an interlocking fusion of organism and environment
whereby one side of this coin is given its very character by the other side
(Mead 1922, 157). This can be referred to as the *relational* aspect of

transaction that forms its core. Mead gives the example of an antelope bounding through the Savanna. It becomes that part of the environment known as food only in relationship to some other animal that has the capacity to eat it. Tree bark is not food for us. But it becomes food for a deer that brings to its experience a different set of taste buds, teeth, and digestive tract. Environmentally supplied food, then, is inseparably determined by organismic "sensitivities." In Mead's terms (1922, 159), "food exists as an immediate experience (only) in relation to the individuals that eat it." There is no such thing as food apart from such individuals. In this manner, the dualistic hiatus between organism and environment is overcome.

Relational here is to be distinguished from a *relativity* suggesting that "anything goes." Mead insists on a notion of constraint and objectivity within the relational world carved out for our experience by our own senses, organs, and impulses:

> The causal effect of living organisms on their environment in creating objects is as genuine as the effect of environment upon the living organism. A digestive tract creates food as truly as the advance of a glacial cap wipes out some animals or selects others that can grow warm coats of hair. (Mead 1922, 160)

The relational aspect of transaction reminds us that any talk about environments as separate from the actions and capacities of the organisms that act on them is a dangerous abstraction.[2] The way this fusion is achieved is by viewing environmental objects as those features that *answer to*, or sustain, the particular capacities of the organism to act toward them. Thus, organism and environment, nature and nurture are inseparably joined with each other. Morris, in his introduction to Mead's work (1967, xxi), offers this transactional statement on value: "Value is the character of an object in its capacity to satisfy an *interest* . . . it resides neither in the object alone or in the . . . state of the subject" (emphasis added). In formulating transactional statements of the organism/environment relation, the organism's *interest* is an outcome of its physiological sensitivities and capacities. The three words, *interest, sensitivity*, and *impulse* (capacity), are almost synonymous in this context. Furthermore, they are viewed as a product of the evolutionary transactional process to begin with. Even their source is inseparable from the environmental characteristics that originally shaped them. In the human organism, the distinctive capacity for symbolic reactivity is overlaid on our physical sensitivities. But transactionally, this broadening of sensitivity on the part of the organism must also be recognized as a broadening of its environment. Mead addresses this point in a classic transactional passage:

> The individual organism determines in some sense its own environment by its sensitivity. The only environment to which the organism can react is one that its sensitivity reveals. If . . . there is an increase in the diversity of sensitivity there will be an increase in the responses of the organism to its environment that is; the organism will have a larger environment. (Mead 1934, 245)

THE SIGNIFICANCE OF ACTION IN THE TRANSACTIONAL FRAMEWORK. In the quotation above, Mead implies a point that is critical to his larger argument. Responses are seen as "intervening variables" through which the increase in sensitivity in the above quotation is translated into a larger perceptual environment. That is, sensitivities (interests and capacities) affect the organism's environment only insofar as they "move beyond themselves" in manipulative action to shape adaptive behavior.

Sensitivities that are not objectively enacted remain self-contained. To treat the organism's sensitivities as independent of reality-testing action fosters the very subject–object split that Mead and his colleagues were attempting to avoid.[3] Again, to quote Dewey and Bentley (1949, 69) on transaction: "The interpenetration of the old dualism is revealed by avoiding the tendency to name characteristics of organisms alone, or environments alone, in every case they name the *activity* that occurs of both together" (emphasis added). Such is hardly the language of textualism and its variants.

We make a grave mistake if we overlook the significance of action at just this point. If we focus on the sensitivity (i.e., a digestive tract) as a self-contained entity without attention to its affect on the organism's behavior on the world, we will be drawn into the very subjectivism that Mead labored so hard to avoid. A major problem with this subjectivism and the self-actional perspective it embraces is that it places mind and body in contradictory, diametrically opposed realms that force a choice between one or the other. Again, must we really choose between the reality and significance of continuity or change, abstract thought or sensation, universal or particular? Experience is of both, and the task of inquiry is to illuminate both.

While some thinkers through intellectual history started, as did Descartes, with the subjective knower and tried to proceed from there to understand the "objective" world, others like Wundt started with the objective world in order to discover the nature of inner consciousness.

The problem with these approaches has been that they become "stuck inside of themselves," as it were. It becomes difficult to formulate satisfactory accounts of the other dimension. The subjectivists have difficulty getting over to the objective side of the coin, and the objectivists have difficulty getting over to the subjective side. As a result, they both become one-sided accounts of existence.

Such is the weakness of the self-actional perspective that Mead and his colleagues avoided by their transactional approach. Its relevancy for critiquing much of the "linguistic turn" should be clear. Manis and Meltzer (1978, 12) are alluding to the inadequacies of self-actional models when they describe Mead's quarrel with the tendency shared by rationalists and empiricists to see mind as a fixed substantial entity existing as a box-like container full of images, which mirror an external reality.

Mead's way out of this intellectual morass was to start with action as behavior *toward* something, much as the European thinkers had transcended Descartes's subjectivism by insisting that consciousness is always conscious *of* something. The "intentional" quality of action points to experiences beyond itself (Lewis 1979, 142; Franks and Seeberger 1980). In positing a transactional relationship from the very beginning, the loggerhead created by having to work one's way out of a subjective or objective self-container was eliminated. According to Tibbetts (1974, 116), in order to escape this "bridging problem," the pragmatists rejected the view that the subject–object relation was primarily a cognitive relation. Tibbetts illustrates this by reference to Dewey and Bentley's (1949) plea to discard the term "knower" in favor of "knowings." These processes were then defined in terms of phases of transactionally observed behaviors rather than by reference to cognitive states or other less intensely behavioral events. By taking the act as primary, Mead could define subject and object, perceiving and perceived in terms of phases or dimensions of the act (Tibbetts 1974, 116). By addressing subject and object as phases of action, what were once seen as dichotomies precluding and undermining each other's realities were avoided. By beginning with action as a "neutral datum" that was neither mental nor physical, thought nor thing, the idealism–realism controversy was rendered irrelevant (Tibbetts 1974, 117).

For example, a leading pragmatist, Charles Morris, illustrates how Mead avoids the old hiatus between the intangible universal and the tangible particular. Both are seen as simply different phases of the same act rather than one coming from a preexisting mental realm and another from a separate physical realm:

> Objects have universality in relation to an act capable of being furthered
> by various objects or aspects of objects. The objects have universality in
> relation to the act which they indifferently support; the act has univer-
> sality as the character of being supported indifferently by a range of
> objects. (Morris in Mead 1967, xxvii)

Mead took universality down from its Platonic source in a mysterious realm of eternal forms and conceived of it as a derivative of the
observable world of everyday action. By so doing he sought to avoid the
antithesis of mind and body, being and becoming that has proved fatal to
theorists from Plato to Whitehead (see also Morris in Mead 1967, xxviii).

THE CONSTRAINING CONSEQUENCES OF ACTION AS THE NEUTRAL DATUM. Many
symbolic interactionists notwithstanding, and with appreciation for the
place of creative interpretation and profound relativity in social behaviorism, Meadian thought should not blind us to his insistence on equal
attention to the more objective side of the transactional coin. Mead's
interest in avoiding self-actional subjectivism carries with it *ipso facto*
the necessity of avoiding extreme relativism. Mead used the phrase "acts
indifferently" or "impartially supported by a world that is there" on too
many occasions for them to be an insignificant choice of words (see the
quotation above). Packed into his repeated reliance on these two quali-
fiers is the recognition that the physical world imposes its own terms on
us. These terms stand aloof and over against us. But this very indifference
also produces the recurrence that makes possible human prediction. As
stated before, fully felt meaning is not built up through words alone but
by our own nonverbal actions. By symbolically noting which of our goal-
directed actions are reliably "furthered" by the dependable responses
they trigger in this world, generalized knowledge is created. We do not
create or symbolically construct the indifferent answering of the world to
the actions we bring forth to it. We symbolically interpret them and we
perceive them selectively, but we do not initiate them. If we are to survive
a 200-foot drop into the ocean, we must enter that ocean in one of the
very few ways that its terms allow. However, from ten feet, it will answer
back benignly to any number of entries from belly flops to cannonballs.
Unlike sociologists with no comparable avenue for testing their "verbal
approaches," divers from high cliffs deal constantly with a world not of
their making.

Regardless of Goffman's (1959) legitimate emphasis on the interpersonal management of symbolic interpretations, inanimate nature is
surely dumb and powerful: words do not cajole or deter her; the avalanche rumbles despite our most fervent prayers. Here we live in a world

of real success and real losses—we make mistakes and pay the consequences. We act in accordance with what supports our intents and judge these actions as efficacious by criteria stemming from processes *we do not make*. Divers and skiers relate to environments that are aptly and unproblematically described as objective and real. In such a world, even truths can and must be recognized. In a world of words where meanings are simply consensual, these words are not as relevant. "Objectivity" means only shared abstraction. The criteria to decide what is "real" or "true" are lost.

When Mead brought the universal down from the "heavenly spheres" and placed it in the nonmystical, evolutionary process of manipulation and cooperation, he had to forsake both the subjectivism and unfettered relativism of many current symbolic interactionists and extreme social constructionists. In order to fully understand the objective aspect of Mead's thought, we must see how behavior is constrained by at least three interlocking conditions. They are: 1) prerequisites for survival in the evolutionary process, 2) the limited number of effective means to any end in the world of action, and 3) the constraints imposed by significant symbols in the process of role-taking with objects in the social or physical environment.

Since there is general recognition of Mead's commitment to a Darwinian framework, there is no need to document this here. The constraint this system places on action and the symbols that subserve it has been generally ignored. Even though we no longer live in a social Darwinian environment, as long as we interact with the world, not just "anything goes." Without the criteria of physical and emotional constraint, we can think and imagine anything we want—the symbolic possibilities are limitless. But as soon as we become oriented to instrumental action and/or the manipulative stage of the act, the possibilities become limited. Once we leave the subjective world of inner imagination and commit to intentional actions in a world that responds to us indifferently, we realize that only those actions are valuable that are supported and furthered by forces we do not make. Certainly Mount Everest imposes limitations on actions directed to reaching its peak even with the aid of helicopters, and hunting large animals in the unprotected expanse of the tundra places certain limits as well as demands on the hunter.

Involvement in the manipulative stage of the act, social or physical, most often means we must get out of our skins, out of our own fantasy where our own symbolic possibilities are endless, and into a world that imposes terms on us. If we are to make manifest our symbolic intentions, we cannot just think and do anything. We are limited to that range of actions supported and furthered by the way the social and material world answers back to our actions in it.[4]

Note in the following quote how Mead's rejection of the self-actional model of the disembodied linguist also embroils him in a clear rejection of rampant relativism (Mead 1934, 74):

> If you conceive of mind as just . . . a conscious substance in which there are certain impressions and states . . . then a word becomes purely arbitrary—it is just a symbol. . . . You can pronounce [it] backwards, as children do; there seems absolute freedom of arrangement. . . . If you recognize that language is . . . a part of a co-operative process, that part which leads to an adjustment to the response of the other so that the activity can go on, *then language has only a limited range of arbitrariness.* (emphasis added)

Here we see how Mead realizes the constraints imposed by the indifferent—that is, impersonal—dictates of social cooperation and effective action. It should seem obvious at this point that action here has an intentional quality to it that is directed outward beyond one's own self-reflection and inner fantasy.

But to see meaning and definitions of situations as constituted solely through symbols divorced from their function of guiding efficacious action is to reduce symbolic interaction to the very subjectivist nominalism and radical relativism that a transactional framework was designed to avoid. At a later point we will discuss the critical place of resistance in a behaviorist theory of perception. Leslie White's (1949, 22) phrase "in the word was the beginning" to the contrary, in the beginning is the *act*. Originally, this act formed a purely motor process out of which words were later derived (see also Perinbanayagam 1985). The relationship between actor and the inanimate-object world discussed here as motor activity may seem too narrow in scope for describing the symbolic animal. Further chapters describe current knowledge about how higher levels of cognition derive from sensorimotor activity. It is basic to transaction that the emergence of the significant symbol presupposes an animal already linked together with its kind in socially organized behaviors—that language and thought are made possible only in the prior context of cooperative instrumental activity. The necessity of asserting such priority to avoid a subjectivist position will be clarified below.

In sum, Mead's position implies an important level of action or interaction that is concretely separable from purely verbal activity when he deals with the developmental context of human thought. Insofar as a large proportion of our actions must have an "intentional" quality to them, directed to a "world out there" that answers only to those human actions geared to the indifferent terms that we do not dictate—insofar as this is true, social behaviorism recognizes a fundamental difference between actions geared to instrumental activity and mere thinking. This is imperative for a transactional framework that avoids an exclusive emphasis on subjectivism and nominalism.

Transaction *and the Objective Reality of Perspectives*

Mead (1959, 161) combines his relationalism and his stress on the objective constraints placed on instrumental action in the notion of the "objective reality of perspectives." In order to clarify the place of this concept within a transactional framework, we will again return to Dewey and Bentley:

> If interaction assumes the organism and its environmental objects to be present as substantially separate forms of existence prior to their entry into joint investigation, then transaction assumes no pre-knowledge of either organism or environment alone . . . but requires their acceptance in a common system. (1949, 123)

The "objective reality of perspectives" specifies the nature of this common system. On the one hand, the system is the character of the environment that enables it to receive and support—to answer to and consummate—the intentional actions that the organism brings forward. On the other hand, the common system is also the capacity of the organism to call out such a response to its intentions. Every organism is biologically equipped to pay predominant attention to certain stimuli to the exclusion of others. We have seen that every organism has its characteristic capacity to react to environmental distinctions that the other cannot. The capacity of these stimuli to answer to the sensitivities and actions of the organism is referred to as the *patience* of nature. The principles allowing for this mutuality or patience constitute a perspective: Dewey and Bentley's common system. It is this patience in nature that Lorenz's quote so aptly captures: "If the eye were not sunlike, it could never see the sun." The character of the sun that produces light waves and the character of the eye in receiving these waves form an objective slab that is "there in nature"—what Whitehead and Mead refer to as a *consentient* set. This set, slab, or common system would presumably arise within the evolution of the organism transacting with a sun-filled world. The streamlined form of the shark reflects the flow of water from which it evolved and the chiseled teeth of the beaver reflect the mal-

leability of the wood into which these teeth cut. Such a perspective is
not a mere distortion or "selective bias" that carves out for our attention
only one slice of the totality of a preexisting nature. Perspectives are, of
course, relational, but these relations have been formed in nature and
whether we are conscious of them or not, they are "objectively there."
Objective perspectives are "transactional slabs" enduring in nature
itself, but always relative to the action-capacities of the organisms
enabled by the aspects of the environment that "further" them. Thus, the
perspective carried out by the sensitivities and behavioral capacities of
a fly with its microscopic eyes differs from that of a dog whose long nose
obfuscates the view already blurred by eyes that poorly discriminate colors and whose four legs keep it firmly rooted anyway toward ground
smells. (See Dennett [1996] for a neuroscience point of view here.)
These two perspectives of the fly and the dog differ greatly from that of
homo sapiens. The latter's upright posture, converging eyes on a flat
face, and relatively underdeveloped ear and nose fix them in a world of
splendid variations in color, while impoverishing their organic capacities
to discriminate noises and smells.

Thus, the outside ranges of the worlds made available by these perspectives are *objectively* limited by nature. Every animal lives in its distinct world that, while relative to its capacities, is objectively "there in
nature." The objective reality of perspectives is then inseparable from a
transactional framework. We can see this clearly in Mead's statement:

> The process by which the organism has arisen is . . . one in which the
> organism has determined its field by its dependence between the two.
> This is expressed in the term "perspective." . . . The conception of a
> world . . . independent of any organism is one without perspectives. . . .
> There would be no objects except physical particles, for every other
> object involves abstractions from relations that are as real as those in
> the object and in the environment, and the only ground for such ab-
> straction can be found in the attitude of some . . . structure which main-
> tains itself through a patience of the world to that structure. (1959,
> 163–65)

In the human case, the common system or perspective that made it
possible for members of a society to share worlds did not originate full-
blown from a linguistic capacity that was born of itself. Mead (1959, 167)
clearly roots it in activity independent of, and prior to the emergence of,
symbolic processes. Communication is a social process whose natural
history shows that it arises out of cooperative activities such as those
involved in sex, parenthood, fighting, herding, and the like. Currently,

many argue that language arises out of emotional communications (J. H. Turner 2000).

In this manner, according to Goff (1980), the temporal priority of action as distinct from symbolic thought is established. The importance of the theoretical priority of action in its broadest sense will emerge below.

TOWARD A TYPOLOGY OF ACTION
FROM THOUGHT TO DEED

As in all analytical pursuits, monolithic definitions must give way to specification. Austin (1975) and, more currently, Butler (1997) distinguish types of verbal actions as *performative, illocutionary,* and *perlocutionary* (see the above discussion of Burke's interest in the nonverbal). The specification that is reflected in the following typology derives from our discussion of transaction and Peirce's quote mentioned earlier that the world is learned in two phrases: mastery and limitation, capacity and resistance. The pairs here are obviously implicated in each other. Thus the most important end points on the continuum from the first through the fifth levels of action are arranged according to the amount of resistance to be overcome and concomitantly the amount of competency demanded by way of the situations. Other dimensions include the amount of effort and focalized attention demanded, as well as the situation's potential for surprise and its significance for one's identity. As with all continuum thinking, the boundaries marking the five levels must be somewhat arbitrary and the levels must be seen as "family resemblances" rather than being categorical, with no overlap. These categories are not meant to be reified. Below, it is assumed that human acts are social though our discussion focuses on additional attributes of constraints.

We take our lead here from Dewey's ([1925] 1958) analysis of the fully meaningful experience that he sees as a balance between "doing" and "undergoing." (By the latter, he means "reflection.") In the doing phase of experience the emphasis is on the actor's experience as a locus of cause— of manipulation, of bringing things about, of making things happen. The undergoing phase refers to a self-reflective registering of experience wherein action is delayed as one mentally absorbs the consequences of his enacted impulses and its significance for the self-system: "Unbalance on either side blurs the perception of relations and leaves the experience partial and distorted" (Dewey [1925] 1958, 44). A preemptive lust for action leaves persons with experiences of superficial paucity characteristic of the "sociopath" (Becker 1964). A preemptive focus on reflective

undergoing may produce rich fancies and impressions, but this experience is devoid of sagacious judgment or appreciation for practical realities and the intangible sensitivities of people who have actually "been
there"— who have, in Dewey's terms, "suffered" the real experience.[5]

With important exceptions like panic and prognostication, it is often
easier to imagine than to do. In the world of doing, let us say writing,
unexpected irrelevancies arise that are tempting distractions; digres-
sions suggest themselves in terms of enrichments. These were not present in the image prior to doing. It is devoid of embodied exhaustion,
boredom, finger-cramping, and a stiff back. Actual dealing with these
unforeseen resistances requires greater "perceptibility" than mere
thought. Without actual embodiment, "an experience" in Dewey's sense
remains incomplete.

In the previous chapter we stressed the amount of unpredictability of
immediate contact with the lived experience, or actuality. Thoughts also
surprise us, but with important exceptions we can dismiss or change
them. Deeds, as distinct from thoughts, have to cope with this. Actual
events are usually better or worse than we imagine. As a matter of fact,
they are often better *and* worse at the same time. Sexual experiences
can be a case in point. As our thoughts are committed to writing, problems of qualification and expression come to mind that were not confronted when pencil and paper were taken in hand to write. For example, in the immediacy of writing this text, we have to decide whether it
is necessary to include a sentence granting that life has to have enough
predictability to make effective responses possible. And then we need to
decide whether to be more specific about the *kind* of "subtle" unpredictability we are discussing. The writer stops to ponder the choice of a
word. He is surprised at the need to control his urge to spend pages on
this little exercise. He had none of this "in mind" when he started; yet it
describes precisely the distinction between thinking about writing and
the more intense writing as deed. Now that this much has been submit-
ted to paper, the need to make a further distinction becomes evident that
was not evident before. Writing may be an overt action and share therefore the quality of *deed*, but it certainly needs to be placed somewhere
below the mid-point on a continuum between inner thought and dealing
with what we call social and/or physical reality. There is surely a difference between manipulating words on paper and dealing effectively with
concrete people. An important difference is that when dealing only with
words, one only has to be "careful" to handle one's own idiosyncrasies
and speak to the impersonal "generalized other" of some reference
group. With concrete others, at least two sources of immediate idiosyn-

crasies must be considered: one's own as well as the other's. It is also of significance that the writer can erase his or her words, but to erase a social blunder is ultimately the prerogative of others.

At least with people, we can negotiate another chance. This is more than we can do with a mountain avalanche, a riptide, or the awful finality of the bullet shot in an instant of rage. It is at this point that we have come again to the importance of resistance—more specifically, different degrees of recalcitrance.

The First Level of Action

On the lowest level of action, we are thinking about something and are often using our active powers to assess alternatives. We either automatically or with awareness force ourselves minimally to be constrained by impersonal rules or logic (e.g., the norm of rational efficiency or those of "due process"). To the extent that we are manipulating these rules consciously, guiding our thought by the terms they impose and using our self-powers, we are engaged in a some "low-level" doing, even if our behavior is internal and not yet made manifest or objectified. Thinking requires effort and can result in physical tiredness. As de Sousa (1987) reminds us, we drink coffee for the physiological value of caffeine in order to stay alert. Even here, thought is embodied to some extent. On this lowest level, the constraints are up to us to ignore or not. We operate more within our own terms.

The Second Level of Action

In placing thought on paper, we usually enter into another level. For most persons, it is harder to write than to simply think, though at times writing can be used to help thought. This observation has been detailed above. While we can be surprised at the point where our logic leads us, writing for audiences other than ourselves increases the motive for role-taking and thus choosing words with more care. It frequently necessitates dealing with the constraints of grammar and vocabulary. It adds a new level of surprise, as viewing our words forces new thoughts to emerge and new decisions to be made. By making the idea permanent, more reflection is possible and more complexities must be handled. In short, more potential resistance must be overcome than with private thought. Writing letters and memos and the like still lacks the quality of concrete face-to-face interaction with another person. Writing to workers that they are being terminated when their offices are nearby can be seen as a "cop-out." One does not have to deal with the feelings of the other person—at least not in that moment. In face-to-face situations we deal with real persons who often place immediate, embodied terms on us and are capable of genuine surprise. This is why television characters cannot be "friends" to the audience, some writers to the contrary. Granted, they can surprise us, but without instrumental consequence. Diaries, of course, should be placed as a subcategory of inner dialogue. After all, no one has to see it—and thus we do not have to deal as much with the "resistance" of others' actual responses.

The Third Level of Action

Talking to others is the public announcement of self. It is the everyday manifestation of who we are. As we have seen, there is a lot at stake. In this sense it is "doing" on the verbal level. Butler (1997) discusses how we injure persons with talk. At this level, we open-up ourselves more to contingencies inherent in the interactive process. Here, unless we are all-powerful, we must control our own idiosyncrasies as well as considering those of others. In relatively egalitarian situations, our effectiveness in announcing our identities is dependent on our social skills and manipulative powers. However, the outcome, insofar as we stake ourselves on others' responses, is once again ultimately in their control. We are always potentially vulnerable to human capriciousness. This can also be true for previous levels, but it prevails more consistently at the level of talk. Surprise is common and puts a premium on our ability to deal with it immediately. The confrontation with the immediate realities of other persons has a unique potential for calling forth change and development in the individual.

The Fourth Level of Action

The fourth level of action can only partially be captured by the word "deeds." It has to do with putting our thought and/or words to work and making them actually happen. Ideally, there is a tendency for task-oriented interactions to challenge the predominance of identity-oriented interactions (Turner 1968). This level involves the practical world of objective application; it is impervious to favoritism; like the avalanche, it cannot be cajoled. With no dispensation to make amends, this world frequently gives us but one chance. Above all, it is the final activity whereby our ideational intentions to provoke specific changes in a world standing indifferently against us are made into actuality. It is important to see that this activity is the final instrumental endpoint of adaptive consummations in Mead's four-staged theory of the act. We will remember that these phases are impulses to action, perception, manipulation, and consummation. The scholar who writes about the world must draw on a sizable amount of competencies and self-powers, but the kind of action referred to in the fourth level must transcend mere writing, which is something we have argued most sociologists fail to do. In this scheme, the phrase "statistical tests of group differences" hides the dearth of actual tests that can only be those of practical application—of using this knowledge to produce desired changes in an indifferent environment and refining our theory on this basis. The "real" test according to the theory of praxis is in the registering of the objective consequences of our actions. Indeed, on the individual level, consequences that are the result of focalized attention, intended effort, persistence, and our own self-powers are experienced differently than events that just passively happen to us (White 1965). An example of level four activity would be that involved with "edgework" (Lyng 1990b) wherein actors seek the most demanding and unforgiving activities in which to test their competencies, including the overcoming of fear.

The Fifth Level of Action

Finally, a fifth level of action can be identified, which brings us to the principal domain of sociological inquiry: the study of institutional patterns of society and culture. We must emphasize again that the distinctions contained within the typology are merely analytic and therefore not to be understood as "objectively" given. Thus, by adding a fifth level to the typology, we seek to distinguish various dimensions or facets of action referred to as "praxis"—understood as reflective action put to work for the satisfaction of human ends. The concept of praxis allows us to understand the concept of "reality" as a human product, but also as parts of the social and physical universe that answer indifferently to human action. Hence, the "objective world" is treated here as one side of a dialectical relationship established by an ongoing process, which is described by Marx (1964b, 157) as the "humanizing of nature and the naturalizing of man."

In conceiving of praxis as intentional action to bring about changes in the social world, we have seen that the ideational forms through which we perceive and know the world cannot be separated from interest-oriented action to achieve specific ends (Ollman 1971). An equally important "moment" of praxis is the social dimension of the act. Rather than separating the individual and society as do traditional sociological perspectives, a transactional conception makes no ontological distinction between these two levels. As human beings interact with nature to fulfill their needs, they engage in action that is naturally and necessarily social. This implies that "reality is not inextricably bound up with *indi-*

vidual activity, but that this activity must be comprehended in terms of its social character" (Goff 1980, 28). Thus the objects of action in our final level are social and cultural structures. While action at the collective or structural level can reveal the same transactional features that characterize action at less emergent levels, the institutional realm offers us much greater complexity than the domains heretofore considered. This complexity can be attributed in part to the fact that the institutional domain subsumes all of the other levels of action. When individuals engage in collective action to solve survival problems by participating in a division of labor and other institutional structures, they not only deal with the resistance of a world of material forces, but also the interactional world of individuals cooperating to achieve collective goals. Thus the individual's experience in the institutional domain represents the most pronounced confrontation with an objective world of resistance to his or her actions. Indeed, the resistances of the institutional order can be properly conceptualized as the realm of "social constraints" existing in dialectical opposition to "spontaneous" human action, a dialectic emphasized by both Marx and Mead (Blake 1976; Lyng 1990a).

From a transactional perspective, a key problem in analyzing the institutional order is to understand how social and cultural forms either solve or fail to solve problems of human survival, and to identify the social processes that give rise to either of these outcomes. What drives the institutionalization process, in this view, are collectivities seeking to apply, elaborate, or modify the stock of existing cultural knowledge and socialized capacities to deal with unique problems arising in particular historical epochs.

As with problem solving at all levels, the historically specific reality to which these collective efforts are directed responds indifferently to the institutional action and the various knowledge systems that inform this action.

CONCLUSION

Much more can be said about the nature of the institutional patterns that constitute the fifth level of action in our typology, but the present discussion is sufficient to achieve the primary purpose of this chapter—to distinguish types of human action in terms of their transactional characteristics. If action proceeds and in a real sense affects perceptions, we must come to grips with the differences in resistances that types of action must overcome. This discussion represents only a start in that direction.

From a transactional perspective, it is understood that we perceive
most clearly what we have the capacity to act toward. We selectively
perceive that which answers to the "telos" of our actions or tendencies.
Our active behavioral repertories greatly influence what is most salient
in our awareness. This is another sense in which behavior is prior to perception. The reflective registering of consequences from the behavioral
world of praxis feeds back to create change in self-knowledge. A typology of action allows us to analyze the various modes of experience and
perception that result from a preponderance of personal (and social/cul-
tural) choices in favor of one level of action over another (see chapters
5 and 8). For example, the "hyper-cognized" mentality of our age and its
tyranny of abstraction may well be a case in point. Dewey's assumption
was that as we develop efficacious ways to act towards objects, the
object world is reduced to clarity; perceptions are made more refined,
more lucid, and richer in quality. If the "higher" levels of action call out
our capacities in a different and perhaps more demanding way than
other types of action, then we can hypothesize that perceptions will be
made more sagacious thereby (see Becker 1964).

NOTES

1. The very opposite extreme occurs in poststructuralist theorizing that min-
imizes, and sometimes obliterates, the self. This is to us a form of textualism
wherein "language speaks the person" and so on. There is, of course, truth in this
observation. But to negate the person is a consequence of the "all within discourse" axiom. Transaction roots the self significantly in manipulative action
(see also the neuroscientist Damasio [1999] and Lakoff and Johnson [1999]).
Only *bodies* guided by selves act on the world outside of discourse.

2. This is precisely what textualism does: It focuses on language and even
concepts as self-contained and irrelevant to the objective constraints found in
the world of manipulative action. The viability of the term "objective" hardly has
a place in this kind of untempered subjectivism.

3. Herein is a not-too-implicit criticism of the linguistic idealism that Rorty
questioned in parts of the linguistic turn.

4. The process of role-taking, of course, has allowed us the distinctively
human capacity to get outside of ourselves in order to mesh our own actions
with terms imposed by both physical things and other people. Effective action
requires that we implicitly respond to our own conduct prior to the response of
the object to us. This is the general principle of a voluntaristic model of behavioral control: self-control means that we respond to our own actions in a very
prescribed and objective way—namely, that way in which the external person or
thing would respond. Only then can our self-responses be used to monitor and
guide our own behavior in effective ways. In sum, both social custom and the

indifferent nature of the physical world impose limitations on efficacious actions demanded by a behavioristic scheme. Current theorizing has become more sensitive to the embodiment of social interaction and implies qualifications in specifying situations that foster such deliberate self-consciousness, as do some forms of role-taking. If the demands and speed of social interaction make "athletes" of us all, deliberation must be a "sometimes" affair. Role-taking is also often intuitive. Nonetheless, as reflective animals, we are indeed capable of deliberate role-taking with others as well as with physical objects. It is a process critical to our social character.

5. This qualitative difference between mentalities largely forged through "making things happen" in an impartial world of application and mentalities formed primarily by playing words on other words is emphasized by Dewey more than Mead. Though we allude to it in this chapter, various ways of conceptualizing this difference are elaborated on in chapter 5 and by using examples from neuroscience to emphasize its importance.

◙   ◙   ◙

CHAPTER FOUR

A Relational View of Subjectivity and Objectivity

This chapter redefines objectivity in a way consistent with our transactional theme. By so doing, objectivity may become more compatible to those who appreciate the subjective component of life and think beyond dictionary definitions. We will then apply our redefinition to a general view of emotion that is no longer seen as the opposite of the objective, but as having objective as well as subjective dimensions. The many meanings of both terms necessitate knowing which of their various senses are being used at the moment. Therefore this chapter spells out these senses. The importance of both words is only matched by the confusion they create, because their diverse meanings usually remain outside of awareness. We need to see how the same statement is objective in one sense, but subjective in another. To speak of *the* subjective and *the* objective can be useful simplifications as long as we remember that they take on meaning only in terms of each other and that we can seldom, if ever, find them in their pure forms. A completely detached analysis having no subjective interest to speaker or listener—that is to say, about which no one cared—would be of dubious use to anyone and, as we shall see, quite impossible anyway. This is not the place for categorical thinking.

In this chapter emotions are seen as real, insofar as they offer harsh resistance in the face of the actor's efforts to change them. We may be mistaken about how we *label* our feelings, but the feeling is an embodied and thus real experience. This characteristic of emotion is followed up in chapter 6, which is about the body as transactionally subjective and objective. The lack of coherent meaning for objectivity, subjectivity, and reality has caused confusion in the Western world concerning a variety of important subjects ranging from scientific objectivity to emotion. This is especially true when emotion is seen as a self-actual, solely psychological process unrelated to anything outside of itself.

Looked at transactionally, the particular subjective experience of the passage of time and objectively measured time, clearly presuppose each other. Without an abstract, impersonal conception of 50 minutes, how could we know that our classes may "fly by" for engaged professors, but "creep by at such a petty pace" for some of our less engaged students. In this case, the whole notion of the subjective as idiosyncratic would be impossible without presupposing the objective 50 minutes from which "flying by" and "creeping by" are measured as different. In a transactional scheme, objectivity and subjectivity are so intertwined it is impossible to keep the discussion of one separated from the other. Lorenz (1977) notes the somewhat confusing origin of the two words. It is a mark of their imprecision that they have exchanged meanings since the age of scholasticism. In our present usage, the word *subjective* means the experiencing, thinking, feeling agent, as opposed to the objects about which the agent experiences, thinks, and feels. Literally, subjective used to mean "that which is thrown under" in the sense of a foundation on which the whole world is based. It is strange that for the most vital, most dynamic force there is in the world, we should have found no better term than *subjective*, a passive participle! How is it that from this word "subject," denoting the foundation of all knowledge and experience, we derive the adjective "subjective," defined as illusory, fanciful, arbitrary, and prejudiced? And how, in what is obviously a misguided devaluation of the subjective, have we arrived at our higher estimate of what is popularly called *objective*, or, which is the same thing, corresponding to something real? *Objicere* means to "throw towards." An object is something thrown in our path, something that opposes and obstructs us. This "resistance" to our desires will become extremely important in the discussion below of the objective. Despite the fact that the subjective and objective are only analytically inseparable, the subheadings below indicate the many meanings of both. In what follows, the subjective is illustrated by the emotional, but as the reader will see, neither the subjective nor emotion is seen as purely separable from some sense of the objective.

Popular Meanings of Subjectivity and Objectivity

There is no limit to the irony of the use of the term *objectivity*. It connotes firmness and lack of ambiguity, yet its meanings are anything but. Its various usages have to be taken in context, usually without awareness of what we are doing so that we are insulated from its ambiguity. At the same time, rhetorically, it has a type of everyday morality to it. How many times have we been urged to be objective, compared to being subjective? The later does occur, but hardly as frequently as the former. The first tip-off that this powerful rhetorical word is so deceptive and incoherent comes when one reads its dictionary meaning. For example, the *Random House Dictionary* refers to knowledge of "the world independent of our knowing apparatus" as if this were a possibility at all. True enough, the object is constructed intersubjectively and experienced as independent of interacting individuals. However, this contradicts the dictionary definition, since the "constructed" aspect of intersubjectivity is not independent of us, and the objective is defined as the world as it is beyond any human construction. A second leading usage of the term is that it is opposed to the subjective, but when you look up the definition of the subjective, the problem only worsens. The subjective means the opposite of the objective and vice versa in a clearly circular fashion. It is evident that the dictionary is not a philosophy book but simply one of usage, because it ignores all we have learned from the time of Greek thinking about epistemology and what we currently know about the brain.

In all these overlapping definitions of objectivity is the notion of resistance stressed in the last chapter. Pragmatically, the real is that which offers resistance to our push. This is not just material resistance but the constructed resistance known as "social power." Regardless of their overall subjectivity, emotions are objective in this sense. Katz (1999) writes of their dialectical nature as being "something we artfully produce and yet experience as forces that take us over independent of our will." "Ego-alien" is a term frequently used for the fact that emotions resist our efforts to control them. These implications of the objective are elaborated upon below.

SENSES OF OBJECTIVITY

Independence

For over 25 years one of us kicked trash cans against the walls in his classrooms without warning time and time again. He blew-up balloons, scratching them with a pin to ensure that they would burst inevitably but at no particular time. The use of the unexpected was to drive across the point that these activities were the result of factors initiated outside of the students' will. The noises were unaffected by their desire that they would stop. These things happened to them passively, breaking through their active selective perception. Only in this external initiation and indifference to our own desires does the definition of the objective as "independent from anything human" make some questionable sense. Noise, as the reader has seen, owes as much to our human senses and brains as it does to the existence of sound waves.

Impartiality

Impartiality follows from the above and is inseparable from the discussion of indifference. Just because an abrasive noise is so unresponsive to our wishes and thus impartial, such stimuli affect each normal student's eardrums similarly and are analytically separable from their various symbolic interpretations. First comes the surprise for which the students are not prepared. Then comes the interpretation that the professor is making an intellectual point. In over 25 years not one student left the classroom, even though the crash of trash can against the wall or in some cases the ceiling, was thoroughly abrasive. However, it is just this determinant, predictive character of the world that enables us to develop reliable means to act toward it and allows its responses to conform to our wishes. As was suggested in the last chapter, this is the foundation for efficacious action or the building of necessary feelings of control and competence.

Matching

De Sousa (1987) is one of the few scholars that discusses the different senses in which objectivity can be taken. The closest one to independence has to do with "matching," which he views as a metaphor. The match is between mind and environment in the process of gaining knowledge. This metaphor is obviously the image behind the "tabula rosa," "correspondence," or "copy" theory of knowledge that pragmatists and others including current neuroscientists have found inadequate. However, as with so many uses of the word *objective*, we must not throw the baby out with the bath. Our perceptions may not mirror the world, but they give crucial information to adaptive functioning. Given some modicum of attention by the person, events initiated outside of our desires and control will be registered. And though the sensory part of the brain adds its own character to what is initiated independent from us, something occurs that we could refer to as generally isomorphic between sensory preceptors and an impartial world. This is true even if our minds do not register an "uncontaminated" picture of the "objective" side of this occurrence.

The matching metaphor is usually behind our notion of perception; that is, the way objects and events in contact with our senses appear to us. The objective sense of perception is the way it links us to the world of stimuli; the subjective side is that our own senses and concepts play a large part in what we see. Nevertheless, the basic function of the senses is to connect us to the environment. The senses may not provide us a mirror picture of the world because, as we shall soon see, they are "transducers," but they reliably respond in determinate ways suggested in the objective reality of perspectives.

Organism and environment are determined transactionally as described in chapter 3. Thus a "relational," as contrasted to a "relativist," notion of objectivity remains consistent within a transactional framework. Recall the example of the tree bark answering back to the digestive capacities of the deer to use it as food. What an illustration of canceling the opposition but keeping the tension! The tension is created when either the organism cannot accommodate to the environment or changes occur that are noxious to the organism. However, the determinate and thus the objective quality of the relationship should be clear. The relational match is between the bark and the deer's digestive system.

Perception can be "interceptive," which pertains to the registering of sensations arising from or initiated within one's body. This will be discussed under the subjective "quale" of emotion. In the context of this section heading, however, perception is "exteroceptive," that is, associated with an external orientation to environmental objects after allowance is made for selective perception and the transactional relationship between organism and environment.

The matching metaphor of objectivity, if properly qualified along the lines above, is important to a study of emotion that attempts to do justice to its adaptive quality. While emotion is not to be reduced to perception, it is similar to perception insofar as it gives us a relational type of information about the personal relevancy of what is happening "out there" to what we care about "within" (Hochschild 1983, 219). Another crucial similarity between emotion and perception stems from their selectivity: Emotion is notorious for the exclusiveness with which it abstracts a small sliver of our world but, as de Sousa (1987) argues, it can illuminate that sliver very well—with great nuance and subtlety.

Hochschild's suggestion that emotion be considered as another sense cannot be taken literally, because this would ignore important differences between the two—differences that highlight the social nature of emotion. The latter usually has a character of objective intelligibility that subjective sensation does not share (Coulter 1979). The purely sensual sting of the bee may leave a welt that is at least at the moment more than symbolic interpretation. The sting of a social insult depends exactly on such linguistic interpretation. This "sting" can be much more devastating than that of a bee. Emotion also contrasts with sensation, because of the former's "intentional" nature—that is, it is (objectively) directed toward something outside of itself. The briefest acquaintance with Hochschild's work makes it clear that she is quite aware of these differences. More important to her, however, is how emotion is nonetheless analogous to perception. Emotion simply adds to exteroception a subjective aspect, namely, personal involvement that in its intensity becomes embodied and felt. De Sousa views emotion as mimicking perception, and indeed, as a kind of perception of what is worthy or valuable. He refers to it as personal axiology.[1]

Successful Action

De Sousa's metaphor of successful action is the ruling image behind both popular and sophisticated notions of pragmatism. It conveys an earthy practicality—the image of success. If it works, you are "making something happen!" You may not know just why, but that can wait. The objectivity inherent in successful action lies in the assumption that the world is responding impartially and thus reliably to our own actions. Again, as soon as we shed the safety of the self-contained world where ideas simply play on other ideas and move into the manipulative stage of the act, we increase the stakes with which we play the game. Here, our words must subserve effective action and have a limited range of arbitrariness. Serious error is possible and objective reality-testing is at a premium.

In this metaphor, efficacious action takes priority over the popular mirror image of matching, but not what was just referred to as "isomorphism." Here, the world is known transactionally by the way that it responds to our actions upon it. To the American pragmatists, objectivity was not a matter of how accurately the "camera of the mind" takes pictures of the environment, but how we can act effectively on an impartial world.[2] Reality becomes known in terms of its consequences for human action. Knowledge is a strategic assessment of what action-possibilities an object affords. Though thoroughly practical, the active part we play in constructing this knowledge is readily discernable and vivid in the success model. Perhaps the different emphases reflected in these metaphors are best illustrated by Mead's summary statement: "Stimuli are means, tendency is the real thing." Our own interests select for perception those stimuli in the objective world that we use to consummate these interests. Mead elaborates on the relationship between tendency and consummation: "[T]he later stages are present in the early stages . . . in the sense that they (the images of consummations) serve to control the process itself" (Mead 1967, quoted in Swanson 1989, 6).

In this model, action, or what Mead referred to as "precipitant acts," is prior to and determinant of stimuli. In contrast, the matching model starts with the stimuli as initiator. One of the crucial points of de Sousa's work on the rationality of emotion is how it acts as "tendency" that organizes the world in advance for our actions on it, as well as connecting us to it. We will take this up in more detail later.

Swanson (1989) has neatly summarized the relevancy of the success metaphor of objectivity for emotion. He points out that all of the common affective concepts had a central place in social behaviorism:

> There is the ultimately valuable condition found in the completion or "consummation of the act" [Mead 1967, 186–87]. There is their value of things as their relevance for blocking or facilitating behavior. There is emotion [Dewey 1894; 1895] as the consummatory experience of value or perhaps with one's living with the actual or anticipated consequences of that experience. (1989, 6)

In another vein, the psychological and sociological literature on efficacy-based self-esteem (a phrase with obvious implications for success) presents strong support for Whitehead's (1958) statement: "The sense of reality is the sense of effectiveness." However, this sense is emotional in quality.[3]

To show how the subjective is intertwined with the objective success model, Dewey (1910) and more recently Swanson (1989) remind us that the affective component in belief is crucial to effective action. For Dewey, a belief is more than having a dispassioned idea of what is true. Like the efficacy feelings discussed above, belief is close to motivation because it sustains the effectiveness of action. In it's positive function it is thought to be laced with anticipation, confidence, and hope. According to the two above-named authors, "a plan without commitment and confidence is not belief" (Dewey [1910], as quoted in Swanson [1989]). Belief implies that a particular line of action will be successful; it is the affective dimension of the teleological purpose of the human act. We place our believed consummation in the future, and its image "reaches back" to pull us more confidently into this future. To look for one's lost keys with the idea that they might be anywhere diminishes focalized attention and purposeful effort. We might look in the right place, but not close enough to see them. To have the confidence to narrow down alternatives and to think of where they probably are, means that we will be energized to dig around, thinking the whole time, "I just know they have to be here somewhere." This belief is not just idea; it is conviction about a future outcome. Conviction allows full identification with our actions, from religious activity to looking for keys. Subjective emotion, then, is implicated with the objective feature of the success metaphor.

One of the limitations of the success dimension of objectivity is that we can be right for the wrong reasons, and we could be unaware of this until it is too late. Wearing garlic cloves around one's neck to "ward off the demons that cause colds" may work, but not in the isolated parts of Siberia or Duluth where there are fewer people to give you germs anyway. Without the theorist who wants to verify the thesis beyond its momentary success, this dimension of objectivity (like all others) remains incomplete. In sum, whereas with the success model the manipulative phase of the act is dominant, the matching metaphor focuses on the determinant quality within the sensory dimensions of perception.

Directness

By means of our senses, we are directly linked with the world of the here and now. This means that sensation derives from some tangible source, since things located in the here and now offer independent resistance to our push as discussed above. This direct linkage is a cause-and-effect, inevitable connection between our physical environment and ourselves. Such is the nature of all sensation, and even considering perception's subjective selectivity, the limits of each animal's senses offer the range from which it selects. The trash can and balloon overpowers this selectivity in everyday cases, gurus and meditators notwithstanding. It is perception's direct tie to stimuli in the present that makes perception associated with the empirical. This distinguishes the senses from conception, which in humans draws on intangible, symbolic interpretations. These symbols have an arbitrary tie to their referent from the point of view of impersonal nature and from sensation's cause-and-effect linkages. (See the reality-based dimensions of the concept and the tie between senses and concepts in the next chapter.)

The Publicly Shared World

While the above senses of objectivity are found in general discourse among laypersons, the metaphor underlying objectivity as shared worlds may be more limited to philosophers and sociologists. According to Northrop (1948), Heraclitus captured this abstract notion of the objective some time ago: Those who are awake have a common world; those who are asleep turn in their own private worlds. Northrop updates the same insight as follows:

> [A]s Albert Einstein and most expert scientists who have examined with care the methodological foundations of scientific knowledge clearly recognize, the belief in an objective, public world with scientific objects in it the same for all observers, is a *theoretically inferred* not a purely empirically given knowledge. (1948, 43 [emphasis in original])

The metaphors of independence and directness presuppose solitary actors passively absorbing a world of stimuli. Both are social only in that we can share knowledge and interpret our singular experiences through language. The success model assumes an actor actively impinging on the world by solitary actions brought forward. It is indeed ironic that the world as it really is—the *ding an sich* of Kant's "noumena"—is a completely hypothetical construct created like all language as an emergent from social interaction. The world independent of human intelligibility, thought to be the most thoroughly objective world is instead created out of the intersubjective necessities of human talk and social cooperation. What is assumed as *read out from* the world by stimuli is in actuality *read into* it by the symbolic interaction of a collectivity.

Sociologists may more readily recognize this type of objectivity as an essential part of Simmel's answer to the question of "how society is possible?" For example, O'Neill (1973, 94) refers to this notion of an objective world as based on the "naïve and massive everyday assumption that there is a world which, despite the variety of viewpoints and circumstances, we nevertheless think we hold in common." Indeed, it is to this abstracted common world and its platitudes that we refer to our differences in order to settle them within its limits.

Emotion, while admittedly drawing on linguistically shared worlds for its intelligibility, contrasts starkly with the extrasensory, distanced, hypothetical realm of abstracted objectivity. Here, we must distinguish between the symbolically constructed, intangible products of extrasensory thought like rules of grammar or mathematical systems and the embodied process of thought, tinged as it is with confidence, efficacy, determination, care, love, caution, anxiety, joy, or despair. The ideational products of thought, being disembodied abstractions, have permanence not known to concrete events locatable in space and time. Thus the products of thought have the permanent character implied by objectivity even if they are mind-formed constructs. Geometric systems being hypothetical do not wrinkle with age and melt away like winter's snow. Being atemporal and aspatial, such systems do not change even though they become replaced. Such systems ranging from those of due process to the rules of warfare remain impersonally but intersubjectively available to any mind willing to follow the rules that comprise their structure. By disregarding the personal and idiosyncratic, agreement is more possible and the resulting consensus further confirms the character of objectivity within the intersubjective. This is why the term "preobjective" is used to denote human experience before, or outside, of language. Once again, we see why the disembodied consensus model of objectivity is insufficient, a point we emphasize when critiquing Habermas in chapter 7.

Contrasting emotion to the above pushes us to recognize two different and almost antithetical ways in which we talk of "the real." One is the hypothetical, abstractly generated kind of reality that is essential to intersubjective objectivity and science. At the same time, insofar as it is hypothetical, it is a human creation, a product of thought that is projected, or as we say above, is "read into" the world. This is at the same time what many understand as being subjective. To refer to it as real is an illustration of Berger and Luckmann's (1967) warning that in any act of objectivization, reification is only a step away. The objectivization involved in intersubjectivity and the world common to all of us removes us as far away as possible from the immediate world of the senses and as far away as possible from the "reality" of the here and now. We have hopefully shown the irony in referring to this world as "real." This abstracted reality ignores the fact that children abandoned to the streets, having known no adults who care for them and not exposed to the adequate modeling of the emotions of guilt or sympathy, *must* live in a perceptual world different from children from caring families. Perceived worlds are different worlds for each individual. The world of scientific abstraction is one of intangible principle, even as we apply it to the control of the tangible world. If some of us have expected more certainty from the objective than is realistic, we must come to terms with our unrealistic expectations, not turn our backs on this crucial term. Confusion regarding the objectivity created by intersubjectivity will always surface unless we recognize a further irony. Intersubjectivity's formulation of the world common to all of us is critical in producing the stability necessary for individual health and the maintenance of society. But such fixity is gained only by an immense abstraction from actual perception and lived experience. This abstraction, while making society possible, inevitably creates an image of a self-sufficient universe having nothing to do with knowings of any sort. This image is an every-day version of Kant's noumenal world in and of itself independent of per-ception. While this simplification may be necessary for our practical, everyday worlds, its inadequacy for scientific levels of knowledge has been increasingly recognized through the course of the past century. As critical as intersubjective objectivity is, we need to be aware of tenden-cies within it that are antithetical to a transactional framework.

More on the Relationship between the Objective and Subjective

When an idea becomes "realized" in Dewey's sense of embodiment and personal significance, we include an important subjective reality that is lost in the hypothetical common world (see chapter 5). In the real-ity of emotional realization, the idea is no longer "distanced" and hypo-thetical. This experience, like any other concrete particular, is unique and cannot be shared. The concreteness of emotion, its authenticity and personal reality, is rooted in tangible bodily experience. This is alto-gether different from objectivity won through hypothetical worlds, which in ignoring the very real, lived experiences of concrete individu-als also ignores human value. Chapter 5 will detail this further.

One contribution of sociology to the question of "what emotions are" is in detailing how intersubjective objectivity enters into them, but only as enablers. To talk of the social aspect of emotion is to talk of thought as the enabler of the objective component of emotion. As we have seen, an important meaning of the objective is that it transcends the exclu-sively idiosyncratic.

In reaction to the James/Lange suggestion that emotion was the interception of changes in the viscera, Cannon had argued effectively that the viscera were too insensitive and changed too slowly to explain the diversity of emotions. Not only do different cultures appear to have emotions not experienced in other cultures, but specific types of emo-tion die out, enter the scene anew, and increasingly diversify through history. The taken-for-granted culturally shared ideas from which we draw our very personal idiosyncratic emotions vary in cultural space and historical time. It is this socially relative differentiation of emotion that must be explained in terms of linguistic classifications. As Hochs-child (1983, 223) explains, "we do not name feelings after physiological states for good reason. . . . Physiological differences are not pronounced enough from one feeling to another to account for the wide variety of emotion names we have in our language."

There is mounting evidence from neuroscience that basic emotions exist wherein biology plays a predominant part, but the neuroscientist Brothers (1997) disagrees. Culture also gives a basis for identifying the social and objective aspects of emotional experience, because as Wood (1986, 197) observes it is the very personal appropriation of collective and culturally conditioned appraisals. Even if anger, fear, happiness, and sadness turn out to be "hard-wired," as J. H. Turner (2000) argues, culture influences when and how emotions are warranted and expressed. The evidence on cultural variation is too abundant to be ignored and is not at issue. Here especially we need to practice seeing similarity within variety. This does not contradict Linda Wood's claim that what transpires individually and privately is appropriated from the public-collective realm. She continues, following Harré (1986), that emotion can be individually realized but collectively or socially defined. Again, the sense of objectivity involved is that of the intersubjective objectivizations or the differing classifications of a particular culture giving intelligibility to our feelings.

Just as every observation is really a thought/observation, every emotion is a thought/emotion or an embodied thought. Calhoun (1989), Rosaldo (1984), Hochschild (1983), and Averill and Nunley (1992) are among those thinking that the key to making this symbolically given common stock become embodied is our sense of personal involvement and engagement (Franks 1989).

Important as these linguistic sources of intelligibility and cultural lexicons are, we must understand that taken alone, they leave out just that part of our subject matter that we think of as emotion. They supply an important half of the story, but not the decisive half. Cultural enablers of emotion do not capture its sensual, ineffable subjectivity. They leave out just what we know is unique and distinctive about emotion. It is the subjective part of emotion that constitutes it as real happenings rather than mere symbols about happenings. We may be reminded at this point that objective understanding by itself moves nothing. For the part of feeling that is moving and compelling we must turn to its subjectivity. But the subjective will always be dialectically joined with the objective. In this case we are made capable of subjectively caring about being objective because we authentically want to know what works.

SENSES OF SUBJECTIVITY

Following de Sousa (1987), we will now present four meanings of the subjective. We will continue to use emotion as predominantly subjective remembering its objective dimensions; for example, that it draws from the objective character of shared language. The rational character of emotion also hinges on its similarity to perception. Emotion tells us the personal relevance of what is happening in the situation. The fact that emotional "information" is about our most personal biographies makes it all-the-more important and rational, rather than less important. Despite the fact that perception, like emotion, is riddled with subjective dimensions, both are still necessary to individual survival as well as that of social structures. It is rational, after all, to care about one's self and one's close others. As Damasio (1994) has clearly shown, emotion is also "rational" because it is necessary for successful decisions in everyday life.

Phenomenal Qualia

"Quale" has to do with what it feels like to have a certain emotion. Its focus on interception makes it a radically subjective concept and must be handled gingerly. As Dewey (1894) understood, the particular "feel" of being angry may be intellectually abstracted from a readiness to act in a hostile manner, but such a "feel" certainly has no existence by itself detached from situations; nor is it a full-fledged emotional experience. In and of itself, quale would produce sheer spasm or seizure instead of emotion. In music, the term "timbre" refers to the quality of sound produced by a particular instrument. A "c" note on a tuba will sound "brassy," whereas the same note on a flute may have an "airy" or "light" quality to it. These qualities are sometimes referred to as the "flavor" of a sound. To describe these flavors as "airy" or "light" communicates fully only if one has objectively experienced the sounds of these instruments for themselves. The qualia of sensations are subjective, because they are nonverbal lived experiences and change within and between individuals. Any college freshman trying to see how much beer he can drink is aware of the change of its quale as the drinking progresses. Even a tipsy person can figure out that it is not the beer that has lost its luster.

Quale then, names and separates out the ineffable quality of sensation. By definition, language, being abstract, has no ability to do this. We addressed this in chapter 2. Words by themselves cannot conjure up the actual feeling of love or clinical depression. If one could express a particular quale in certain words, we could produce a particular sensation just by saying it: we could produce the taste of the best meal ever by just describing it, or we could verbally drum up some other sexual experiences and be in eternal ecstasy.

Quale is commonly referred to as what adds emotional glow and warmth to cold, or neutral, perception. It gives emotion its "bite" and its embodied nature that cognition alone does not. Here again, the subjective and objective are clearly implicated in each other, because it is this subjective "bite" that stands over against us, resisting our wishes. This reflects a crucial character of the objective. Quale is a term more often used by persons interested in the physiology of emotion and the brain. While it may seem outside the purview of sociology, we will suggest later that it is not. When we discuss a person's depression we hopefully do not experience the abject dread, hopelessness, and complete debilitation that forms the quale of that depression for the person. What quale refers to is not intersubjective; it does not transfer between people as does $2 + 2 = 4$. With some exceptions, when we remember back on our sorrows and joys, the things we cannot bring into our present are just these qualia. Again, this is because of its dependency on the concrete, real physiology of the moment. This physiology is vital to the contextual quality of human affairs. To urge a clinically depressed person to remember, and take substance from the good times, is only to imply the speaker's lack of understanding. This is just what the depressed person's embodiment can no longer do.

A subjective depression may originate in personal problems, but the biochemical process created by these problems takes on a life of its own. In becoming a reality *sui generis*, this new process often becomes responsive to a new level of biochemical treatment. A different layer of physiological reality has been imposed—a layer that gives a whole new momentum to the dire beliefs that set it in motion. If beliefs are intangible, the effects of this physiology are decidedly less so. Without the notion of quale, we may miss the fact that something real in terms of biochemistry is happening. This is true regardless of how variable this chemistry may be for each person, or between each emotional episode. None of this implies a physiological reductionist approach to emotional differentiation.

Projection

Along with its fierce selectivity, projection is a major subjective source of error in emotion. Because of current prejudices, the numerous errors in cognition are ignored when contrasting it with emotion. The mistake in projection usually involves attributing properties, whose sources are solely in us, to other objects. Unfortunately, such projection is usually reinforced by one's utter conviction that it is correct.

An important type of emotional error connected with projection is the way it can become involved in self-fulfilling, defensive emotional sequences. This is especially common in interpersonal quarrels and self-deception. This is a critical area of research in an age that places great value on intimate relations that fail at a rate inconsistent with this value. Take the common situation of a man that has been out late drinking and has not notified an inconvenienced and concerned wife. Confronted with her anger, he thinks, "Well, I kept thinking I'd break it off so I didn't call. I don't feel emotionally inconsiderate, why can't she give me my space?" Without great cogitation, some words may follow these thoughts that seem to fit his sense of things: "Give me a break, Jesus, I've busted my butt for you . . . I mean, how can you wonder if I really love you?" Now his words are that of a victimized person, which fit his feelings of being "boxed in." Now that he has turned the tables and become the victim, do we really expect him to voice his complaints in anything but a convincing manner? Not hardly! By now the man has played his own part in constructing his emotion as his authentic ego-alien reality. It would be an understatement to say that this "accurate" but subjective *interception* can be easily combined with his exteroception to produce emotional projection as error as well as hurt feelings on both sides.

Let us attempt a broadening of the use of projection by elaborating on the self-actional view of the person discussed in the previous chapter. Elias (1978, 256–62) discusses projection when he suggests that our pervasive feeling of isolation in an era of subjectivization makes us predisposed to reify the boundaries of self in our intellectual models. This distorts the interactional penetration of selves that is sociology's task to describe. Our emotional conviction of the appropriateness of the metaphor of "inner" self as true and real appears to be inherent in our overdone notion of the individual as isolated and self-actualized. It seems to fit. What it fits, according to Elias (1978) and Baumeister (1986), is our own existential experience of isolation in an alienated society, as well as the sharp boundaries we feel as we constantly check our impulses in the service of "civility" (Elias 1978). The emotional source of the metaphor's plausibility is intellectually misplaced.

Relativity and Relation

Perhaps the most decisive blow to the objective realist's position is the notion of the senses as transducers. This clearly illustrates the objective reality of perspectives discussed before; namely, how the capacities of the organism determine its reality by its bodily-given vantage point. This discussion paves the way for an understanding of how emotion transforms intersubjective, objective nature into a peculiarly human and individually perceived world. A transducer takes information from one system and changes it to accommodate to another system. Your word processor does this when it changes text from Word Perfect 5 to Win-

Word. Chlorophyll changes light rays from the sun into nourishment for plants. With color-blind people, a particular light wave appears differently from the majority of others. If one happened to see as green what most of us see as red, the color-blind person would learn to stop on the majority's experience of green and to go on the majority's experience of red. Since that person would reverse the names and call his subjective green "red," no one, including the person thus afflicted, would necessarily know that there were differences between himself and others in the subjective and private experiences of color. Because our senses project what is peculiarly human into the world's appearance, perception is seen as primarily subjective in disregard of its previously described objective dimensions. Some erroneously think that transducers distort this world. Note, however, that the "real world" here is viewed in self-actional terms. We have seen that the objective and determinant quality of "transduction" is real if placed in a transactional framework of relation. The elaboration on transducers below, will continue with this emphasis. Here, emotion will have to give way to sensation as illustrative of the subjective.

 Without the "transformer" that we call the eye, electromagnetic energy states would be just that—energy states, not color. Pause and think of that vast difference between electromagnetic waves and color. To have the human experience of color, you need a transducing human eye and brain. Stimuli alone are not enough to fully explain sensation. Compressions of air of different intensities lack the quale of actual noise until they hit an eardrum and cause the kind of vibration that the ear can change into noise (Christian 1977). At the point of this vibration it is not yet noise. A number of things have to happen before the final stage of awareness: Three small bones must pick up the movements of the eardrum; one bone rests on a membrane at one end of a spiral-shaped organ; inside this organ are hair cells with bristles surrounded by fluid. As the sound wave (compressed air) must be relayed by the bones to the bristles, a wave activity develops just like the wave generator used in a marine science lab or museum. But it still is not the subjective experience of sound. These waves brush the tips of hair cells against another membrane, which creates an electrical spike. As a consequence, positively charged chemicals must carry these spikes to the brain. Notice the vast difference in the three stages from objective stimuli to its complete transformation to human subjective sensation. We have gone from compressed air in the first case, to bristles touching membranes, to electrical charges. Even the electrical charge is not noise. That vast transformation happens in the brain. The tree may fall in the forest and it certainly makes compressions in the surrounding air. But without some ear to change compressions into sound, it is not yet noise (Christian 1977). We need the objective compressions of air, but just as important is the "transduction" that our bodies supply. Ignoring the critical part our senses play in this process and seeing yellow as an independent part of the grapefruit itself is a common error.

Our language completely ignores this transformation of nature into a distinctively human perceptual world and routinely commits this error. We say that the apple is red or the music is lovely or the lemon is sour. The part our own biology plays in the process is totally ignored. These sensations are results of the determinate relationships between the senses and these things and events; they do not belong to the objects themselves.

The fact that our senses are transducers drives a final stake through the heart of traditional correspondence theory and its assumption of objectivity as mirroring the world as it is independent of us. As noted above, perception does indeed correlate with the external world and our ears and eyes change as it changes. Indeed, they are linked with selected stimuli in an objective and necessary manner as with the isomorphism given through the objective reality of perspectives. But all this gives in terms of knowledge is how the world appears to our distinctively human preceptors, not how the world "is" in the traditional sense of "objectively." It tells us how the world affects our awareness. It tells us only about this relationship. The emotional quality of experience adds an even more distinctive and critical dimension to how the world appears to us. A gloomy day to us may seem like a cozy day to new lovers. But as we shall see, even the emotional, with all of its subjectivity, is absolutely essential for human existence.

The following quote from Hannah Arendt (1958) uses the words of the leading astrophysicists of this century to summarize how our scientific knowledge does not produce any mirror image of the world as it is, independent of how our senses change it. If scientific knowledge has its subjectivity, this may temper the pejorative way we view emotions' subjectivity. It will help in understanding the quote to view scientific instruments as extensions of our senses: Assemblages

> The modern astrophysical world which began with Galileo and its challenge to the adequacy of the senses to reveal reality have left us a universe of whose qualities we know no more than the way they affect our measuring instruments and in the words of Eddington—"The former have as much to do with the latter as a telephone number has to a subscriber."

Instead of objective qualities, in other words, we find reflections of our own instruments instead of nature or the universe, in the words of Heisenburg, "man encounters only himself."

As the above implies, humans perceive a very human world cast in particular ways by their own senses, and, as we shall see, by their own languages. But we must think carefully here. If we are looking to our senses to give us pictures of the way things are, we are simply asking too much of them. What man encounters is not literally only himself, but his limited and peculiarly human *relationship* with the world. The senses and our instruments do after all respond to regularities we do not control and are in that sense objective.

Perspective

Every experience and every choice is made from a certain point of view or agency. We can never attain "the view from nowhere" (de Sousa 1987, 147). If there are "perspectival truths," then each of us knows something that even an omnipotent god could not know. This refers to a most profound type of subjectivity—it becomes especially so when we talk of the ineffable nature of quale. At the same time, it does not imply any more irrationality to emotion than does relational subjectivity. We have seen that there is no such thing as hypothetically experiencing emotion, but it bears repeating here. In this sense, emotion is profoundly existential, as the adjective "perspectival" implies.

To find a story sad or thrilling, one cannot simply be told that it is, like we tell someone an object is hot and they believe us. Belief is not enough here. Naturally, a good storyteller increases the chance of producing emotion in us. But in the final analysis, we must authentically feel this for ourselves. We must be disposed to do so. While we draw on the public scenarios and moral orders for our emotional experience, we forge them into our private beings by means of a very personal wholehearted appropriation. The private, appropriative act involved in emotion is derived from the perspective of our particular individuality that no one else can share.

The function of role-playing therapy is to induce the emotion that imagination cannot summon. One time, at a convention round-table session, one of us asked someone from the University of Chicago if it was alright to call him Ben (as gleaned from his nametag). His response was, "Go right ahead, David." And my feeling was as automatic as it was pristinely unambivalent: "You don't know me!" It remains unclear if he had intended that impact, but it is likely that he did. One's imagination alone could not have made the point that the author's utterly surprising but perspectival emotion allowed.

THE SOCIAL CONSTRUCTION OF THE SUBJECTIVE AS REAL

Ironically, in ignoring emotions' biology, we also lose something really unusual and distinctive about the dialectic relationship between the subjective and society. Berger and Luckmann (1967) have described the "three moments" in the social construction of reality: The first is externalization, wherein some internal thought or feeling is given visible, public form. On the individual level of emotion, which should be thought of in terms of these three moments, this externalization is emotional expression. The next moment in the social construction of reality is when this object loosens its ties with its creators and takes on a life of its own. Berger and Luckmann refer to this as "objectivization." Again, on the individual level, this is emotions' particular quale, which creates its "ego-alien" character. Wentworth and Ryan (1992) have warned us that emotions' biological reality—its convincing quality, its objectivized ability to act back on the individual who authored it—lies in this very feature. It is what remains from a "specificity theory" that is compatible with, and necessary for, a brand of constructionism that has yet to clearly surface. This is a perspective that refuses to set artificial academic boundaries between biology and sociology and honors the task of not reducing emotion to cognition. Emotion is socially constructed, but it becomes real in this process.

For Berger and Luckmann, what individuals in interaction have created has been severed from its authorship and acts back according to its own laws on the children of those whose collective action unwittingly brought it into being. Once objectivization has begun, reification, as we have noted, is only a step away. How true, for the essentialistic view of "real, natural emotion" is construed by the traditionalists to be the core of the "inner," true self (Morgan and Averill 1992). The final stage is when the dialectic has come full circle and its knot is tied. This is the moment of internalization—the stage where each individual in his or her own way (Wentworth and Ryan 1992) uniquely appropriates the objective order. The social is made into biological reality (see chapter 6). Emotion and the embodied self is this final step in the individual–social dialectic.

As Goffman (1959) may have told it, the principles that uphold the social order are sometimes broken by some unhappy act. Real blood courses into real faces, and once again the solitary actor pays his or her social dues with his or her most separate being.

CONCLUSION: WHY IS THE SUBJECTIVE THE LAST TO BE DISCOVERED?

In this conclusion we will come full circle to make important elaborations on Lorenz's notion of the subjective as foundational—so much so that we miss it in passing. Children only slowly move to an understanding of the subjective—their own feelings and those of others. They start calling themselves by their third-person name and only with time move to referring to themselves in the more abstract, first-person "I." Yi-Fu Tuan (1982) and Westen (1985) are among the many scholars pointing to the preoccupation of nonliterate societies with the objective and a relative lack of focus on themselves as separate from their groups. Only in literate, complexly differentiated societies do we see a movement toward a keen awareness of the individual self—its value and prerogatives.

As we saw in chapter 2, the subjective is foundational in the positive sense that the former is the necessary lens through which we see in contrast to the object seen. In spite of the fact that our scientific focus is on the object of observation, the way our eyes are constructed comprises the foundational starting point that determines how that object will be seen.

There is another, slightly different way in which the subjective is foundational. When I look at you, when you look at me, the last things we are aware of are our own eyes. We literally cannot, in that precise moment of looking, see the eyes that enable us to see. In fact, in spite of their all-importance, they are the very last things we will reflect on unless we can't see well enough or our eyes cause pain. Even then, we would not realize the implications we are drawing here (Ostrow 1990). Likewise, Katz (1999) insists that emotion is the invisible foundation for selves and their thought. We know how people are the last to know their own emotion: "I'm not jealous, but that leading journal you just published in has gone down the drain."

We need also to elaborate on the "ego-alien" character of the objective. You will remember that Lorenz joins us in emphasizing the part resistance plays in defining the objective. Those particular emotions that compel us against our will take on this character regardless of their clearly subjective aspects. The numerous, if over-emphasized cases, however, of schizophrenics that hear frightening voices commanding them to do terrible things are also subjective in that they are idiosyncratic. So we must consider other senses of objectivity that include more than this kind of resistance. It must be shared or potentially sharable by others, not merely because of symbolic consensus but because of the regularities of our transactions. This leaves room for creative achievements that are only later recognized as such. We must remember, however, that the old adage "Can five hundred thousand Frenchmen be wrong?" must be answered with a resounding "Yes!"

This chapter has offered a redefinition of subjectivity and objectivity that sees them as being implicated in each other relationally rather than oppositionally. Both terms are too important to cast aside. If you ignore one of them, you miss important things about the other. We have offered a more inclusive approach to each by identifying the different senses that can be ascribed to them. Only with this type of specification can we transcend circularity and contradiction to give equal value to each term. This allows even the most reluctant to accept at least certain senses of objectivity. Of course, this leaves out the powerful concern of how we may appear to our colleagues. Nonetheless, without giving credence to objectivity, we can hardly turn unambivalent attention to the notion of a real world redefined relationally. As we observed in chapter 3, objects are created by the acts they indifferently support.

The core of the objective to us is resistance in some form. Without actions there are no resistances. Symbolic resistances are stressed, because the intersubjective notion of the real world beyond our impressions, common to all of us, is a symbolic belief essential to being human but symbolic nonetheless. Autistics only survive because of the "intersubjective objectivity" of others.

To incorporate objectivity stemming from material resistances to our acts and wishes we have presented Mead's (1959) "objective reality of perspectives." Here, perspective is not merely used as a conceptual viewpoint, but as the viewpoint given by our upright stance, free hands, flat faces, and enlarged brains. Both perspectives—one given by our socialization and one given by our bodies—produce their own type of resistances.

If, in our professional work, we can give up on our belief of a self-actual world independent of our particular means of knowing, the objective and the real shed those absolutist features that made them so unacceptable to many. The symbolically real becomes real in its consequence, and the materially real becomes real through our bodies.

NOTES

1. "Axiology" here refers to the individual's construction of personal values. This is accomplished through emotional processes.

2. While this will seem obvious to many readers, Maines has pointed to a tendency to view such accuracy as the only focus of some ethnographic projects.

Here, poetry becomes a tool to come closer to lived experience. This seems to us similar, at least, to the old historicist assumption that if you describe things well enough, some meaning will jump out of the data. It also privileges the subjective in such a way that its dialectic relation to objectivity is lost. We mean not to disparage poetry of all ethnography; but once again, we see the extreme of textualism alive and well today and the rebirth of a one-sided dualism that chooses the subjective over the objective.

3. According to R. W. White (1965), consequences of intentional actions, focalized attention, and directed effort are experienced in ways different than unintended happenings. White (1965), Smith (1968), and Bandura (1986) point out that such acts end in the subjective feeling of "efficacy" that is of reward value in itself. White believes that the feeling of efficacy is one of our most fundamental affects. It forms the basis of persisting attempts to achieve whatever mastery we can over the environment and to enlarge our sphere of competence, which is so central to self-esteem. Not only is emotion placed as central to the consummation of competent acts, but also it provides the motivational basis for the infant's interest in reality-testing and the objectivity therein.

◧　◧　◧

CHAPTER FIVE

Cognition and Linguistically Given Distance

Aided by our previous discussions of transaction and the subjective/ objective frame, this chapter will return in a different way to our critique of nominalistic positions within the "linguistic turn." As we have suggested, the clearest example of nonverbal reality is our phenomenological experience of bodily feeling, the one thing that talk is not. The distinction between the verbal and the nonverbal is relatively clear when dealing with the qualia of feeling. Unfortunately, it is more problematic when dealing with such things as the world confronted in motor activities, our "pictures" of the universe, or the workings of social processes— that is, the social and physical, external world. The difficulty with our understandings of these "objective" worlds is, as discussed in chapter 4, that they are commonly understood as being fixed and self-actual, existing independent of human perception. Reality, or the objective world, becomes a highly abstracted reification.

Implicit in this, of course, is our main theme: The "realities" of application that can refine our sociological understandings too often go unrealized. As we have argued, this severely limits the sense in which sociology is an empirical field.

In this chapter, we make an argument against extreme relativism that strengthens and completes our earlier case. We base what follows on a fully embodied theory of mentality.[1] We suggest how concepts that originated from our bodily activity in the world can become problematically separated from it. This is true regardless of the neurological ties to motor activity remaining even in our higher level abstractions. In the extreme cases of those that literally live in such worlds, the potential pathology is a type of "disassociation" wherein talking the talk becomes more real than walking the walk. In such life-worlds, the felt reality of our selves and transactions easily pale.[2] The neuroscience experiments by Damasio (1994) are used to demonstrate why very intelligent patients—masters of symbolic manipulations—are nonetheless unequipped for real-life demands. The chapter concludes with the implications of this study for keeping the tension between acts of words and deeds, as well as the need to refine abstract theory by testing it in the real world.

This chapter offers ways to explain the paradox hinted at above. Our concepts can be the very means of our connection to the world, and at the same time they can foster our removal from it. Unfortunately, our reluctance to fully appreciate the importance of a world beyond discourse is greatly aided by our traditional and still-dominant theories of cognition, which only incidentally relate to physical, embodied activity, if at all.

This chapter also reviews some of the less-attended half-century attempts to balance the misguided notion of "pure" cognition divorced from action and purified of the emotion that compels us to this action. The illusion of pure, disembodied cognition as the sole vehicle of knowledge has been a major force in our inability to think of the possibility of an embodied transactional notion of objectivity, reality, and a more viable notion of truth.

The *extrasensory*, seemingly otherworldly nature of linguistic symbols and the concepts they convey are produced by our very worldly social brain and the practical problems of action it had to solve in its evolutionary past. Our goal here is to show that intellectual thought for its own sake can distort lived experience and separate us from it rather than uniting us with it.

PURE COGNITION ON A PEDESTAL

The exalted place granted pure cognition has long been held in suspicion among those with romantic leanings. Only recently have hard-nosed technical scientists like LeDoux (1996) been strong voices in the critique. To the layperson this may seem preposterous, but in no way do these authors or LeDoux discount the importance of cognition and its sister, human speech. Our ability to change our own environments is precisely due to this cognitive capacity. However, cognition, especially conceived by the old cognitive sciences as separated from emotion and the body, is most worthy of critique regardless of its lofty position, and even more so because of its association with human distinctiveness, however defined. By taking a critical look at what is usually only applauded, we discover additional reasons to glimpse a broader reality than that *completely* determined by our own subjectivity.[3] The discussion of the relational character of subjectivity in the previous chapter should prepare us for this journey and help maintain our transactional stance.

The Disembodied Symbol in Post–World War II Social Psychology

Most sociological approaches to human mentality emphasize the detachment of linguistically formed symbols from necessary, cause-and-effect relationships with their nonverbal referent. Usually, the next step is to stress how symbols critical to thought simply refer to other symbols in a purely detached discursive system.[4] To emphasize the degree of this "otherworldly" detachment, the difference between linguistically formed concepts and sensation is frequently stressed. Sensation, we have seen, typically results from processes initiated outside of our own agency and viewed as objective even though *attention* to it may belong to the organism.

Sensation is contrasted sharply with the symbol in this perspective for several crucial reasons: first, it ties us to the "here and now," while the symbol frees us from the moment, allowing reflection that recreates such immediacy in our minds long after it happened. Now we have the original event and our mind-formed event that we can act *on* and manipulate hypothetically. As Leslie White (1949) wrote in his influential essay on "The Use of Tools by Primates," both homo sapiens and ape have the makeshift tools of the moment, but only homo sapiens have the permanent and continuous concept. For White, the ape lives in a small world that is spatially confined to the range of his senses and temporally limited to the moment, with a dose of anticipation and reminiscence. As a consequence, after using the tool it is cast aside, with no pieces saved for the next time. In contrast, White (1949, 46) says that humans create a new symbolic world, where *possibility* overcomes the *actual* and environmental mastery is increased:

> This world of ideas comes to have continuity and a permanence that the external world of the senses can never have. It is not made up of the present only, but of a past and a future as well. Temporally it is not a

succession of disconnected episodes, but a continuum extending
to infinity in both directions, from eternity to eternity. . . . This inner
world of ideas in which man dwells seems more real to him than the
outer world of the senses.

The simplicity of White's argument (and others like it) was no doubt
one reason for its widespread popularity.[5] Additionally, arguments that
imply categorical distinctions between humans and other animals are
reliably received with relief and applause by nervous humans. Many
social psychologists between the 1950s and the 1990s saw the *extrasensory* symbol as categorically distinguishing humans and other primates
in disregard of Leibniz's warning that "nature takes no leaps." We are not
suggesting that the popular treatment of the symbol's "disconnect" from
the sensed world was incorrect, but rather that it left out any developmental relationship to embodiment. It also left out a full appreciation of
Mead's manipulative stage of the act. As Becker (1964, 15) points out, we
are so enamored by the symbol that we think all learning involves stuffing one's head with symbols. Most parents and educators, at one time or
another, have to confront how ineffective this is. We forget that it is the
organism itself that must edge forward. Fully felt learning comes when
we use words for ourselves that result in satisfying actions. As we presented Shalin's arguments in chapter 2, mere intersubjectivity, seen as
nothing more than consensus or social agreement, leaves out what we
learn by contact with the world. We learn best by doing, not by passively
incorporating other people's symbols. Becker (1964, 15) puts the symbol
and organismic relationship clearly:

> Man has been so well aided by symbols in his helpless exposure to
> nature that it seems as though *organisms* exist in a *symbolic* world; that
> somehow they are subservient to it. But symbols share in an organismic
> world; the symbol is a part of flesh and blood behavior.

The disembodied consensus model can be seen as a major culprit in producing Dennis Wrong's (1961) oversocialized conception of man.

In light of current neuroscience, the almost exclusive emphasis on
the extrasensory nature of the symbol only exacerbated the chasm
between mind and body, a problem that White hurriedly addressed in his
next essay on mind as bodily process. But this was hardly sufficient and
was largely ignored. The lasting implication of White's work was the creation of a self-actual and disembodied theory of mind that lead to
extreme cultural relativism. Here, viable notions of reality, objectivity,
and truth are most difficult to achieve. The hypothetical—we want to

say the *unworldly*—cast to our understanding of the symbol is strongly encouraged by focusing on the nonepisodic, continuous nature of human mental experience. Granted, this seems supported by the atemporal and aspatial nature of our concepts. Here, the devil must get his due because this detachment is a strength, even though Becker and Marx warned that it can become a weakness. Chapter 3 has shown how measured time actually violates the lived experience of passage by stopping it in our mind's eye. Likewise, we see objects in "terms of space," but we do not "see" space. Space has no actual sensed quality even if it developed out of our bodily experience with movement toward objects. We have previously discussed how these extrasensory concepts are "read into" the world. Taken by themselves, they do indeed have an unworldly quality. In the felicitous words of Dewey and Bentley (1949), "even the oldest concepts do not wrinkle and shrink up with age." Of course there is more to the story.

The Fusion of Concepts and Sensation: Bringing Concepts Down to Earth

Contrary to the above understanding, we find from neuroscience that sensation is as abstract as the verbal in the sense of being taken from a larger whole. According to Lakoff and Johnson (1999), the most important thing to understand about the categorization, and the resulting simplification involved in all concepts, is that the whole process is an inescapable consequence of our *bodily* makeup. Mind and body are transactionally joined. The necessity of abstraction, even on the sensory level, is clear. The human brain has approximately 100 billion neurons and 100 trillion synaptic connections. Perceptual information is commonly passed from one dense ensemble of neurons to another using a relatively sparse set of connections. Activation distributed over the first set is far too great to be conveyed to the smaller set of connections. It is thus necessary for the sparse set to group individual data into simpler categories. When we see trees, we see them as *trees*, not the totality of individual objects. The same is true with rocks, houses, windows, doors, and so on. Lakoff and Johnson (1999, 18–19) argue that, granting cultural variation, our bodies and brains determine what kind of basic categories we can have: ". . . the peculiar nature of our bodies shape our very possibilities for conceptualization and categorization." In this small phrase they also challenge the simple idea in some social psychologies that all dimensions of cognition can be explained within language, even though language is obviously critical for making these "transactionally" determined cognitions organized and useful.[6]

Given this general finding on the abstract nature of sensation, Lakoff and Johnson turn to the fusion of concepts and sensations. This is in stark contrast to the gulf between them described by White (above). In our previous discussion of the senses as transducers it was clear that the ineffable qualia of color—its lived experience—was as much a result of the peculiarities of the organism's color cones and the connecting brain circuitry as it was of external wavelengths of reflected light. However, in the original discussion of transducers, we neglected a further complication: under different conditions the wavelengths of light coming from a banana, for example, will differ considerably. This is a consequence of the light of dawn or dusk or whether it is a sunny or cloudy day. The interesting thing is that regardless of this variation, the color of the banana will be made relatively constant; that is, this consistency depends on the brain's ability to compensate for variations in light source. Two different reflectances can both be perceived as the same red. The category *red* contains central red as well as bordering hues such as purplish, pinkish, or orangey red. The resulting color concepts are simplifications that act perhaps much like "ideal types."[7] In sum, even sensation has its nonverbal but abstract concepts.

Basic-Level Concepts: Cognition Rooted in Worldly Activity

Linguistic concepts have to do with grouping the perceptual world into likes and dislikes. Concepts are so important that they are used as synonyms for categories, classifications, universals, generalizations, and linguistic groupings. To the naïve observer, the linguistically formed concept of cow is simply the same as the particular cow and therefore there is no problem about the source of such categories. Epistemological problems arise when we confront the cultural variation that in fact exists in conceptual groupings. Cross-culturally, linguistic classifications are clearly seen as involving more than what the empirical world of the senses give. The same tangible object is, transculturally, often categorized very differently. Granting conceptual commonalities stemming from transcultural manipulative experience, cultural groupings become obviously "read into" the world. They can no longer be seen as reflecting the given order. The idea of linguistically formed "projections" does not fit a position that assumes that our concepts are read out from the world. However, we need to ask why it is that on the practical level of life, these concepts do seem to mirror our worlds so directly. Here, as noted in chapter 4, objectivity, reality, and truth seem straightforward. The car either starts or it doesn't and the cat is on the mat or he isn't.

We have implied above one answer to the philosophically unproblematic character of life on the practical level: that many of our concepts have evolved to optimally fit our sensorimotor experiences of manipulating entities and adjusting to critical differences in the natural environment. Following Berlin and Kay (1969) and Mervis and Rosch (1981), Lakoff and Johnson (1999) describe the body-based properties of "basic level categories." These categories revolve around our perception or gestalt of "shapes." Sensation and mental imagery are heavily involved in basic-level categories. There are four conditions that characterize such categories: First, they are the highest level in which a *single mental image* can represent the entire category. While you can get a mental image of a chair, it is not possible to get one mental image of the category furniture—furniture including the many different shapes of chairs, tables, or beds. We can have an image of trains, boats, and planes, but not a mental image of the more general term "vehicle." Second, it is the highest level at which all category members have *perceptively similar* overall shapes. Third, it is the highest level at which a person uses *similar motor* actions for interacting with the particulars of the category. We have no specific motor programs for interacting with all pieces of furniture; we do with chairs, tables, and beds. Finally, it is the level at which *most of our knowledge is organized.* You can know many things about cars, but little about trains, tanks, and airplanes subsumed under the general category of "vehicles." How different this is from varieties of textualism where symbols only refer to other symbols!

Basic-level concepts are basic in the sense that they take priorities over lower and higher levels. Obviously, atemporal and aspatial concepts like time and space have no shapes whatsoever and are at a higher level. Also, lower-level concepts like different kinds of yams within the basic level are harder to recognize. According to Lakoff and Johnson, basic-level concepts are understood earlier by children, enter languages earlier in their history, have the shortest lexemes, and are identified faster by subjects.

Basic-Level Categories and Common Sense

Basic-level concepts derive from motor programs and mental images as well as gestalt perception involved in shapes. They make the traditional, empirical, and rationalistic assumptions that the categories of our minds fit the categories of the world quite plausible because they make effective action possible. These categories are the source of our most stable knowledge, and the technological instrumentation of science allows us to extend this stable knowledge. There are also basic-level actions for which we have mental images, such as swimming, walking, and grasping. Here, the link between human categories and divisions between things in the world suffices for the practicalities of everyday life. Metaphysical realism seems to work primarily at the basic level and makes sense to practically minded people. Evolution has not required us to be as accurate above and below this basic level. This is the level that matters most for our survival. It is the level in which our bodies most contribute to our sense of what is real.

This approach to conception breaks down the popular dichotomy between perception and conception. In the light of neuroscience, concepts in general can no longer be seen as purely mental and wholly separate from our abilities to see and move (Lakoff and Johnson 1999, 37, 463). To further undercut the sensation/conception distinction exaggerated by Leslie White, it is quite plausible that the same neurosystems engaged in bodily movements correlated with perception also play a central role in conception (see also Damasio [1994] and Franks [1999, 172]). According to recent findings, the idea is plausible that abstract thought arises out of neural projections from the sensory-motor parts of the brain to higher cortical regions. This fits nicely into the pragmatic notion that action is prior to thought on the developmental level.

Nonetheless, following Becker (1964), Laing (1960), and Marx (1964b) we will next suggest that one of the limits of higher level cognition is that it can so easily be used in a way that *removes* us from action in the real world. This is especially true if cognition is seen as existing in the lofty position usually granted it—for its sake alone, cut off from human action. We shall see below that neuroscience has much to say on this score as well.

Cognition and Distance from the World

It is a point of irony that an empirically oriented science can know the world only by getting as far away from it as possible and projecting onto it a peculiar leverage given solely by the extrasensory products of brain and its mind. Again, this may seem to contradict Lakoff and Johnson's (1999, 95) point that regardless of the necessarily abstract nature of concepts and their apparent removal from the sensed world, *we never were separated or divorced from reality in the first place*. The reasons for this are in the text above regarding basic-level concepts and common sense. What we have left out of their position is that higher-level concepts are formed by metaphors taken from our experiences with motor activities. We "hold" to our philosophical positions like we "hold" to a ball or a desired object. Higher-level spatial-relation concepts, for example, use the metaphor of the container. When we say "the bee is in the garden," we are imposing an imaginary container (Lakoff and Johnson 1999, 117). We assume the same container when we are *in* a "funk." A container is something that puts resisting borders on our sensorimotor movements. If we see a cat as being behind a tree, we are imposing a front and back on the tree that only makes sense in terms of our own position. Trees, being somewhat round, do not have fronts and backs.

Nonetheless these concepts are worldly, since they derive from our motor actions on the world. Lakoff and Johnson's emphasis is that science is made possible by our embodied activities on the world, not our transcendence of them. This is not to say that our overall mentality cannot become detached in a way that keeps us encased in our own words and fails to "somatically mark" features of the world outside of our verbal "spell" (Damasio 1994). In this section we elaborate on features of cognition that allow this detachment to happen.

It is through brain science that we can specify ways that the brain contributes its own "unworldly" character to perception, even if these extrasensory capacities were originally forged in evolutionary survival-struggles with the environment. By understanding this apparent contradiction, we can understand the importance of a truly behavioral approach to cognition, thought, or talk.

Concepts, Abstractions, and Linguistic Classification

The old empiricist theory as described by Cassirer (1953) was that concepts arose through repeated experience of similarly sensed shapes (likenesses). These similar sensations give rise to a habit of mind whereby the individual differences of sensed particulars cancel each other out and the similarities reinforce each other, becoming ingrained as concepts in the mind. The criterion for grouping things together, therefore, is determined by the naturally given fact that some objects are inherently similar to each other. This is the epitome of the self-actional, dualistic view of the mind as a blank tablet writ on by the environment.

According to Cassirer, the "most simple" reflection will show that similarity and dissimilarity themselves do not exist side by side with colors and tones or sensations of pressure and touch. We may debate the degree to which this realization is "simple," but observing the effort taken to understand the different classifications of the world will help make this clear. As stated before, by the time familiarity and linguistic habit have done their work, one culture's obvious similarity is the other's incomprehensible outrage. In short, the linguistic decisions about criteria for groupings are hardly matters of mere observation.

In recognizing the very large part that a particular language plays in determining what ends up appearing so obviously as "the same things," we cannot forget that the many linguistic choices are made from a pool of empirically available items. Our arrangements are not empirically groundless. We do arrange material things by means of empirically available criteria, *it is just that any of these empirical criteria will do, and that the possibility of sensible arrangements is so vast.* Logically, however, the *choice* that linguistic categories make among countless equally empirical similarities cannot, itself, be a matter of simple observation. That choice is read into the world by the linguistic process or the universal regularities of motor behavior. (Figure 5.1 will help clarify the interplay between empirical factors and cognitive-linguistic factors involved in determining the specific classification.)

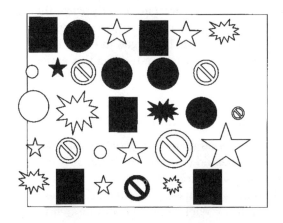

Cultural Arrangements

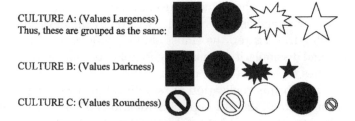

CULTURE A: (Values Largeness)
Thus, these are grouped as the same:

CULTURE B: (Values Darkness)

CULTURE C: (Values Roundness)

FIGURE 5.1 *Attributes of Things Prior to Categorization*

In this figure, linguistic categories are groupings of objects and events, both mind-made and nature-made, into likes and unlikes, similarities and dissimilarities. These are known as "classifications." Each culture groups things differently. As seen in the cultural listings above, obvious differences are ignored or "subsist."

These values become *criteria* for groupings. Note that classifications are tied to empirically available attributes. Once the classification is set up, they are read *out* of the world. "Nature" gives us any number of choices. Different languages choose only one criteria for the grouping and then make it look like nature did it. The impersonal, emergent cultural *choice* is read *into* the world. As Cassirer (1944) insisted, human and/or cultural choice is not of the same order as sensations. The type of social constructionism implied by linguistic relativism does not ignore the objectivity gained through sensation.

CLASSIFICATION AS RADICALLY SELECTIVE. The development of classifications, then, involves a radical abstraction wherein one of several potential similarities is mentally separated from the object and seen as defining its totality. The concept of race is a case in point. In this country, for example, skin color in many cases defines the whole person, obliterating the myriad of individual differences that could be seen as being significantly more important.

It has been commonplace to point out that literal fidelity to the given order, free of such mind-formed abstraction, is totally antithetical to sense-making. As William James (1953) states it:

> Is not the sum total of your actual experience taken at this moment and impartially added together utter chaos? The strains of my voice, the lights and shades inside the room and out, the murmur of the wind, the ticking of the clock . . . do these make a sensible whole at all? . . . It is an order that we have nothing to do with but to get *as far away from as possible* . . . we break it into histories, we break it into arts and we break it into sciences and we begin to feel at home.

Separating the Inseparable and Stopping the Unstoppable

The following succinct statement can express the extent to which high-level cognition violates the given order: *our minds separate the inseparable and stop the unstoppable.* For example, we have seen in chapter 2 how numerical dates and calculations of time literally stop the lived experience of time as continuous passage. To say that we cannot go back in time can hardly raise an argument. Yet cognition ignores this truism when we refer to the year 1785 at 5:30 PM and stop time dead in

its tracks to revisit the precise moment—at least mentally. Likewise and
to the same extent, we separate the inseparable, mentally breaking the
actual fluid of water into very different components of one part hydro-
gen and two parts oxygen. By means of what we call "analytical," as
opposed to "empirical," distinctions, we conceive of time and space as
totally separate considerations; we distinguish between heat and pressure, which are obviously aspects of the same process of the accelera-
tion of molecules. We separate perception into cognition, sensation, and
emotion as discreetly distinct processes. This chapter is virtual testi-
mony to these purely mental separations, but whatever mind-games
these separations play with reality, these violations have been essential
to the analytic aspect of deliberate thought and the making of science.

Linguistic relativity makes evident the indeterminacy of the symbolic. To continue our catalog of the ways cognition violates reality and
thus, ironically, wins practical control by escaping details, we go back to
Burke's reminder that every selective categorization ignores more than
it highlights. Discrimination, he says, is by the same token lack of discrimination (Burke 1968, 426).

Even with color concepts we "separate the inseparable." But here we
are talking of another level of conceptualization. According to Lakoff
and Johnson (1999, 96) basic-level concepts are extended to abstract theoretical domains. Despite the fact that we can *think* of the color red independent of any red object, red only really exists as an attribute of something else, like the sun or an apple or the color of blood. Some languages
do not make distinctions between blue and green, but interestingly
enough in light of sensory concepts, it is easy to teach people in these
cultures how to see these differences. Redness per se, as a linguistic category, is an idea that we detach from its real existence as an attribute we
place on material things. Any time we think of a color per se and then
paint it on a color chart, we are treating it as a thing apart from concrete
objects; we are "separating the inseparable." Only in the mind does red
exist as a *self-sufficient thing unattached to objects.* It takes up no particular space; it is located in no specific time. Being totally intangible, it
resists no physical push. It does not, in actuality, hover around independent of immediately perceived objects—except in our minds.

Likewise, there is no tangible thing like shape, independent of objects
that have shape, except in our minds. The general ideas of shape and
color per se are just two examples of an almost infinite number of so-
called "qualities" of things that our abstraction-generating brains make
into detached mental entities.[8] The advantage of their "unworldliness" is
that we can arrange them mentally in any number of ways and can think

of them as mere redness or roundness undistracted by their empirical existence as qualities of complex objects. To be able to think of "sound" in general rather than being stuck with only the notion of a particular and actual sound may be merely an imaginative exercise, but it is extremely advantageous. Only after we can make such false separations are we in the position to develop *theories* of sound. Although sensation is tied to the world of cause and effect, many generalizations, universals, or classes are purely products of linguistic mentality. The *choice* of criteria needed to group particulars is tied to this nondeterminate symbolic order. It underlies a balanced social constructionism's legitimacy.

For example, Newton could see a likeness that was not evident to any one else at his time. Allegedly, this likeness was between the apple falling from the tree and the orbit of the moon around the earth. What made these two empirically diverse things alike was his hypothetical notion of gravity. Certainly, to see these as examples of the same thing, he had to get as far away from the real tangible world as possible. Whatever the real exigencies of Newton's insight, it appears that the essence of high-level cognition is its creative and free-floating flexibility, its transcendence of the empirical world, its ability to separate the inseparable. This is what gives the human a lever to "step back" and figure things out rather than to be engulfed by experience. Here, the extrasensory devil must be given his due.

Precise renditions of the world's details are not cognition's forte despite our conviction that the closer and more precise we get, the more we know. Of course, precision and accuracy have a vital place, but they cannot be seen as characterizing the cognitive enterprise. We must appreciate the irony of the situation. In order to control the environment, we need to get away from it. Cognition derives from our transaction with the world, but higher-level abstraction unapplied to the world does not necessarily bring us closer to it, nor is it in itself a way of connecting with it. Connection is about effectively acting on the world. Cognition allows us to greatly simplify and analyze, thus giving control. As important as control is evolutionarily, by itself it leads to neither understanding nor wisdom. And, once again, even when we are successful in using analysis to produce efficacious action, we can always be pragmatically right (able to make intended things happen) for the wrong reasons.

On the Poverty and Scope of Mathematics

The clearest example of the poverty of abstraction and its "disconnect" from the world of actual particulars is, of course, mathematics. For years one of us has informally surveyed his students, young and old, on this matter. The vast majority of them see math as concrete rather than abstract, demonstrating how little is recognized about the use of these words. Math seems concrete to them because it is practical, familiar, and unchallenged in its authority. When informed, they readily concede its abstract nature. For example, few have difficulty seeing the poverty in the descriptor "one entity." This tells us next to nothing except that out of billions of other things, there is one of them. Even here, it does not tell us if there is *only* one. Think of the reality, emotional and otherwise, left out of the observation that the human death rate in the United States is approximately nine out of a thousand a year (Population Reference Bureau 2000). So at least 281 million deaths occur annually. The poverty of these abstractions is further hidden from us because we classify them as having the status of "objective fact," with all the ontological and epistemological authority implied in the term. If we justifiably laud the cognitive powers of such seriously selective abstractions, we should also recognize their dangers, since the actual particulars with their subjective experiences are omitted in each case. What they give, however, is tremendous scope enabling foresight, planning, and control.[9]

Remembering our theorem about dealing with dualisms, when we break down the antithetical contrasts between mind and body, organism and environment, we must also retain their differences and thus their tensions. The example of mathematics shows clearly how we can live solely in our own world of abstractions at a cost of losing connection with the world of actuality, especially for an "over-cognized" and distanced society such as ours.

Analysis and cognition has been used in just this way—to steel one's self from the realities of the world. This was Bruno Bettleheim's technique for survival in the Nazi concentration camps. He occupied himself by analyzing the mentality of the guards and the general situation so that he could exert whatever little control over the situation as possible, thus keeping somewhat at bay the emotional realities of the situation. Scheff (1979) has discussed the inadequacy of such over-distancing to mental health in his theory of aesthetic balance.

BALANCING ABSTRACTION WITH EMBODIMENT

Numerous theoretical attempts have avoided the over-distanced aspect of cognition that lacks the power in itself to move us to actions. These concepts describe the frailness of cognition that are balanced by the neuroscientist Damasio's notion of "somatic markers." First, however, we present efforts outside of neuroscience to achieve this same balance.

We include them to demonstrate the various ways that others have critiqued living in the world of detached thought and to share their various insights. Briefly describing these attempts should also make the meaning of Damasio's somatic markers more clear.

Concepts that "Subsist" and "Exist"

A similar slant on the otherworldliness of cognitive abstraction is given in the distinction revived by Becker (1964) between ideas that gain a psychological "hold" on us as compelling, and those that only "subsist" in the outer edges of awareness. The latter evoke only the most minor attention. In the earlier example of the calculation of death rates, the personal anguish associated with these rates only "subsists"—it is present, but so "faintly" that it hardly warrants attention. In most contexts these realities are held to be irrelevant. Damasio implies a similar phenomenological continuum between ideas that "subsist" and those that "exist" in his "somatic marker" hypothesis.[10] Some ideas—those that subsist—require a minimum of sensory feeling while some—that fully exist to us—provoke a great deal of such feeling. The idea of "freedom" and "the right to bear arms" among many U.S. citizens is a case in point. One advantage of concepts that "subsist" and therefore extract little out of us is that we can respond to them in such similar ways. Numbers in the abstract are a case in point. The personal (and therefore the room for disagreement) is minimized. As we have observed, such abstract terms—namely, those involving little personal identifications and meaning—are critical in establishing intersubjective objectivity because with them we are not immersed in our own particular experiences. Nonetheless, even with these important advantages, such "noninvolving" abstractions alone are not adequate for moving through our actual worlds, as Damasio's research with his brain-damaged patients described below will illustrate.

On the Promiscuity of "Pure" Cognition

Cognitions that only subsist do not compel action that is "suffered" and "undergone" on the level of "doing"—terms used by Dewey (1920, 86) and Anselm Strauss (1959). Consistent with our main theme, the experiences of others, both spoken and written, can certainly prove helpful as challenges arise, but no amount of linguistic description can "teach how you yourself will evaluate. You yourself must do, suffer, and undergo" (Strauss 1959, 25). Here, Strauss clearly assumes our distinction between mere verbalization and a more demanding type of action that includes the subjective "suffering"—the emotional and physical stresses—that only the actor can experience (since classification leaves out the particular). It is the emotion evoked by words and images that make them exist more fully in our mental experience and thus compel us to action, Purely cognitive understanding by itself moves nothing. It is the more emotional end of the continuum between "pure" cognition and extreme emotion that moves us to actual "doings" and commitment.

In contrast to cognition, the commitment involved in emotion connects and engages us with the world. Emotion gives personal involvement. We can "know," but do we "care"? Cognition is flexible because it need not carry felt commitment. We have seen how concrete objects can be grouped according to any number of abstract criteria. In this sense cognition is "promiscuous," especially compared to emotion (de Sousa 1987). We can group things one way at one moment, another way the next. We can change our cognition from one second to another in a way that emotion does not usually allow. It is difficult to love someone one second and hate them the next.

Cognition's power lies in the very opposite direction. It sacrifices emotional commitment for the flexibility of the mind-game when action in real life forces us to make either/or choices. For example, debaters and lawyers are particularly practiced at taking a variety of positions and arguing them out logically without necessarily believing any of them. Beliefs, being at least cousins to emotions, fix us. They take a "hold" on us in a way that pure cognition does not necessarily do, although we clearly get committed to certain thought patterns. Nonetheless, we do not merely think we might hate someone. The song that says "If you can't be with the one you love, love the one you're with" suggests a promiscuity of emotion that is contrary to its essence and is, instead, very characteristic of "pure" cognition. A word, name, or number can be attached to anything. The mere word "love" can apply to ice cream, country, sunsets, or our lovers. Love and hate as emotions attach to particular people. We love our particular daughters and sons. They are irreplaceable. De Sousa (1987) refers to this "irreplaceability" using the legal term "nonfungible."

In contrast, the power of cognition is that the term "apple" applies to all past apples, even those existing before humans inhabited the earth, and all future apples. The term "dollar" attaches equally to all particular bills defined this way by legitimated authorities. One is as meaningful as the other and are thus interchangeable. This quality is described in law as *fungibility*. The power of word-formed thought is not that it reflects a singular accurate picture of a totality, but that it so easily takes us out of the actual here and now. In one grand swoop it allows consideration of *all* actual examples of its class. If cognition is to be our crowning strength, we must see it for what it can do and also for what it cannot do. Cognition's lack of attachment to the objects and events of the world gives flexibility and control, but commitment and engagement with the world is made possible through emotion.

On Cognition Without Emotionally Given Realization

You can know something in the sense that it subsists in your mind, but not realize its significance. To realize something is to have it fully exist and to include its human significance in its understanding; for example, "now I realize that she really meant what she said." Realization, which often involves overt feelings, is tied to what we know now as "emotional intelligence" and is more encompassing than pure cognition.

Randolph Cornelius (1996, 150) tells a story of a bomber pilot during the Vietnam War. He had gone about his job as he was trained to do, flying by the book, arriving at a set of coordinates drawn on a navigational chart and following written procedures that he had internalized for various situations. Dropping bombs was experienced as a case of pulling the switch, just part of a procedure. Afterwards, this pilot had occasion to visit a village that he had bombed. Here, he learned the rest of the story and it changed his life. He came face to face with the full scope of what he had done to maim and kill innocent civilians young and old. His understanding was no longer of the sort that "by itself moves nothing." Emotionally tinged realization has to do with an important part of reason if reason is to be something other than preoccupation with the cheapest, quickest, and most guaranteed means to a goal. But even here we are proud of its stern "objectivity" that supposedly eliminates all human bias except its own.

This is particularly evident in moral considerations wherein abstract knowledge of right and wrong "moves nothing." As Seeberger (1992) suggests, mindless adherence to such "rational efficiency" creates not a thoroughly rational human being but a psychotic. In a television documentary, when asked about his actions before his execution, the serial killer Theodore Bundy said in effect that he "knew" what he did was wrong. There was no emotional evidence of remorse or genuine compassion for his victims. In our terminology, Seeberger is saying that there was no *realization* of what he did, though his words voiced the correct discursive answers. If Bundy's knowledge is seen as complete and genuine because of his so-called objectivity, then we need to redefine knowledge.

In one of the early classics in the sociology of emotion, Shott (1979) made the point that without the role-taking emotions of sympathy, embarrassment, shame, and guilt, we lacked the authentic, bodily given constraints on which morality depended. We needed more than cognition, Shott argued; we needed to add the compelling nature of emotion that made us genuinely not want to do such things. Without these emotions, cognition alone would only give more effectiveness to sociopaths and con men.

Somatic Markers and the Insufficiency of the Purely Symbolic

Damasios's neuroscience thesis of somatic markers ties together many of the older notions discussed above. It is directly germane to the place of emotion in the reasoning process and the important difference between "talking the talk and walking the walk," a phrase Damasio himself uses. Important in his whole scheme is that real life, as opposed to thought for thought's sake, forces choice, as we have noted above. The place of emotion in such decision making, however, lies much deeper than what has been described above in our discussion of realization. To understand this, we first need to appreciate what is referred to as the "insufficiency of pure reason" or in our terminology, the insufficiency of the purely symbolic. As Oatley and Johnson-Laird (1987, 30) stress, emotions "rather than being left out of models of human thought are *central to the organization of cognitive processing*" (italics added).

If overt, behavioral life demands decision making, pure thought gives only a scattering of possible choices. Choice implies preference. Out of the myriad of ideas and facts available, how do we objectively determine what is relevant to our choices? Consistent with traditional meanings of pure reason and objectivity, to determine the best course we would have to drop our "biases" and give equal consideration to all possible consequences and relevancies. But do we really have time to give equal weight to whether the price of tea in China or the weather will be affected by our action? According to de Sousa (1987, 193), this infinitely vast store of possible considerations gives rise to the "philosopher's frame problem"; namely, we need to know how to retrieve just what we need from this vast store and *not* consider what we do not need. *We need to know whether a consequence is relevant before drawing it* (de Sousa 1987, 194).

Emotion supplies this necessary bias by limiting what the organism will view as worthy of consideration. We tend to reject insights and suggestions from people we do not like, and we learn the hard way that this does not mean that everything they say is wrong. This is one reason why it is essential to practice emotional intelligence, but even there, the insufficiency of pure reason is enough to take pure cognition down from its pedestal of perfection.

For Damasio, negative and positive experience "marks" many ideas with a somatic state. This affective marker determines whether an idea will be center stage in our minds, or whether we will enter it into our decision making. Certainly, somatic markers become relevant to our discussions on realization and to what makes something authentically and spontaneously right or wrong for us. According to Damasio, and consistent with de Sousa's answer to the "philosopher's frame problem," somatic markers drastically reduce the number of options in choice making and are a special instance of feelings generated from the secondary emotions, which include those that Shott views as necessary for social control.

Evidence on the Inadequacy of Pure Cognition to Deal with Real Life

Antonio Damasio's research on patients physiologically deprived of certain emotional feelings provides the most telling empirical evidence that cognition alone is inadequate for actual life. To act, as we have seen, we must choose, and to choose, we must have something more than cognition and the capacity to manipulate words.

Damasio (1994) tells a convincing story of how he concluded that more than cognition was essential for rationality. He starts with the historical case of Phineas Gage. Gage was a well-mannered, competent foreman who had the unsettling task of drilling deep into rocks for the purpose of stuffing dynamite in the bottom of the holes. One day the dynamite went off prematurely and shot the rod through the bottom of his right jaw and outside of the left, front top of his brain. Amazingly, he lived! But he was never the same man. He became incorrigible—surly with caretakers and impulsive in financial matters. He became a social and financial disaster.

The classic case of Phineas Gage was the foundation of Damasio's long-term medical project. Over and over again he gathered cases of patients with similar lobe damage to the brain's prefrontal cortex. Behavioral similarities in these patients to Mr. Gage's were striking. Whatever the source of trauma, changes in thought patterns, lack of emotional capacities, and noxious behavior were linked to damage to the top-front gray matter of the brain. Injuries differed only in which sides of this middle-top region were affected. The biological name for this area is the "ventromedial prefrontal cortex." This is the area in which thought and general arousal, already intertwined, are fine tuned into the social emotions (guilt, shame, embarrassment, sympathy, etc.).

The first patient Damasio introduces us to is Eliot, a highly successful lawyer and "family man"—that is, until a tumor attacked his ventromedial cortex. While both sides were damaged, the condition of the right side was worse than that of Phineas Gage. As with many of Damasio's patients, Eliot passed with flying colors all the psychological tests administered. Most pertinent to his story was his very high performance on various intelligence tests and on a test that measured levels of morality. Of course, all of these were paper-and-pencil tests. Eliot could "talk the talk" in the lab. He knew cognitively what to say and what to write. He just couldn't "walk the walk." In real life he lacked emotional intelligence and his moral judgment was sorely lacking. His marital life disintegrated and a successful business career was in ruins. Eliot was down and out. But he didn't care.

Most important was the fact that he had only rudimentary feelings about anything. He could vent impatience and anger, which would abruptly dissolve. As Damasio listened to the tragic story of Eliot's social and business demise, he was almost moved to tears. But not Eliot; he could not have cared less. He could talk about emotions, but they did not move or compel him. He had no pity for himself or others. Emotional realization was nonexistent. His words were without the "somatic markers" or the "limbic glow" that would make them fully exist. Lacking effective role-taking emotions, his social life was ruined. Lacking feelings of value, he could not prioritize well enough to make appropriate judgments. Decision making is the hallmark of rational choice making. But feelings set saliency: they determine what we care most about. Choices, we have seen, depend on this.

Finally, the future did not exist for Eliot, at least not a future that constrained action. Long-range consequences were mere thoughts, if that. They were not somatically marked. Perhaps they "subsisted" in the mind's periphery, as empty, shadowy afterthoughts instead of in the emotionally given spotlight of emotionally tinged experiences. Uninhibited by futuristic apprehension or moral concern, Eliot went for immediate gain. Unfortunately, there was no lack of sleazy business partners ready to offer just that.

Eliot's behavioral symptoms of social incorrigibility and his inability to make successful choices were basically repeated in twelve other such patients treated by Damasio. They also had Eliot's myopia for the future. This group of patients revealed one other characteristic: They would compulsively list possible choices. For example, several patients would spend all their time in the waiting room listing all of the available times for their next appointment. But after all of this, none of them could make a commitment to a particular time. They simply could not choose. Lacking the somatic markers of emotion, they had no answer to "the philosopher's frame problem." They could formulate, but never implement. Again, they could "talk the talk" but not "walk the walk."

Damasio's last effort to understand his injured patients involved creating a gambling game that would reveal the subtle deficiencies of his subjects. Four decks of cards are placed in front of the patient; they are labeled A, B, C, and D. The purpose of the game is to lose as few as possible of the 2,000 play dollars allocated, and to win as much extra as possible. Turning the cards may result in earning some money, or both earning and losing money. Players turn cards from any of the four decks until the experimenter stops the game. No one but the experimenter knows the length of the game, the loss or gain in any card. Any card from decks A or B pays $100; decks C and D pay $50. Sometimes the player is shocked to learn that the $100-paying decks require a high penalty, as much as $1,250. Decks C and D sometimes require a much smaller penalty of less than $100. True to life, "there is no way for the player to predict at the outset what will happen or to keep in mind a precise tally of gains and loses" (Damasio 1994, 213).

Normal subjects show an early preference for the highly rewarding decks A and B, but within 30 moves switch to C and D. Bit by bit they develop the intuition that in the long haul decks A and B are more dangerous than C and D.

Ventromedial prefrontal patients were very different. Somatically marked apprehensions of the long haul did not move or compel them. Halfway through the game they were bankrupt, as they were in real life. Experience in playing the game taught nothing. Remember, these were highly intelligent, attentive players. Patients with serious damage to other parts of the brain caught on, whereas the ventromedial patients did not. After paying a large "fine" for choosing decks A and B, Eliot and others like him avoided the penalty decks just as others did, but unlike the others, they would soon return to the bad decks. They were sensitive to punishment; it just didn't last. They did not lack an abstract future— what they lacked was a future that they cared about. Since this makes intelligent people into very poor rational decision makers, Damasio (1994, 218) suggests that the images constituting future scenarios are weak and unstable. In our terms, they merely "subsisted."

CONCLUSION

Damasio's clinical studies test hypotheses independently formulated by fields as different as artificial intelligence and philosophy. So ends the most persuasive argument available to our knowledge for the embodiment of reason and the inadequacy of pure cognition (purified of emotion and behavioral influences) to equip a person for actual life. The "all within discourse" axiom makes it difficult to deal with the demands that real life put on Damasio's patients, who had to act in a world that demands more than what pure thought for thought's sake could provide. All of his patients, as well as Phineas Gage, were constantly symbolizing, defining, and interpreting their worlds. However, they needed more than this, and our social psychological theory must give proper emphasis on what this "more" is. Making instantaneous choices is a demand of the behavioral world that must be seen in transactional tension between the verbal and nonverbal. We also need to understand the place of emotion in dealing with the demands of a world beyond our words.

In this chapter, we have seen that the "read-in" aspects that forced the "issues" of epistemology are actually *brain*-given rather than world-given processes, although higher-level abstraction is made possible by our worldly transactions. We have shown how our so-called objective abstractions can get out of hand unless balanced by emotion and some degree of praxis. When we consider that the brain only functions in the context of other brains and environments, we escape both "self-actional" thinking and erroneous reductionism that sociologists associate with brain studies.

To return to the discussion of abstract knowledge and pathology, Damasio (1994, 178) writes that the effect of a sick culture on a normal adult can foster the so-called "objective thinking" that values only itself and gives somatic markers to one thing above all—profit and its resulting wars. We would add the emotion widely known as "corporate greed." Damasio himself fears that "sizable sectors of Western society are gradually becoming other tragic examples."

Neuroscience's contribution to our knowledge of emotion makes us confront, instead of hide, the necessary value judgments in the land of "sweet reason." Emotion is the creation of personal values; it is personal axiology. There will never be an escape into the nirvana-type land of logical finality, because logic does not stand alone—not unless we are just "talking the talk."

NOTES

1. Here we follow Lakoff and Johnson's *Philosophy in the Flesh* (1999), which borrows from second-generation cognitive science instead of the old version that reified and disembodied cognition. In our opinion, these authors fill-in the neuroscience details needed to refine the social behaviorism of Mead and the Chicago pragmatists. This is true especially in their assertion that activity is

prior to thought developmentally, generically, and in time sequence. The neuro-scientist Damasio (1994) is also helpful in this regard.

2. This was a major theme of the late Ernest Becker (1964); however, he saw it as the foundation of pathological "schizophrenia." If not carried to this extreme, his thesis fits well with Marx and Peirce. Self-powers grow as they overcome resistance. In order to be, there must be an object outside of one's self. Of course, academics develop self-powers in manipulations of symbols whether they be sociologists, mathematicians, or philosophers. But symbol objects are different than person objects and material ones. R. D. Laing (1960) is cited at this critical point by Becker. To Marx, philosophers exemplified individ-uals who almost exclusively related to symbol-objects. Alienation to Marx was any style of thought that divorces one from action and separates itself from the involvement of the total individual (Becker 1964, 124–25). As we shall soon see, involvement implies emotion. Much of this chapter is our own way of detailing the point made by Becker, Laing, and Marx.

3. Cognition, so frequently associated with the objective, *becomes* subjective when seen as purely "mentalistic." In this context, as we have mentioned, cog-nitions are seen as existing self-contained, in our own heads, unrelated to action.

4. This oversimplified and partial comparison with some forms of poststruc-turalism points to enough commonality that similar implications are drawn. The world external to the symbol is largely erased and the way is paved toward a totally relativistic, ungrounded social constructionism.

5. White's most influential article was, perhaps, "The Symbol: The Origin and Bases of Human Behavior" (see White 1949). We alluded before to how this left out nonverbal behavior or gesture as the origin of speech. We use White, how-ever, only because he wrote clearly and was reprinted so often. He was only part of a large group making the same argument. A description of primate tool-use that is less categorical can be found in Lindesmith, Strauss, and Denzin (1991), but even they could not present a thoroughly embodied discussion of symbols and the concepts symbols convey because the information was not available at that time. This does not minimize the widespread effect of the overly symbolic framework that has ignored the importance of embodiment in social psychology.

6. They also call into serious, if not decisive, question the validity of analytic philosophy and the correspondence theory of knowledge.

7. Cognition's birth in the peculiarities of the human body destroys the tra-ditional understandings of its ability to connect us to a universal nature outside of our *ümwelt*—the world carved out for our attention by our capacities, sensi-tivities, and motor repertories. It seriously questions whether the logic and structure of our minds are the same as the "principles" that guide the "self-actional" universe. Abstract reason appears to be a character of humans alone. But if seen in light of the "objective reality of perspectives"—that is, as a rela-tion between the body and the environment—we can still retain the reality and objectivity provided by this "transactional slab." It is just that we are objectively stuck inside of this "transactional slab," as it were; we only perceive that which answers to our capacities and is "patient" of our transducers.

8. While the Greeks reified these categories of qualities into fixed essences, we place them in human language.

9. As noted above, many philosophers insist that there is common ground between the principles of the world and our brain-given mentality. Many see this connection as mathematical. Others see this mutuality as pure reason. Here, our brains and reality are moved by the same principles. This is certainly a comfortable idea. From what we gather from our senses as transducers, we are too limited to accept such a mutuality. For example, our brains will seek out and create reasonable patterns where there are none (Gazzaniga 1998). The exaltation of cognition, and by implication high-level abstraction divorced from emotion, body, and activity into the principles guiding the universe, can be seen as presumptuous. It has created a dangerously imperceptive "normal schizophrenia" behind our rational-efficient culture.

10. Damasio, as much as almost any philosopher or psychologist, has demonstrated the importance of the body in cognition. The exception to this is, of course, Lakoff and Johnson. Some ideas, like mathematical ones, involve so little of our bodily given feelings that they seem not to be derived from our organisms at all. This misconception is encouraged by the fact that conceptions are seen as extrasensory, atemporal, and aspatial. The most detached abstraction is still "bodily." The difference is only in the degree and the parts of the body involved.

PART TWO

Applications to Selected
Sociological Fields:
An Embodied Approach

◙   ◙   ◙

CHAPTER SIX

Toward a Transactional Sociology of the Body

In this chapter we continue to strive for a more coherent notion of reality, objectivity, and truth by incorporating the human body further into our transactional framework and sociological theorizing. This stance towards the body contrasts sharply with the orientation of classical social theory and contemporary sociological thought. The sociology of the body has been a late arrival as a legitimate field of sociological study and the body has received only minimal attention (Turner 1984). This is curious when one considers the paradigmatic importance of human action to sociology. It should be self-evident that when we speak of the action of individuals, we are really referring to the actions of their *bodies*. Unfortunately, most twentieth-century sociological theory has been blind to what should be obvious to everyone: The body is the vehicle of human action and all selves are embodied selves (Damasio 1999).

Proceeding from this last point, we endeavor to orient the sociological imagination to the reality and objectivity of the body and show why it must be seen as a basic unit of analysis. We supplement our transactional interpretation of work in the sociology of the body with theoretical concepts and empirical evidence from other fields of study such as medical sociology, epidemiology, criminology, the sociology of risk, and neurosociology. Applying the relational view of subjectivity and objectivity to the body allows us to see it as both subjective agent and objective reality—

as the vehicle of transaction and a socially inscribed object. This perspective is supported by the rapidly accumulating evidence from research in medical sociology and epidemiology, which points to a strong relationship between social factors and health status. The evidence is reviewed with an eye to what it indicates for the transactional approach to reality and objectivity. Next, we demonstrate the analytical power of the transactional framework by showing how existing work on the body can be reframed in relational terms. While much of our discussion has focused on the determinacy of sense perception, here we stress how embodied selves come to terms with the feature they share with all other dimensions of reality—the indeterminacy of the natural world. Finally, we conclude by discussing how our analysis challenges traditional dualistic thinking about the relationship between nature and culture.

THE CORPOREAL BODY, THE SOCIAL BODY, AND THE SUBJECT–OBJECT RELATION

In order to develop a transactional interpretation of the body's significance for reality and objectivity, we must return to our typology of action discussed in chapter 3. It is possible to extend the earlier discussion of the typology by looking more closely at the body's implication in all forms of action, including thought and talk. Asserting that all action is embodied is to say that every form of action depends upon processes that are governed, in turn, by the lower-level actions of organ systems, tissues, molecules and atoms. Hence, when human beings act in the physical and social worlds, the organic agent of that action is the body—in sociological terms, the body is subject in the sense of agency.[1]

However, it is also important to understand the body as an environment to be acted upon—the body as object. Acknowledging that "bodies are used purposefully by the consciousness within them" (Frank 1995, 50) is not a slip back into the disembodied conception of human actors that has dominated modern sociology. Rather, it merely directs attention to the multidimensional nature of organic action systems, a complex structure in which each level forms an environment for acting entities (symbolic processes, tissues, chemicals, atoms, etc.) at some more reduced level. Thus the action of neurotransmitters crossing synaptic gaps of millions of neurons underlies "intentions" within a conscious mind that are actualized and resisted by other body systems. Insofar as these more emergent body systems impose terms on the thought processes involved in the formation of purposes, they exist in objective relation to subjective consciousness, even as the body as a whole stands in *subjective* relation to the ecological and social environments acted upon by human beings. These considerations point to the inadequacy of subject–object dualism in relation to the body. The corporeal body can only be viewed properly as simultaneously subject and object.

The transactional framework thus insists on a view of human thought that is captured by conjoining the terms "embodied" and "consciousness." Embodied consciousness is the process of the embodied mind becoming conscious of itself (Frank 1995, 51). Frank believes that this idea can serve as the starting point for significant advances in social theory: "Only on this grounding can theory put selves into bodies and bodies into society" (1995, 91). This idea is crucial for the development of a fully transactional perspective, but it only captures one side of the coin: theory must also explain how society is put into bodies.

To better understand the process of embodied awareness and the penetration of the corporeal body by the social environment as an aspect of this process, we must return to the type of transaction we identified as praxis. Understood as the actualization of intentions to alter a world that responds indifferently to these acts, praxis is a crucial concept for exploring the ontological status of embodied consciousness. As Mead argued, "the body becomes most conscious of itself when it encounters *resistance* . . . which is to say, when it is in use, acting" (Frank 1995, 51 [emphasis added]). The body's capacity for the manipulation of objects to achieve specific ends is the foundation of the double-edged process by which environmental objects are constituted and sensitivities and capacities are broadened. But the purposeful manipulation of objects is problematic: the objects (people and things) of one's attention and action do not always respond as one anticipates. Thus action undertaken by the body meets with resistance, which forces a refinement of the action and further development of the bodily capacity or sensitivity. The body becomes most acutely conscious of itself in this way.

As embodied selves transact with elements of the material world, they make use of internalized strategies and knowledge available to them as members of social–cultural systems. Problem-solving efforts have an impact on both the body and the social world. On the one hand, the implementation of structural strategies "both reproduces and transforms those structures in interactive response to the problems posed by changing historical situations" (Emirbayer and Mische 1998, 970). On the other hand, the bodies engaged in this action are *inscribed* by the structural patterns involved in problem solving. Acquiring a full repertoire of socially prescribed action patterns is the means by which we develop our species potential and form a conscious embodied self. The action patterns to which we refer belong to the world of Durkheimian "social facts" that shape both the bodies and minds of human organisms.

Thus, in transactional terms, we can conceive of the body as an acting subject within a social environment made up of social facts. But we must also appreciate that social facts should not be reified. They exist only insofar as they are objectified in the form of the embodied interaction of living people. People experience the external world through their transacting bodies while, at the same time, they experience their bodies by means of the action patterns and perceptions provided by the sociocultural system. This is the second meaning of the assertion that the body is both subject and object: we *are* bodies (body as biological subjective agent) at the same time that we *have* bodies that act in socially prescribed ways and are constructed through existing cultural categories (body as social object). A similar claim can be made for the self: we *are* social selves (social facts are appropriated by and shape the subjective body) at the same time that we *have* social selves (the body objectifies and transcends social facts). Hence, bodies become social and the social becomes organically objectified.

In order to clarify the transactional interpretation of the body's objectivity, we will shift to a discussion of concrete empirical evidence relating to the key themes. Although research conducted by empirically oriented medical sociologists and social epidemiologists has not been related in any systematic way to transactional models of agency and structure, we believe that some of the accumulating evidence from these fields strongly supports the view presented here. Consequently, we will draw on this evidence to demonstrate how culture and social structure become inscribed in the actual organic tissues of the body in a process involving the socialization of the body and the corporeal objectification of the social.

THE SOCIAL REPRODUCTION OF EMBODIMENT

The proposition that social forces are as important as biological forces in the formation of bodies is supported by a growing body of evidence. Researchers in many different fields have documented variations in body structure and physiological functioning across social groups, between whole societies and various group formations within societies. The discipline of social epidemiology provided some of the earliest evidence of this sort by identifying variations in the distribution of disease and disability by age, gender, race, class, and other sociological categories. Initial efforts to explain these variations focused on issues of differential access to medical care and social-group variations in health care practices (compliance, health-seeking behavior, etc.). However, recent research has pointed to the intriguing possibility that the different rates of mortality and morbidity may be a consequence of social-group variations in physiological functioning. It is unclear precisely how social factors are related to these physiological variations, but one possibility is that action patterns tied to specific institutional locations could have a direct impact on biological function. This opens up a new space in which biological and medical events can be observed.

Social Location and Biological Function: The Evidence from Epidemiology

People transacting with elements of external reality in everyday problem solving confront pragmatic challenges that are structured by the institutional environment: the specific problems they address and the ways in which they approach these problems are a product of the institutionalized roles enacted. Consequently, all of the biologically based sensitivities and capacities involved in problem solving are organized by the broader institutional imperatives reflected in various role-pattern sets. Action systems operating at many different levels within the body (cognitions, emotions, muscles, etc.) are activated and integrated by the demands of a particular problem to be solved, but the problems that become the focus of human attention and action emerge through institutional processes. In this way, social institutions indirectly shape bodily function. Moreover, because role patterns are not only components of social institutions but are also organized into social strata defined by gender, ethnicity, and class, we would expect to find differences in biological function across these strata, as revealed in the social epidemiological data. Once again, the mediating terms in the social determination of such biological differences are the kinds of general problem-solving complexes that typically arise within each stratum.

The transactional approach to social-group variations in health status can be utilized further by considering an exciting new line of interdisciplinary research on population health. In a recent review of findings from several different fields, ranging from epidemiological studies to genetic and neurological research, Evans, Barer, and Marmor (1994) shed some light on the complex causal connections involved in health status variations. Consonant with the perspective presented here, these authors view the body as a product of both social and biological forces. Indeed, Evans, Barer, and Marmor note that recent studies make an even stronger case for structural variations than did earlier research. For example, the massive Whitehall study led by Marmot (1986; Marmot, Kogevinas, and Elston 1987) has helped to clarify the socioeconomic factors that are most important to health status by including indirect controls for some of the suspected variables. The subjects of this study, British civil servants (N = 10,000+), represented an ideal population for studying the social determinants of health: as civil-service employees, members of all occupational strata had an adequate standard of living (in absolute terms) and they all could access health care within the National Health Service.

Examining age-standardized mortality rates over a ten-year period, Marmot and his associates found a clear gradient across the status hierarchy of occupational categories, with death rates among males in manual and clerical grades three-and-a-half times higher than male death rates in senior administrative grades. With material deprivation and access to health care controlled, it appears that the critical social factor behind the gradient in mortality was the phenomenon of "hierarchy." This led Evans, Barer, and Marmor (1994, 6) to conclude that "there is *something* that powerfully influences health and that is correlated with hierarchy per se."

This is not the place to attempt even an initial sketch of a biosocial model of the relationship between hierarchy and health status, but it is possible to orient the data to a transactional interpretation of how the power hierarchy imposes itself on human bodies. Our premise is that all of the social, psychological, and biological action systems related to the observed health differences are keyed to the problem-solving imperative within the human species. Indeed, even the basic "fight–flight" model of the stress response supports this premise. The set of action systems involved in this response—neurological systems related to perception of a threat, physiological changes that mobilize resources, immunological changes stimulated by biochemical and neurological factors—is focused on the immediate *task* of ensuring the survival of the organism. Hence, even in the absence of problem-solving complexes that introduce many other factors into the process (control, prediction, etc.), the biological changes that affect health are influence by the fleeing or fighting requirements of human prehistory.

When we move from this fundamental survival task to the problem solving within complex societies, the relationship between the social and biological dimensions becomes much more complicated. One important complication relates to the problems created by the fight–flight response itself, namely, the increasing maladaptiveness of this evolved capacity within the social contexts of modern life. The product of millions of years of evolution, this trait was adaptive in the environments occupied by human beings for most of our evolutionary history. However, for members of postindustrial society, the mobilization of the body for feats of physical exertion is generally irrelevant to genetic fitness. In a social environment that demands increasingly sedentary lifestyle patterns, the physiological response to perceived threat generates a potential for which there is no release. We are just beginning to understand the complex neuroimmunological processes that account for the damage to health caused by this unreleased potential.

If the irrelevance of the basic fight–flight response to modern problem solving has had important consequences for the human body, the broader social and cultural patterns that circumscribe problem solving within modern societies may also have an impact on body function. One way to make sense of the Whitehall data is to consider variations in work conditions across the hierarchy of occupational groups. In recent years, researchers have devoted significant attention to social psychological factors involved in various types of work, with variations in stress receiving perhaps more attention than any other factor. A wealth of data on the precursors and health effects of stress presently exists, but little progress has been made on developing general concepts for organizing the vast amount of data currently available. Evidence is accumulating on the relationship between hierarchy and stress in human and nonhuman primates, connections between the neurological and immunological systems in stress-related illness, the effects of social support on stress, and many other dimensions of the stress response. A biosocial framework for integrating this evidence is now sorely needed. The concept of "praxis" may be a key component of such a framework.

This possibility is suggested by another line of study that is relevant to the relationship between hierarchy and illness: research focusing on the health effects of the work environment. While workers who occupy positions lower in the administrative hierarchy may experience more stress that those in higher positions, the more important factor in the experience of low-strata workers may be their lack of control over work conditions. Recent research indicates that individuals are less likely to experience ill effects in highly stressful work if they also experience control and novelty in the tasks they perform (Karasek and Theorell 1990). This finding would help to explain the phenomenon of "eustress"—high-level stress that seems to impart psychological and biological benefits to people who experience it. Individuals who value and actively seek out high-stress situations (particularly high-risk occupations and leisure sports) often report that having direct personal control over the tasks to be performed is critical to their enjoyment of the stress-ful activity (Lyng 1990b). Hence, one could argue that the key factor mediating between hierarchy and health status is *not* stress per se, but rather the opportunity to experience praxis in one's work; that is, putting one's creative cognitive capacities and manipulative skills to work in solving practical problems.

The issue of control over the conditions of work is directly relevant to the Whitehall findings on the relationship between hierarchy and health status. A key feature of hierarchical arrangements within bureaucratic work environments is variation in control over work, with workers in higher grades typically exercising more control in their problem-solving activities than do lower-grade workers. Thus it is possible that the gradi-ent in mortality and morbidity across the occupational hierarchy may be due, in part, to varying opportunities for independent problem solving. As one moves down the hierarchy, control in problem-solving activities decreases, shifting from an "internal" locus to various "external" loci such as clients/customers, supervisors, production technology, bureau-cratic formulae, and so on (see Edwards 1979). Labor becomes increas-ingly "alienated" in the classical Marxian sense and workers are offered fewer opportunities for the development of biopsychosocial capacities through praxis. The tension resulting from unconsummated transaction potentials may be comparable to the unreleased potential of the fight–flight response in members of postindustrial society who live sedentary lives filled with perceived threats to their well-being.

Reality, Objectivity, and the Social Inscription of Bodies

The epidemiological data presented here offers compelling evidence of the social determination of bodies, as well as the other side of the transactional coin—the organic objectification of social structure. In reviewing these data, we find strong empirical support for our claim that social structure makes its way into human bodies, shaping and deter-mining bodily tissues and physiological functioning. Group differences in health status can be taken as a measure of socially induced variations in body structure, which may arise from important differences in the problem-solving strategies related to class, gender, age, race, occupa-tion, and other social-group affiliations.

Although we focus on the social inscription of the body in this chap-ter, it is important to also appreciate how corporeal transactions consti-tute the social and material world. As the subjective agent of transac-tion, the body emerges as a socially inscribed object in the course of constituting the objects of its natural environment. Thus it is possible to say that *material reality*—the body and its natural environment—is constituted through the transactions of embodied selves. The objects of the natural world are carved out of obdurate reality by the attention and action of embodied actors who occupy specific positions within the social order. Social-group differences in health status may emerge as objective consequences of the corporeal reality created by these transactions. Moreover, these same transactions also constitute *social reality*. As the existing stock of social knowledge is used in everyday problem solving, these structures are reproduced and transformed, and the body in transaction with natural objects leaves its imprint on the social world. Thus the reality that we confront as human beings, in both the material and social sense, can be seen as the emergent product of social actors' embodied transactions. The body's constitutive role in reconstructing social reality will be discussed in the next chapter.

At this point, however, our concern is to get beyond the conceptual limitations of research that does not deal directly with the body but rather focuses on concepts such as "health," "illness," "physiological functioning," and similar abstractions. In the spirit of the pragmatist tradition that inspired our transactional approach, we want to avoid as much as possible the "tyranny of the abstract" (O'Brien 1989) in favor of "stick[ing] to the concrete" (Rorty 1985, 173). Here, our goal is to construct a narrative about the body's relationship to objectivity, reality, and truth. We now turn to work that is explicitly committed to such a strategy as well as developing an analytical framework for the sociology of the body.

THE BODY AS A PROBLEM

The new interest in the body is moving sociology into an area that has been generally off-limits in the past. As we have noted, traditional sociological conceptualizations of the human actor have excluded the body as a problem worthy of theoretical attention. The Cartesian distinction between mind and body put the biological and social sciences on different pathways and created a disciplinary divide that has been difficult to bridge. However, the limitations of sociology's "body-less" conception of the actor are now beginning to be recognized, primarily as a result of the pioneering work of Bryan Turner and some of his British colleagues (see Featherstone, Hepworth, and Turner 1995).

Within this developing field, the work that is most directly relevant to our transactional perspective is Arthur Frank's (1995) impressive review of theory devoted to the body. This work is particularly useful for our analysis, because of the way in which Frank frames the central problem to be addressed regarding the body. Responding to the efforts by Turner (1984) and others in this area, Frank criticizes the structuralist bias in defining the key problem of the body for sociological analysis. He points to Turner's implicit use of Parsonian functionalism (albeit functionalism with a critical twist) as a reference point for analyzing bodies in terms of the "social-order" problem. Beginning with the body as a functional problem for society, Turner identifies four "societal tasks" that all societies must fulfill in regard to bodies: reproduction, regulation, restraint, and representation. These tasks all relate to the problems of governing bodies for purposes of meeting social system needs (Frank 1995, 42–45).

In stating his reservations about this kind of approach, Frank adopts a position that reflects the basic tenets of our transactional approach and the pragmatist ontology from which it derives. He questions the usefulness of positing social-system "needs" and "tasks" and points out that these concepts are best related to the body itself. "*Bodies alone have 'tasks.'* Social systems may provide the context in which these tasks are defined, enacted, and evaluated, but social systems themselves have no 'tasks'. . ." (1995, 48 [emphasis in original]). In accordance with the pragmatist injunction to "stick to the concrete," Frank argues for defining the problems of analysis from the perspective of actual living bodies rather than reified theoretical abstractions like the social system. "I propose . . . to begin with how the body is a problem *for itself*, which is an action problem rather than a system problem, proceeding from a phenomenological orientation rather than a functional one" (1995, 45). This pragmatic shift opens up new possibilities for sociological analysis: "The point of a sociology of the body is not to theorize institutions prior to bodies, but to theorize institutions from the body up" (1995, 49).

What follows from this shift in orientation is a typology of body usage constructed from the "four questions which the body must ask itself as it undertakes action in relationship to some object" (1995, 51). These questions define the four continua that serve as the parameters of the typology. The questions are: (1) Will the body's performance be predictable or unpredictable? (the problem of *control*); (2) is the body lacking or producing? (the problem of *desire*); (3) is the body monadic/closed or dyadic/open to others? (the problem of its *relations to others*); and (4) is the body's consciousness associated or disassociated with its own corporeality? (the problem of its *self-relatedness*). The polar extremes of these continua can be combined to form a matrix of four cells designating styles of body usage (Frank 1995, 51–54). The body styles included are the disciplined body, the mirroring body, the dominating body, and the communicative body.

As we will see, Frank's typology can serve as a powerful organizing device for bringing together various theoretical perspectives on the body into a coherent analytical framework. However, as useful as this framework is for understanding the body's transactions with objects of its environment, it is flawed in one important way and must be modified to function effectively for our purposes. Consequently, it will be necessary to address this flaw before discussing how Frank's concepts inform our understanding of the body's status as subjective agent and socially inscribed object.

Frank's pragmatic turn is an important step forward in orienting sociological inquiry about the body to the problems of reality and objectivity, but the primary limitation of his approach can be traced to its failure to fully embrace the pragmatist ontology. In constructing his typology, Frank assumes that the four questions the body asks of itself are all of equal importance. On the contrary, the overriding experience of corporeality is captured by the dialectic between the subjective and objective aspects of the body: the sense of both *being* a body and *having* a body simultaneously. Indeed, these two dimensions cannot be separated in actual experience, because it is in the action of the body as subjective agent that we discover it's ego-alien unpredictability. The latter experience—the sense of the body as external to us and a part of nature—forms the key problem of the body.

As a part of nature, the body's spontaneity and unpredictability reflects what pragmatists see as the defining quality of this reality: its indeterminate character. As Dewey (1946, 351) notes:

> Any view which holds that man is a part of nature, not outside it, will certainly hold that indeterminacy in human experience, once experience is taken in the objective sense of interacting behavior and not as a private conceit added on to something totally alien to it, is evidence of some corresponding indeterminateness in the process of nature within which man exists (acts) and out of which he arose. (Quoted in Shalin 1992, 257)

Thus "objective uncertainty" is the essential nature of the emergent universe, and the body reflects this uncertainty no less than any other aspect of the natural world. Moreover, the pragmatist ontology accounts for determinant relations and order that arises in the midst of indeterminacy by referencing the transacting agent:

> It is up to concrete reasoning—always an interest-bound, socially anchored, situationally specific undertaking—to lift the world from its natural state of indeterminacy and turn it into a meaningful, manageable,

semiorderly whole. This objective whole maintains its predictable properties insofar as we sustain our interest in it, as long as our determined
collective efforts last. (Shalin 1992, 258)

Within this framework, transaction is the means by which human
actors "terminate indeterminacy" by bringing out some of the potentialities of a situation and "render[ing] obscure its other possible determinations" (Shalin 1992, 258). Herein lies the key problem of the body for
human agents: Because we cannot act without our bodies, we are forced
to confront in every action the reality of the body's objective uncertainty.
As an aspect of indeterminate reality, our bodies do not perform just as
we want them to. Hence the body possesses an indeterminacy that must
be terminated, although this end can never be fully realized. Every termination "brings out some potentialities and renders others obscure."
Corporeal contingency is the body's primary problem and the focus of
ongoing efforts to terminate or control it through transactions with
other elements of the environment.

Examining Frank's scheme from this ontological standpoint, we see
corporeal contingency now as something more than one problem among
several equally important issues that bodies must resolve in transacting
with external objects. As we have suggested, transaction is the means by
which determinacy is achieved in the context of an indeterminate reality—a reality that includes the body itself along with every other aspect
of nature:

Whatever determinacy we encounter in the world is . . . of our own making. We terminate indeterminacy in deed and in situ, using the terms
supplied by a community, and we do so as participant-observers who
are part and parcel of the situation we seek to comprehend. (Shalin
1992, 258)

Transaction links the opposing poles of determinacy and indeterminacy
in both our bodies and the rest of the natural world, insofar as the body
determines itself at the same time that it determines the objects of its
environment. Any scheme for connecting body styles to transaction
must give priority to corporeal contingency as one aspect of this fundamental dialectic in human experience.

With this last point in mind, we can now reconsider Frank's body-
usage scheme. We propose to conceptualize each of the body styles—
the disciplined, mirroring, dominating, and communicating forms—as
specific strategies for terminating corporeal indeterminacy. And while
all four body styles are linked by this common problem, they are distin-

guished by the kind of transactions that are used to deal with corporeal contingency. Thus for the disciplined body, *production* is the medium of transaction; for the mirroring body, *consumption* is its medium; and for both the dominating and communicating bodies, *social interaction* is the common medium.[2] Using this modified version of Frank's scheme as our assumptive framework, we will now discuss how each of the styles of body usage informs our understanding of the concepts of objectivity, reality, and truth.

The Disciplined Body

For the disciplined body, the primary transactional moment is the relationship between self-conscious intentions and a body that responds either predictably or unpredictably to these intentions. Thus the primary issue for the disciplined self is coming to terms with the contingency of the body—overcoming the body's *resistance* (which derives from its contingency) to one's intentions. The key to understanding this body type is to appreciate its connection to the central imperatives of modern bureaucratic/industrial/scientific societies. Although Frank's discussion of the disciplined body makes minimal references to Marx and Weber— understandably so, since neither theorist has much to say about the body, the predominant themes of the Marxian and Weberian analyses of modern industrial societies are directly relevant to the social constitution of disciplined bodies. The "productivist" orientation of both of these classical theorists led to distinctive analyses of the structural forces shaping production activities in modern societies. A significant amount of scholarship has been dedicated to explaining and debating the differences in Marx's and Weber's approaches to this problem, but it is clear that they share a common view of the disciplining effects of industrial production techniques.

Weber's focus on the rationalization process is clearly the most useful perspective within the classical canon for understanding the origins of the disciplined body. If, as Weber proposed, the central imperative of Western societies has been the steady expansion of formal rationality over all aspects of social and economic life, one important consequence of this trend has been the increasing efforts to discipline the body (see also Elias 1978). In the sphere of production, the goal of enhancing calculability, efficiency, predictability, and control over the productive process has required that the body be subjected to increasing managerial scrutiny. This is true of bodies engaged in manual labor as well as mental labor, because any unpredictability in bodily performance results in the loss of efficiency and reduction in profits. Hence, industrial and postindustrial managerial strategies have devised many ways to produce regimented bodies, from personal-supervisory control and machine discipline to "scientific management" and bureaucratic control (Edwards 1979).

In the early stages of industrial capitalism, the disciplining of the body was most often externally imposed and met with a degree of resistance from workers. However, since the work regimen offers a solution to the body's key problem—the need to terminate its own indeterminacy, the disciplined body also became a desired ideal for many members of bureaucratic-capitalist society. Indeed, the disciplined body's capacity to respond to corporeal and structural demands simultaneously makes it difficult to draw a clear line between imposition and choice in the constitution of this body style. The decline of manufacturing labor and the rise of professional work resulted in an even more pronounced shift to self-imposed discipline and the acceptance of the disciplined body as a normative standard. Even with the greater degree of autonomy and control over work conditions enjoyed by independent professionals, maintaining the efficiency and predictability of one's bodily and mental performance is a standard to which most professionals adhere.

In discussing the rationalization process in bureaucratic capitalism, it is important to maintain the focus on the transactional dynamic that mediates between the institutional arrangements of production and the actual living bodies participating in these arrangements. As suggested by the transactional conception of agency, embodied actors employ institutionalized routines and discourses in solving pragmatic problems—in this case, the task of producing goods and services. These transactions of production involve routines and discourses such as various bureaucratic formulae, occupational knowledge-bases, managerial designs, and material technologies. In the course of these transactions, the agent and the objects of production are mutually constituted, while the institutional routines used by agents are simultaneously reproduced or transformed. This is the process by which the principles of rational-efficiency come to inscribe a disciplined body: a body that is a calculable, predictable, efficient instrument of production. However, by terminating corporeal contingency in terms of the regimens of alienated labor or other rationalized forms of work, certain organic potentials remain unrealized. In the Marxian formula, the unrealized potential of the body/agent spurs a search for alternative expressions of "species-being"; namely, other ways of terminating corporeal contingency. This is where we can consider another of Weber's major foci in analyzing the growth of formal rationality: the rise of the rational disciplines of scientific knowledge.

Orienting our analysis to this latter focus brings us back to Frank's treatment of the disciplined body. Although he does not frame the problem in terms of the transactions of production, as we do here, one does find an implicit recognition of the productivist dimension of the disciplined body in Frank's analysis. In discussing the cognitive mapping of the body by disciplinary discourses, he notes that: "[Discourse] disciplines not only make bodies productive in terms defined by some other, whether king or factory owner. Disciplines can also be used by bodies themselves to achieve productive ends of their own" (Frank 1995, 58). Frank's examination of the link between rational discourses and the disciplined body allows us to relate another important rationalization pattern to the rise of this body style.

Extending the logic of our argument, it can be said that as workers become increasingly alienated from the disciplining routines of the workplace, they begin to look for other ways to realize the productive potentials of their bodies. The rationalization of culture and the growth of the human sciences created new possibilities for social actors to direct some of their productive energies inward and pursue programs of self-transformation. This reflects one of the major complexities of the modern age. In addition to producing organizational strategies, technologies, and discourses that increase the productivity and efficiency of workers, the rationalization process has also yielded new opportunities for the "improvement" of bodies and minds through the application of science to human problems. Thus social actors have other alternatives for addressing the problem of corporeal contingency: they can make use of disciplinary discourses that define ideal models of "health and well-being," exercise regimens and diets being cases in point. With the growth of the human sciences and other disciplines of human "improvement," it is possible for the body to focus its productive efforts on itself as well as economic products.

Frank offers a critical perspective on these rational disciplines of improvement by drawing heavily on the work of Michel Foucault, who he sees as "the theorist of the disciplined body" (1995, 56). Foucault's wide-ranging studies of the "technologies of domination" focus on the surveillance and regulation functions of rational disciplines dedicated to both individual bodies and populations. Disciplines such as clinical medicine, psychology, and criminology yield intervention strategies that allow for the regulation of the internal and external body, while demography and urban planning are tools for more effective surveillance of populations (Turner 1984). Ultimately, these disciplines become the basis of a "panoptic system" that serves to make bodily actions and functions more predictable and controllable. Foucault's critical insight about the nature of power and domination is that the expressions of both are registered most fundamentally in their effects on bodies.

If, for most of human history, power and domination have resided in control of the forces of violence and the use of violence against bodies, modernity has been witness to the rise of power and domination exercised through the regulation of bodies by disciplinary discourses. This historical shift has consisted of a transition in the primary site of domination from the body as injured flesh to the body as regimented function, but in both cases domination remains fully embodied. Foucault's conception of the disciplined body fits with our productivist theme. The inscription process he describes is achieved through efforts of bodies to (re)produce themselves in forms dictated by the human sciences. This view is reflected in Frank's (1995, 56) interpretation of Foucault's later work:

> Foucault seems to have reached the idea that a theory of domination must begin with the body dominating itself. From an extensional societal perspective we may see domination as imposed, but to understand its effectiveness, we must also understand this domination as chosen. Bodily domination is never imposed by some abstract societal Other; only bodies can do things to other bodies. Most often, what is done depends on what bodies do to themselves.

Thus we see that actors endeavoring to produce their bodies in the context of rationalized Western culture is the basis of a central paradox of the modern era: that is, efforts by embodied actors to achieve progressive self-transformation become acts of self-domination. Consideration of this paradox raises the issues of objectivity and truth again, specifically in relation to the disciplined body. The question to answer in making sense of self-domination is: "How can actors be duped into participating in this project?" Foucault's answer accords with our claims about the key problem that bodies must address. What we have referred to as the body's need to terminate its own indeterminacy is expressed in Foucauldian terms as the desire of embodied actors to find their own "truth." Frank (1995, 57) states that "as we recollect Foucault at increasing distance after his death, the desire of human beings 'to understand themselves' may emerge as the central presupposition of his philosophical anthropology, just as the notion of 'technologies' may form the core of his institutional analyses." In these terms, the search for ways to come to grips with the contingency of the body is a search for the body's truth, a search that must take account of the various "truth games" available to embodied actors within the existing culture.

The truth games of bureaucratic-industrial society are the rational discourses and techniques of science (biomedicine, economics, psychiatry, biology, etc.), which, as we have seen, serve to regulate human bodies and minds in terms of the ideal constructions of "health," "normality," "equilibrium," "well-being," "self-actualization," and the like. The fact that embodied actors seek the truth of their own bodies in the established truth discourses of their culture should come as no surprise, even if playing these truth games and extinguishing corporeal contingency with these moves leads to self-domination. A transactional reading of this process suggests, however, that when truth discourses are imported into bodies and succeed in inscribing the flesh therein, they become more than truth "games." When bodies can be made to conform to certain discursive principles and a unification of knowledge and corporeal reality is thereby achieved, the principles in question become "pragmatic certainties" rather than mere moves in a discourse game (Shalin 1992, 258). Discursive systems that are objectified in the actual organic tissues of living people are not arbitrary symbolic constructions. By functioning as vehicles for expressing the particular truths of the body, these discourses are truth systems that meet the standard of pragmatic validity. For example, the "body-as-machine" metaphor promoted by the biomedical model captures a certain truth about the body insofar as artificial joints and other replacement parts can be incorporated into bodies in functional ways, even if this metaphor fails to realize other bodily truths (see Fox 1994).

If corporeal truth is found in the transactional link between knowledge and the objective reality of the natural body (the body as a part of nature), then a further implication of our transactional interpretation is that not all discursive systems are valid in the pragmatic sense. Discourse games that are incapable of inscribing the body fail to meet the crucial standard of pragmatic certainty, despite their institutional dominance or claims of scientific validity. Consider, for example, the limitations of formal biomedical theory as a disciplining discourse for the body. In defining "health" as the absence of disease and offering a complex system of disease categories tied to clinical symptoms and signs, the biomedical text has limited relevance for the everyday body practices of common-sense actors. People can experience "illness" when no disease is present or maintain good "health" in the presence of disease. It is true that the biomedical perspective structures the healing practices

of medical professionals, but even in this usage clinicians confront pragmatic difficulties that can be overcome only by adopting ad hoc diagnostic and treatment practices. It is well understood now that the actual
diagnosis and treatment of disease by practicing physicians relies only
in general terms on biomedical theory and depends more directly on
practice styles unique to individual physicians or local and regional
physician networks. Research on these "small-area variations" in medical practice (see Roos and Roos 1994) not only challenges the claimed
precision and standardization of biomedical diagnostic and therapeutic
procedures, it may also indicate the limitations of formal biomedical theory as a text for terminating the contingencies of the illness experience.

In making this argument we do not mean to imply that biomedical
medicine has limited impact on the constitution of modern bodies. We
would suggest that just the opposite is true: widespread biomedical
intervention in the body is one of the distinguishing features of the modern age. However, medicine's impact on modern bodies has more to do
with the application of biomedical *technologies* to the resolution of medical problems than it does with the imprinting of bodies by biomedical
theory/text. Modern bodies may be prodded and poked, cut upon, and
chemically altered by biomedical practitioners to an unprecedented
extent today, but the biomedical text has little influence on how individuals seek to maintain good "health." For instance, Crawford's (1984)
phenomenological study of health practices indicates that contemporary
Americans do not conceive of health in biomedical terms at all. His well-
educated, middle-class subjects rarely discussed health as the "absence
of disease," but rather conceptualized it primarily in terms of "control"
(self-denial) or "release" (unfettered consumption), concepts that, in
Crawford's view, reflect more the production and consumption imperatives of capitalism than any form of medical discourse. Moreover, the
fact that increasing numbers of biomedically trained physicians are
incorporating concepts and therapies associated with "alternative medicine" into their practices may also be read as a sign of the inadequacy of
biomedical concepts for making the illness experience meaningful to
their patients (Kleinman 1988).

As the case of modern medicine demonstrates, even a discursive system receiving the kind of powerful institutional support accorded to the
biomedical paradigm can fail to meet the standard of pragmatic truth. In
spite of the impressive advances in the treatment of *disease* that have
occurred in this century, the biomedical text has been less successful in
the treatment of *illness*.[3] The irrelevancy of biomedical concepts to the
meaningful experience of health and illness accounts for why this text

has largely failed to imprint bodies and become objectified in the living flesh of human beings, although the technologies associated with the biomedical system do leave their mark on bodies. Thus the transactional analysis challenges the relativist implications of postmodernist interpretations by allowing that discursive texts can be pragmatically *false* as well as pragmatically true.

Our goal in discussing the disciplined body has been to show how transactions associated with production can terminate corporeal contingency in terms of objective bodily forms that reveal corporeal truths. As we have seen, these transactions of production can involve either labor regimens associated with the production of goods and services or the discourses of the human sciences focused on producing "improved" body/selves. However, as we noted earlier, production is just one of several forms of transaction that brings order to the indeterminate reality of the body and the rest of nature. Another important medium of transaction that leads to this outcome is consumption. This is the realm in which we find the termination of corporeal contingency in the form of the "mirroring body."

The Mirroring Body

The disciplinary regimens of modern culture can terminate the objective uncertainty of the body, but it must be noted once again that solutions to this key problem are always fleeting. Since every solution brings out some corporeal potentials but eliminates others, bodies always resist, to some degree, efforts to inscribe and order them. When the termination involves a disciplinary regimen, the body's resistance is sometimes expressed in the form of an opposing desire for unrestrained hedonism. But even in this expression of resistance we find additional possibilities for another kind of social inscription related to one of the central imperatives of late capitalism—that of the consumer ethic. The fact that bodies can be socially inscribed in these two opposing ways— through disciplining routines of production or the satiation-seeking activities of consumption—reflects a central contradiction of contemporary capitalism. As Crawford (1984, 92) describes it:

> Americans are the objects and subjects of two opposing mandates, two opposing approaches to the attempt to achieve well-being. The opposition is structural. At the level of the social system it is a principal contradiction. The culture of consumption demands a modal personality contrary to the personality required for production. The mandate for discipline clashes with the mandate for pleasure.

We now examine how the structural mandate for pleasure figures into efforts by social actors to extinguish corporeal contingency and how the body is inscribed in the process.

In Frank's analysis, the mirroring body is classified in terms of the four continua of his typology of body use. However, in our transactional interpretation of this work, the key parameter of the mirroring body, like the disciplined body, is the transactional relation most essentially involved in its constitution—transactions that extinguish corporeal contingency. While the disciplined body is constituted primarily through transactions between a self and a body made to respond predictably, the mirroring body arises out of transactions between a self and objects to be consumed. As Frank (1995, 62) notes, the "mirroring body finds its paradigmatic medium of activity in consuming, but consumption is less about actual material acquisition than it is about producing desires." In our analysis, "producing desires" through consumption is read as giving form to bodily potentials, the termination of the body's indeterminacy through the externalization of desire.

In the transactional framework, embodied selves and commodified objects are mutually constituted in the act of consumption. On the one hand, the body is produced through its reflection in consumer goods: "As the body sees the object it immediately aligns itself in some fit with that object; its desire is to make the object part of its image of itself. Thus the object becomes a mirror in which the body sees itself reflected" (Frank 1995, 62). On the other hand, the commodities that become mirrors for the body are created as objects through the body's transaction with them. The thing that ultimately determines whether any particular object becomes a mirror for the body is an act of appropriation by an embodied consumer.

In conceptualizing consumption in this way, consumers are seen as active agents in creating the identity-relevant goods that they purchase in the marketplace. It would be a mistake to assume that the commodities in which bodies are reflected are mere "fashion" imposed on passive consumers who can be endlessly manipulated into purchasing goods promoted by fashion producers. In late capitalism, the consumer is actively involved in the process of making commodities into something significant for the body.

In the case of corporately produced objects, consumers invest the product with a certain kind of value through the embodied use of the object or fashion. This is perhaps most clearly revealed in the constitution of clothing as a signifying commodity. In contrast to the old adage that "the clothes make the (wo)man," it is more important to appreciate how the (wo)man makes the clothes. Since clothing is ultimately designed to enclose bodies, the meaning of any apparel depends on how it is worn—how it appears with the body inside of it. Thus a pair of jeans hanging on the rack carries no intrinsic meaning, but how this article of clothing is worn—tightly or loosely, low on the hips or high on the waist, pants legs too long or too short—gives it substance as a signifier of identity, class, ethnicity, age cohort, occupation, and other group affiliations.

The creative "embodiment" of clothing and other commodities is particularly important for groups seeking to set themselves apart from the dominant culture. One way that "subcultural" styles are created is through the embodied use of objects in nontraditional ways. For example, when members of the "punk" subculture inserted safety pins in their cheeks, they appropriated an object used for mundane purposes and assigned it new meaning by using it as jewelry. This kind of embodied use of commodities is the principal means by which subcultures are constructed. As Dick Hebdige (1979, 103) notes: "It is basically the way in which commodities are *used* in subculture which mark the subculture off from more orthodox cultural formations."

While consumers directly produce commodities in this way and express their bodies in the process, the act of consumption creates the commodity in an indirect sense as well. The body reproduces itself by appropriating objects in consumption, but often what is produced in consumption are signs rather than material objects. "Desire can only operate on objects by turning them into signs. The commodity is less a real thing than it is a sign of itself, because it is the sign we desire" (Frank 1995, 64). Poster (1988, 3), in another expression of this idea, states that "consumer objects are like hysterical symptoms; they are best understood not as a response to a specific need or problem but as a network of floating signifiers that are inexhaustible in their ability to incite desire." Regardless of how one conceives of the commodity, either as an object with a practical use-value or as an expressive sign, its objective significance is found in the embodied actor's transaction with it, a transaction in which the body/self and the commodity are mutually determined.

Once again, the transactional approach to these issues offers a significant contrast to postmodernist interpretations. Among theorists identified with the postmodernist tradition, Jean Baudrillard is probably best known for his attention to the culture of consumption. In analyzing the constitution of the body in consumption, Baudrillard pushes well beyond Frank's concept of the mirroring body. Rather than merely reflecting itself in the objects it consumes, Baudrillard sees the postmodern body/self becoming assimilated into "hyperreality." The hyperreal is the product of consumer culture gone wild, in which signs have become completely self-referential. In this context, it is no longer possible to distinguish between signs and the reality they represent. Media-produced simulations become more real than reality itself and people immerse themselves in consumer culture in search of the most powerful simulations of desire. This search takes them deep into a black hole of meaninglessness, inertia, and apathy, where the body ceases to be reflected in consumer objects, but rather becomes "a pure screen" for the display of a meaningless mix of dominating signs (Baudrillard 1983, 133). In the hyperreal culture, corporeality vanishes as a form of resistance.

In pronouncing the death of corporeality, Baudrillard engages in a radical form of constructionism in which notions of objectivity, reality, and truth clearly have no significance. It appears that Baudrillard's postmodern musings have fallen into a relativist abyss so deep that he can no longer comprehend the possibility of resistance by human agents. From the perspective of transactional sociology (and the pragmatist tradition from which it emerges), Baudrillard's extreme relativism is due, in part, to the limitations of his method of inquiry: his reliance on a form of theoretical reflection that remains entirely disembodied. Frank makes this criticism in response to Baudrillard's claim that jogging and marathon-running involve nothing more than a fetishistic performance and the pursuit "of the mania for an empty victory, the joy engendered by a feat that is of no consequence" (Baudrillard 1988, 21):

> There are insights here . . ., but Baudrillard is limited by the disembodiment of his own vision. His eyes see scenes without the rest of him being embodied in these scenes. He is the remote-control video probe from another world, seeing but never inquiring, incapable of joining in. . . . He cannot perceive the marathon as, in the full sense of the pun, a human race. He cannot hear runners talking to each other, much less drawing energy from their communal effort. . . . Baudrillard's problem is that he has no *Verstehen* for the embodiment which is being preserved and achieved, seeing only "an empty victory." (Frank 1995, 65)

Baudrillard's lack of *Verstehen* blinds him to the objective nature of embodiment and perhaps helps to explain his inability to see the body as a site of potential resistance to consumer culture. In arguing above that bodies exist apart from cultural texts, we pointed out that any termination of corporeal contingency offers only a partial fulfillment of one's desire to know the full potential or "truth" of one's body. This is readily apparent from one's participation in any fully embodied experience, including the experience of consumption. Every participant in the consumer culture of late capitalism experiences the unfulfilled promise of shopping nirvana: one can never buy enough to be completely satiated. Indeed, this profound sense of frustration rooted in the body is a key source of the magic of consumer capitalism. It is the basis of an internal mechanism that propels the system to steadily expand until economic resources that fuel the desperate search for material fulfillment are exhausted. More importantly, it clearly indicates that bodies can never be completely circumscribed by the signifiers emanating from the marketplace, an insight that appears to be lost on Baudrillard.

While Baudrillard's postmodernist analysis generally disdains any notion of tension between texts and body/selves, not all theorists of consumer culture dismiss the objective uncertainty of the body. For Pierre Bourdieu, the body is the primary locus of the consumption imperative, but it retains a degree of "otherness" in relation to this imperative. In the same sense that individual "will" cannot impose itself entirely on the body—we cannot make our bodies act precisely as we wish, the body cannot be completely circumscribed by what it consumes. Thus, while the problem of domination has no significance for Baudrillard because there is nothing to be dominated in his system, this is a key problem for Bourdieu, who maintains a keen awareness of the body's capacity for resistance.

Bourdieu (1984) sees domination expressed substantively in the form of bodily conditions shaped by distinct patterns of consumption. These patterns of consumption reflect variations in taste, which become the primary means for making class distinctions and establishing relations of domination and subordination. Moreover, taste is one facet of a more basic set of dispositions that Bourdieu conceptualizes as "habitus," the deeply rooted schemata by which people interpret and evaluate the social world. Habitus is dialectically related to the social "field," such that the habitus of any particular person is conditioned by social structures reflecting the individual's location in the social order. Reflecting the transactional view of the body/society relation, Bourdieu sees *practice* as the mediating term between habitus and the social world. While habitus is structured by the field, habitus also contributes to the constitution of the field.

The body is reflected in the consumer goods purchased in the marketplace—class is inscribed onto the body through consumer practices—but bodies are also capable of resisting absolute determination by consumer culture. Bourdieu emphasizes this latter point by highlighting the contingent character of habitus. Despite the fact that habitus resides deep within the individual, "below the level of consciousness and language, beyond the reach of introspective scrutiny and control by the will" (Bourdieu 1984, 466), it does not entirely determine thought and action. Habitus establishes tendencies and proclivities in thought and choices of action, but people engage in a process of practically analyzing their options relative to situational circumstances. Hence, in consumer practice, it is always possible to exercise a degree of creativity in the use of the objects purchased so that the body that is mirrored in the object is more than (transcends) the object itself. This, of course, is the very process through which the objects of consumption are constituted, just as they constitute the bodies that appropriate them.

Thus we come full circle in our discussion of the body as an active agent in its own creation. Irrespective of what is consumed—whether it is food, identity-defining products, signifiers of desire, or products that reflect class tastes, the body functions as an ontological force in creating, through the act of consumption, the very objects that it consumes and incorporates into its own being. Transaction is the key to understanding this reflexive process: Only by transacting with objects in consumption do the objects produced by others become food, clothing, expressions of desire or identity, which alter, shape, or determine the bodies that consume them. This analysis emphasizes the two-sided character of consumption: actors terminating the indeterminacy of their bodies and creating themselves in the process, at the same time that they inscribe the objects they consume. And as two poles of a dialectic, the body and the objects it consumes exist in a state of tension: the body is capable of resisting absolute determination by the objects it consumes, just as these objects offer resistance to complete assimilation by the body. This dialectic is critical to understanding the nature of domination and the possibilities for freedom from domination.

Thus far, we have argued that the objective uncertainty of the body accounts for both the principal problem that the body must address at the level of lived experience, and its resistance to domination by the production and consumption practices it seeks as solutions to this problem. It appears, then, that corporeal contingency is paradoxically both a source and a solution for problems of the body. In regard to the issue of domination, an additional paradox related to the indeterminate character of the body can be identified: Corporeal uncertainty is not only a source of resistance to domination, it is also the force that can compel one body to dominate another. This brings us to the last medium of transaction through which embodied selves seek to terminate the body's indeterminacy and the two remaining styles of body use in Frank's typology. In what remains of this chapter, we direct attention to the interpersonal transactions undertaken by the "dominating" and "communicative" body styles.

The Dominating Body

In an age when production and consumption practices have become the center of social life, it seems strange that the threat of bodily injury or violent death at the hands of another person continues to be a critical concern of members of postindustrial society. The prevalence of this threat, no doubt, is partly related to the character of consumer-capitalist society itself. In a system that encourages high levels of consumption while denying sizable populations of people a way to realize this ideal, satisfying one's material needs by participating in violent criminal enterprises continues to be a viable consumer strategy for some. This point notwithstanding, we suggest that the continuing problems of violent crime are related to more deep-seated forces than any set of rational calculations about how one may increase one's consumption power. Following in the tradition of Katz's (1988) phenomenological approach to violent crime, we propose that the principal motivations for violence are to be found in experiential dynamics of violent encounters. However, we go beyond Katz by tying this experience to the persistent problem of the body's indeterminacy, viewed here as the ultimate force behind violent interactions between embodied social actors. If corporeal contingency can be extinguished through the regimens of production and the consumption of commodities, it can also be terminated through various forms of embodied interaction with others, including interactions involved in physically dominating other bodies.

In the usual departure from Frank's schema, then the overcoming corporeal contingency is taken as the central problem to be solved by dominating bodies. The dominating body and the disciplined body share this problem, but while the disciplined body responds to its own contingency by constituting itself in disciplined activities, the dominating body seeks out contingency in others and constitutes itself by overcoming other-contingency. The essential transaction involved in this process is revealed in a quotation that Frank takes from Klaus Theweleit's monumental work on bodies titled *Male Fantasies* (1987): "For the dominating body 'someone or other had to die so that [it] could live'" (Frank 1995, 71).

Theweleit's case study of the German Freikorps powerfully illustrates the central importance of other-contingency to the dominating body. Created after the First World War to harass trade unionists and leftists, the Freikorps units later yielded several concentration camp commandants and numerous recruits to the SS and SA during the

Second World War. Through diary accounts and other texts written by members of the Freikorps, Theweleit was able to reconstruct the mindset of these "soldier males":

> The real source of terror is the light they themselves cast onto reality. As if magnetically attracted, their eyes hunt out anything that moves. The more intense and agitated the movement, the better. When they spot such movement they narrow their eyes to slits (defense), sharpen their vision of it as a dead entity by training a spotlight on it (deanimation), then destroy it, to experience a strange satisfaction at the sight of this "bloody mass." Their writing process works in exactly the same way. (Quoted in Frank 1995, 71–72)

As this passage suggests, the movement of the other represents other-contingency that must be absolutely dominated. Only by reducing it to "bloody mass" can absolute domination be achieved. The paradox in this transaction is that the dominating body is attracted to the contingency of the other at the same time that it wishes to destroy it. What lies behind this paradox is a projection of internal contingency onto the other:

> The Freikorps soldiers are not epic heroes, sure of their own power. They are as threatened as they are threatening, and threatened by themselves as much as by others. The need to dominate the other is a need to control the projection of the internal contingency which threatens them. (Frank 1995, 72)

Theweleit's data on the Freikorps offers some rich insights about the nature of the dominating body. Another analysis of social types who achieve self-definition by dominating others can be found in Katz's phenomenological study of crime. Katz's central thesis is that many criminal enterprises are motivated less by the criminal's calculation of potential material gains than by the seductive appeal of the criminal experience itself.[4] He focuses on how the illicit activities in many different contexts become vehicles to a transcendent reality. Analyzing criminal experiences ranging from the adolescent pursuit of the "sneaky thrills" and gang warfare to adult involvement in professional stick-up and "righteous slaughter," Katz shows us how the sensual attractions of illicit action mold a criminal career. Although the analysis is not specifically focused on the dominating body, Katz's data shed light on its development and expression in certain types of criminal action.

One social context in which the dominating style of body use emerges as a prevalent pattern is the youth subcultures that flourish in inner-city neighborhoods. Katz defines this pattern as the "ways of the badass," which become the core predisposition of many individuals who eventually take up adult careers as violent criminals. Badasses are distinguished by a form of "toughness" manifested as a fundamental resistance to moral malleability and unwillingness to accommodate the desires or opinions of others. To be tough is to adopt an existential stance that says: "You see me, but I am not here for you; I see you, and maybe you are here for me" (1988, 80). Refusing to be morally or emotionally accessible is also expressed within youth subcultures in the form of "symbols and devices of impenetrability": the stony silent, expressionless demeanor of young toughs in interactional situations or the dark sunglasses that prevent access to the eyes (1988, 82). In both its symbolic and pragmatic forms, toughness involves a commitment to the unidirectional transactions that are the hallmark of the dominating body: others are *used* by the dominating body/selves for their purposes, but the contingencies they confront in other bodies cannot induce them to change.

The dominating body's resistance to intersubjective understanding defines the "essential project" of the badass, which, in Katz's words, is to transcend "the modern moral injunction to adjust the public self sensitively to situationally contingent expectations" (1988, 81). Badasses subvert the normative principle of maintaining respectful comportment in interaction by threatening to "suddenly thrust the forces of chaos" into the other's world (1988, 99). This is a view of the dominating body that takes us beyond Frank's initial conceptualization. Katz's work helps us to see that the dominating body's commitment to generating chaos in interpersonal situations—imposing its own contingency on the bodies it seeks to control—must be treated as a central practice of this style of body use.

The badass's desire for "soulful chaos" (1988, 102) reflects, once again, the fundamental paradox in the dominating body's approach to the world. In dealing with his own corporeal contingency, the dominating body seeks and destroys other bodies that threaten contingency. However, in order to prevail in this project, the dominating body must draw on its own capacity for chaotic action to meet the unpredictable responses of its victims. As Katz states (1988, 100), "the badass celebrates a commitment to violence beyond any reason comprehensible to others." He succeeds by communicating that there are no limits on how far he will go to achieve his ends. He induces *others* to reason when he makes it clear that *he* will not make the calculation. He is always prepared to go crazy if the situation calls for it. Hence, the very thing that dominating bodies fear the most—their own contingency—is what they seek in others and what they tap within themselves to control and dominate contingent others. The ultimate consequence of the transactions between dominating bodies and the bodies they victimize is a cascade of chaos.

When adolescent badasses mature and move into adult criminal careers as professional stick-up men and other kinds of violent offenders, they adopt more intense dominating-body practices. Becoming a professional street criminal means that one must make the transition from badass to "hardman." Like badasses, hardmen are both attracted to and repelled by contingency and chaos in themselves and others. For example, the primary attraction of stick up to the hardman is the opportunity it offers for unpredictability, in both the victim's response and the evolving situational contingencies (1988, 220). Stick-up men often look for ways to increase the risks of the endeavor, by choosing associates with known weaknesses or selecting victims whose responses are particularly difficult to anticipate. The point of these decisions is to create "occasions for dramatizing the superior firmness of [one's] will" in overcoming the unpredictable elements of the situation (1988, 226). The hardman's attraction to unpredictability in associates and victims is rooted is his desire to project his own internal contingency onto them, which he can then control by imposing a cold, hard, violent discipline:

> [T]he hardman's response embraces rather than avoids or succumbs to chaos; the hardman seizes on chaos as a provocation to manifest transcendent powers of control. This way of appreciating chaos dialectically, as a motivational resource rather than as a barrier to a criminal career . . . is [the hardman's] distinctive project. (1988, 220)

Thus when we consider the nature of dominating bodies, exemplified by either Theweleit's Freikorps soldier-males or Katz's criminal hardmen, we find another way to talk about objectivity and reality in transactional terms. Starting from the basic premise that the reality of the body is found, in part, in its objective uncertainty, we have seen how this defines the central problem of the body and how embodied selves seek to solve this problem. The dominating body succeeds in terminating its own indeterminacy by becoming literally a "terminator." By destroying life—turning living, contingent bodies into dead meat—dominating body/ selves are able to deny their own corporeal contingency. Paradoxically, however, dominating bodies achieve this goal by drawing on the same force within themselves that they fear the most: They use their capacity for chaotic behavior and normative transcendence as a means to control the contingency of the other. And herein lies the central dilemma of the dominating body: It cannot escape its own unpredictable desires without acting unpredictably to control the unpredictable potential of other bodies!

Moreover, it is actually *attracted* to the contingency of the other, because terminating other-contingency is the means by which it extinguishes its own indeterminacy. Katz's "hardmen" look for victims and situations that are unpredictable, because coming to terms with these chaotic circumstances enhances the opportunity to transform their own inner contingency into a transcendent reality.

What is the nature of this transcendent reality? In discussing transcendence, Katz makes an explicit connection between the alternative reality and the problem of contingency:

> In his everyday doings, the hardman transcends the difference between how he and others experience everyday situations by insisting that his subjectivity remains firm as he moves into and out of others' worlds. In street language, the challenge arises when others try to take him through "too many changes." When it rains, Jones finds "it fucks with my mind. Maybe I'll have to change to my dungarees, and that messes with my head. . . ." The project is to move, without being visibly impressed, emotionally affected, or spiritually swayed, between "here" (wherever you are "at" at the moment) and "there" (all situations defined by others). . . .
>
> Seen in the form of snapshots taken from the outside, the hardman seems to be a collection of impulsive outpourings of hostile feelings—anger, aggressive instincts, and sadistic inclinations. But after a series of frustrated robberies, lost fights, betrayals by intimates, arrests, and prison sentences, one always has a multitude of reasons for *not* responding from the guts. Just because they are done against the background of reasonable grounds for deterrence, the hardman's aggressive moves carry, in their sensual vibrance—in the heavy awe and felt charge they bring to scenes—the ringing significance of their transcendent project. (1988, 233–35)

As this passage reveals, the transcendent reality created by the dominating body consists of an extreme subjectivity that rejects any possibility for intersubjective agreement. Maintaining one's subjectivity is achieved by drawing on the body's contingent power to create havoc. And now we see an additional paradox in this process: The transcendent reality to which violent criminals are drawn arises out of the same corporeal uncertainty that the dominating body wants to terminate within itself—which it achieves by annihilating the contingent threat of the other.

Although the dominating body is attracted to the indeterminacy of other bodies as something to be destroyed, which reflects the revulsion it has for its own objective uncertainty, interaction between embodied selves can also involve more productive responses to the corporeal contingency of self and other. When embodied actors seek to terminate the contingencies they face in themselves and others linguistically in search of *verstehen*, they adopt a style of body usage typical of the communicative body. In describing this last body style, we turn to the final form of transaction involved in the body's effort to resolve its primary problem.

The Communicative Body

We have used Frank's typology of body styles as our point of departure in this chapter, and the modifications we have made in his analytical scheme have taken us in some new directions. Our discussion of the last body type in the scheme, the communicative body, represents our greatest departure from Frank's analysis of social embodiment. This is because our analytical goals at this point diverge significantly from his interests in the communicative body. While Frank's chief concern with this last body type is to explore the possibilities for an "ethics of the body" (1995, 79), we regard the communicative body as a form of corporeal usage that occupies a central place in the emergent transactions that maintain social life. Examining this body style certainly raises important ethical issues, but its relevance is much broader than the ethics of embodiment.

In describing the communicative body, Frank states that its "contingency is no longer its problem but its possibility (1995, 79). While the communicative body may be distinguished in terms of this normative shift, the "problem" of contingency does not disappear since corporeal possibilities cannot be realized unless the body's contingency is terminated. Like the dominating body, the communicative body terminates corporeal indeterminacy through the medium of interaction, but interaction based on symbolic exchange rather than physical coercion. Beyond the normative considerations emphasized by Frank, then, we propose that the communicating body is also rooted in the process of symbolic interaction.

In Mead's conception of the indeterminate and determinant aspects of the "self"—captured by his concepts of the "I" and the "me," respectively—the unpredictable, spontaneous behavior of the "I" is the wellspring of the creative elaboration of meaning. Although Mead's primary concern in analyzing such behavior was to explain the source of modifications in the self-concept and the possibilities for social change, his analytical scheme can also be applied to embodied selves dealing with the problem of corporeal contingency. Thus one additional way to terminate the body's indeterminacy is through narrative constructions produced in interaction with other contingent, embodied selves in which actors strive to capture what their bodies "know," but cannot fully articulate in linguistic terms. This idea is cogently expressed by Arthur Kleinman, whose work on illness narratives is cited by Frank in discussing the communicative body: "Most of us figure out our own thoughts by speaking them to persons whose reactions are as important as our own" (Kleinman 1988, 50). We would assert that this insight applies to thoughts emerging from *all* bodies—those that are "healthy" as well as "ill."

For the communicative body, interaction between the embodied self and other is a means by which creative intersubjective understanding is achieved—a consensual perspective that is not merely dictated and constrained by existing institutions and discourses, but enabled by them. As Frank states, "it is when narratives are spoken from the experience of the body that they can be shared most readily" (1995, 89). In the preceding chapters, we argued that mere subjectivity, if it is nothing more than social or communal agreement, leaves out our contact with the world. Lakoff and Johnson's (1999, 93) embodied realism posits that we are coupled to the world through our embodied transactions. This suggests that embodied actors belonging to the same society share more than common symbolic universes (Berger and Luckmann, 1967). They share common bodily experiences that reflect the inscriptions of production, consumption, and domination, as well as the body's resistance to these inscriptions. Thus meaning that arises in communicative transactions between social actors derives from a common source—a *collective embodiment* more than merely a *collective consciousness* (see also chapter 4). This process generates intersubjectivity through the production of creative narrative constructions: "dyadic contingency becomes the body's potential to realize itself diffusely . . . producing itself, recursively, through the variations of a life which is no longer appropriated by institutions and discourses but is now the body's own" (Frank 1995, 80).

While the communicative body and dominating body share a common medium, they respond to the experience of embodied interaction in very different ways. For the dominating body, the contradictions between verbal and nonverbal signs (the "given" versus the "given-off") in the other's performance are a reminder of the greatest threat to its own subjectivity—the contingency that resides within itself. In contrast to the dominating body, the communicative body approaches contradictions between the verbal and gestural signs with curiosity rather than fear. What this contradiction indicates to the communicative body is the possibility for constructing more complex meaning structures between itself and other, beyond the meaning being linguistically transmitted at that moment. Moreover, the communicative body expects that by reaching a more complex understanding of the other's contingent nature it will potentially discover a deeper understanding of itself—that is, it can terminate its own indeterminacy in ways that it could not discover on its own. Thus communicative bodies assume that human embodiment can be intersubjectively experienced in terms of both its determinant and indeterminate aspects and therefore it expects that the problem of corporeal indeterminacy can be addressed through collaborative effort.

Additional comparisons between the communicative and dominating bodies help to illuminate both forms. Because dominating bodies fear contradictory signs and communicative bodies are often intrigued by such discrepancies, the two body styles respond differently to varying degrees of contradiction between verbal and nonverbal signs in face-to-face interaction. For the dominating body, the greater the discrepancy between the others' verbal self-presentation and their body language, the more frightening others may become and the greater the felt need to dominate or destroy them.[5]

By contrast, the communicative body adopts the opposite approach to contradictions between verbal and nonverbal signs. Because corporeal contingency (as manifested in itself and the other) can be the source of its creative realization rather than just a problem to be solved, the communicative body does not fear inconsistency between verbal and nonverbal signals. To the communicative body, tension between verbal and nonverbal signs is not necessarily an indication of communicative incompetence. What is signaled gesturally by the other, even if it initially appears to be discrepant with what is expressed linguistically, can be an additional source of meaning capturing the nuances and subtleties of experience that cannot be fully verbalized (Turner 1999). This is why the communicative body favors face-to-face interaction with other embodied selves as compared to the disembodied forms of communication that have become prevalent in the modern age. By making use of a tacit form of embodied semiotics in face-to-face interaction, the communicative body seeks to acquire a deeper, more encompassing reading of the other and socially constructed narratives that may be useful in terminating its own indeterminacy.

We have referred to various dimensions of what may be considered as an embodied semiotics in earlier chapters, with the discussion of recent work in the neurosciences, the sociology of emotions, and related fields of study. This work supports our argument here insofar as it demonstrates that only a small part of what is communicated in face-to-face exchanges is transmitted linguistically and deliberately (Katz 1999, 375). While it is not yet possible to describe embodied semiotics in any comprehensive way, we do know enough about this problem to assert that face-to-face interaction produces a richer level of meaning than what can be transmitted by disembodied forms of communication. Rime and Schiaratura (1991) demonstrate that speech is grounded in gesture and when the latter is constrained, speech itself is impoverished. This particular kind of embodiment draws from public, intersubjective understandings of institutionally constrained transactions. These public understandings, being abstract and impersonal, also carry with them a sense of objectivity. At the same time, gesture is foundational in the sense of the subjective that Lorenz (1977) articulates so well. Gesture is not dependent on our awareness and represents an embodied base from which we project meaning. As Rime and Schiaratura (1991, 241) state: "The speaker's gesticulation is one of the facts to which human beings are most often exposed, as observers as well as actors, and yet it usually goes unnoticed in everyday life." The dialectic of subjective and objective involving gesture is similar to the same dialectic with emotion: It draws its intelligibility from the impersonal, highly abstract nature of significant symbols that are appropriated to make sense out of our most personal, idiosyncratic ways of being in the world.

Drawing on the discussion in chapter 4 on the multiple meanings of objectivity and subjectivity, it is possible to identify another sense in which the transactions involved in face-to-face communication represent an expression of objectivity. Since the meaning generated in face-to-face exchanges reflects the common bodily experiences shaped by social inscriptions and corporeal resistance to these inscriptions, it incorporates what the body knows but cannot linguistically express very easily. Thus, while the body is foundational in a subjective sense (Lorenz 1977), it is also imprinted by the production, consumption, and domination practices described in earlier sections and, therefore, is also a part of objective determinate processes as well. This does not mean that the narratives that emerge out of embodied communication possess no content beyond what is dictated by institutions and discourses, since indeterminate bodies always resist these social inscriptions to an important degree. What emerges in corporeal interaction are narratives that reflect the tension between the subjective, idiosyncratic, contingent body, on the one hand, and the objective, socially inscribed, determinant body on the other. It is this dialectic between the subjective and objective sides of the body that Frank has in mind when he says that "for the communicating body, institutions and discourses . . . enable more than they constrain" (1995, 80).

The enabling aspect of institutions and discourses is best understood in terms of the interplay between the inscriptions cultural patterns leave on the body and the contingent resistance that these inscriptions produce. Linguistic symbols exchanged in interaction are most directly influenced by dominating texts, but as we argued in earlier chapters, these abstract symbols are always impoverished expressions of meaning. This is why, analytically, the communicative body is connected to face-to-face interaction. Since the meaning of symbols is determined in part by emotional inflection, gestures, and other embodied signs, the communicative body must reference the full body of the other in its quest to establish intersubjectivity. However, it is precisely this kind of embodied exchange that forces it to confront most directly the contingency of the other—a complication the dominating body wants to avoid.

The contradiction between verbal and nonverbal signs is one of the forces that maintains the flow of the interaction. When one's body language is inconsistent with the linguistic expression of one's personhood and interests, it forces the other to make sense of this discrepancy. Is it an act of manipulation or duplicity? Is the person simply unaware of the signs his or her body is giving off? Or is it a reflection of more complex sentiments than what can be immediately verbalized? We would speculate that the latter condition prevails most often, which means that the interactants are compelled to continue the exchange in an effort to verbally "unpack" the more complex sentiments that the body has signaled. This is an important dimension of the process of "negotiating meaning."

As stated above, institutions and discourses enable the negotiation of meaning, because they give actors a common set of bodily experiences and symbol systems from which to draw, although social-group variations in these inscriptions and symbol systems along class, ethnic, occupational lines greatly complicate the process. But the biggest challenge to intersubjective understanding is making collective sense of corporeal potentials that are obscured by existing practices and discourses. Communicative bodies come to terms with this problem by socially constructing narrative structures that broaden or transcend the boundaries of existing discourses and give expression to embodied sentiments that have not been previously externalized. This process is fully transactional, and therefore social, in the way that Mead (and Kleinman above) proposed: the narrative expression takes form in the act of speaking it to others and its meaning is found, partly, in their response to it. The response of the other is important, because actors assume that, just as they share embodied experiences shaped by institutional practices, they also share the body's *resistant responses* to those inscriptions. On this basis, participants in the interaction seek to develop narrative terminations of corporeal contingency that potentially work for everyone concerned.

In appreciating the objective aspect of embodied communication, we can begin now to understand how the transactions involved in face-to-face exchanges produce an emergent reality that is corporeal as well as symbolic. This perspective on the "social construction of reality" moves beyond the nominalist approach introduced by Berger and Luckmann over three decades ago. Insofar as interactionally produced narratives symbolically express bodily potentials that are unrealized by existing institutional practices and discourses, the resulting symbol systems carve out new possibilities for embodied social life. There is no doubt that social change derives in part from the capacity of human beings to envision new ways of being. But the cognitive visions that lead to change do not emerge out of thin air and take residence in solitary minds. They emerge through the collective signifying practices of embodied actors who reference corporeally based potentialities in deciding what is possible in their lived experience.

Of course, it must be remembered that the process of symbolically terminating the body's indeterminacy typically occurs in the context of bodies seeking collective solutions to problems relating to production, consumption, and interest-oriented activities. This means that the transactions in each of these domains serve as the primary foci for the communicative exchanges in face-to-face interaction. Consequently, practices associated with production, consumption, and the pursuit of interests impact the body in this secondary way, because they often dictate the content of the creative narratives that emerge in face-to-face interaction. Thus structural arrangements in each of these spheres both shape and are shaped by face-to-face communicative transactions, giving rise to an embodied life-world that reflects the problem-solving imperative of human social life.

This analysis suggests that the "reality" referenced in Berger and Luckmann's social construction of reality thesis consists of more than just tacit knowledge or what poststructuralists refer to as "text." While there is no question that existing knowledge or discourse systems have a profound impact on the interpretive practices of actors engaged in face-to-face interaction, the meaning constructed in these exchanges is not entirely circumscribed by existing symbolic systems. The meaning that emerges out of interaction possesses novel, transcendent elements that cannot be reduced to any particular text. Berger and Luckmann would certainly acknowledge as much, but they don't specify the source of these novel elements. We have tried to show how the body is implicated in this problem—namely, the need to extinguish corporeal contingency in interaction. While they share, to varying degrees, corporeal inscriptions that derive from existing institutional and discourse patterns, the body's indeterminacy remains as that part of their corporeal existence that cannot be terminated by these structures. Hence, this contingency can be extinguished only by novel terminations. Those most immediately accessible are the meaning structures generated through the exchange of verbal and nonverbal signs.

Thus meaning arising out of face-to-face interaction possesses a degree of autonomy over existing knowledge systems, partly because it is based on embodied signs as well as significant symbols but more importantly, because it gives expression to contingent possibilities that *resist* existing discourses. Moreover, the unique biographical patterns and interest orientations of interactants make for a wide range of possible meaning structures, although all participants share the common need to terminate corporeal contingency that defies institutional determination. This process gives meaningful expression to the actor's own contingent possibilities at the same time that it externalizes meaning that can be appropriated and modified by other participants in the interaction for realizing their own contingent possibilities. The transactional consequence of this exchange is that actors create possibilities for the other in the process of creating themselves.

In short, the body is an integral part of the reality that is constructed in face-to-face interaction. To elaborate on an earlier point, communicative bodies are able to achieve intersubjectivity not only because they share common symbolic universes, but also because they share a common experience of socially expressed embodiment, in both a determinant and indeterminate sense. This suggests that the body sets limits on the kind of "reality" that can be socially constructed in interaction and calls into question the extreme relativism of the "reality as text" thesis.

THE CONTRADICTION BETWEEN CULTURE AND NATURE

Our description of the different styles of body usage and the basic forms of transaction in which they are rooted gives us a way to talk about the objectivity of the body, while also allowing us to conceive of the body's subjectivity as something that cannot be separated from its objective aspects. Drawing on research ranging from epidemiological studies to interpretive analyses, we have indicated how social forces shape bodies at the levels of physiological functioning, whole-body functioning, and exterior surface. The social determination of bodies is clearly reflected in the data on social-group variations in health status, class differences in taste and habitus, and the cultural differences in emotional, psychological, and behavioral capacities. However, it is also clear that bodies never succumb entirely to social determination, because they embody elements of unpredictability, spontaneity, and creativity. These aspects of corporeality, which are the sources of objective resistance to self- and social determination, spring from one side of a fundamental contradiction in human existence: the tension between nature and culture.

The contradiction between nature and culture has been a dominant theme within western culture and, as we noted at the beginning of this chapter, has received further reinforcement in classical social theory. The absence of body/nature in classically inspired social theory and the privileging of culture, cognition, and reason lent support to a dualistic conception of the nature–culture opposition by making the body into an abstract residual category. As a consequence, the body has not been subjected to analysis as an objective force in the ontological development of social structure (except in the genetic reductionism of the sociobiological perspective). One does find a counter-tradition in social theory, running from Nietzsche through Weber and Foucault, in which the body is regarded as a central reference point for the critique of Christian moral restraint, Western rationality, or panopticism (Turner 1995). But even within this counter-tradition, the body is not treated as a force of objectivity in the transactional sense of this term—as an ever-present source of resistance to human will, while also functioning as the vehicle of transaction with all other objective dimensions of the environment.

As an alternative to the dualistic conception of the nature–culture relation embraced by both mainstream social theory and critical traditions, transactional sociology conceives of this contradiction in terms of an unfolding dialectic in which the body exists as both transacting subject and resistant object. The body dialectic referenced here is a central relation of social life: It is only through the body's transaction with other bodies and environmental objects that recurrent social patterns emerge and acquire an objective existence as fully embodied structures (embodied at multiple levels of the body system from physiological, immunological, and neurological structures to surface structure shaped by muscle, fat, skin, and fashion). At the same time, the body's inherently contingent nature means that it can never be fully inscribed by socially structured transactions. The tautological character of this last statement should not distract us from the most essential point to make about this aspect of the body, which is that it is a primary site of *resistance* to institutions and discourses—a resistance that represents one expression of the body's objectivity. Moreover, this objective quality is something that the body shares with all of nature insofar as the natural objects upon which our actions are focused always resists our push.

A transactional sociology of the body thus takes us in a different direction than the critical tradition represented by Nietzche, Weber, and Foucault. In the latter tradition, bodily features such as sexuality and emotions serve as standpoints from which to critique normative and structural imperatives of dominant culture, but these features enter into the critique only as abstractions. This reflects Mary O'Brien's (1989) "the tyranny of the abstract" in which bodily features and processes such as "sexuality" are hypostasized and thus separated from the actual representations of corporeal resistance found within the lived realities of embodied social actors. As most human beings can attest, the term "sexuality" is an impoverished signifier of the diverse and often disturbingly delightful activities designated by this term. Thus, for example, when men and women living within a heterosexual culture confront the objectivity of their bodies in sensations of sexual arousal for members of the same sex, even as they may be shamed by this experience, we have a case of embodied, lived resistance to the dominant culture. The dissident stance involved in this embodied experience becomes even more obvious when an individual exits the "closet" and participates in organized activities with others who share his or her sexual orientation. But the origin of the resistance is to be found within the body's contingent quality, which is one dimension of its objectivity.

The lived expressions of corporeal resistance assume many different forms, appearing at both the individual and collective levels, and these patterns exist in complex relations with embodied institutions and discourses. As we have shown in this chapter, the challenge posed by corporeal resistance means that the body's contingent nature emerges as a problem for institutional authorities as well as for individuals who confront it in their own bodies. We have also seen that several different transactional strategies are used to deal with this problem. Human science texts and institutional practices that seek to impose a body regiment of good mental or physical health, high achievement, increased productivity, and so on define the transactional strategy of the disciplined body. The mirroring body emerges in dialectical tension with the disciplined body, with both styles existing as "opposed but necessary" forms of body usage required by the production and consumption imperatives of late capitalism (Crawford 1984). In the most pure expression of the dominating influence of these twin imperatives, the opposition between discipline and hedonism disappears altogether. Consumers embrace a "calculating hedonism" (Jacoby 1980, 63) in which they "[sub-jugate] the body through body maintenance routines . . . as a precondition for the achievement of an acceptable appearance and the release of the body's expressive capacity" (Featherstone 1995, 171). In this regimen, one maintains a discipline of weightlifting, running, or other forms of strenuous exercise along with controlled dietary practices in order to "look good and feel good" in terms defined by advertised images of "perfect" bodies.

The mirroring body is reflected in the goods with which it transacts, becoming socially inscribed by consumer culture. Market goods, in the form of things we eat, wear, and conspicuously consume shape the body and contingent desire. It is our capacity for putting material things to particular uses that transforms them into consumer goods, even if these objects ultimately function as floating signifiers.

Social interaction represents another form of body practice that leads to the social inscription of bodies at many different levels. We have seen how bodies are imprinted by acts of domination undertaken by other bodies—transactions of the dominating body. Here, body inscriptions take the form of injured flesh or, in the most extreme case, bodies transformed into "dead meat." However, as with the other forms of body use, the capacity for resistance to domination derives from the contingent character of the body. When the dominating subject seeks to injure or annihilate his or her victim, the latter's body can react in ways that surprise both the attacker and the victim. In the midst of a brutal sexual assault, a formerly compliant victim suddenly strikes back at her attacker in a reflex-like reaction; a child that has been systematically abused by an alcoholic parent sees another beating coming and unexpectedly murders the parent; in Krakow's Jewish ghetto during the Nazi occupation, a group of resisters organizes a suicide mission to strike back at their oppressors. What is often most striking about these instances of resistance to coercion is the unpredictable character of the response: no one, not even the victims themselves, can anticipate the reaction.

Whether considering the complex psychoneuroimmunological changes associated with social support and the stress response or the dimensions of body language related to symbolic communication, the communicative exchanges of embodied actors also have a powerful impact on the bodies involved. However much interacting individuals may want to generate certain meanings through body expressions, they can never fully succeed in this effort, because their bodies often betray the intended message. The smile designed to project warmth and acceptance looks strained; the stern expression that would instill fear looks tentative; the hoped-for graceful move appears awkward. We have seen that the contingencies of the body are a source of resistance to absolute social determination in the interactional exchange and also a reservoir of creative possibilities for making and taking social roles. This creative potential in role enactment is precisely what Mead wished to capture with his distinction between the "I" and the "me" and serves as the foundation for his theory of social change.

What we see in all four styles of body use discussed in this chapter is the fundamental dialectic between social–cultural determination of the body and *resistance* to such determination, which is ultimately found in the body's inherent character as both a cultural and natural object. As a part of nature, the body's actual and immediate engagement with the rest of the natural world is much bigger than any experience carved out by institutional discourses and practices. The lived experience of the body can never be fully circumscribed by social–cultural forces, no matter how totalizing the institutional environment it occupies may be. Thus the body is the starting point for analyzing patterns of experience that oppose the dominant forces of the social system. It is the location of the negative space created by system colonization of the body, experienced so often at the individual level as unfulfilled need or desire and at the collective level as emergent social possibility.

The ultimate goal of this chapter has been to highlight the central place of the body in the ontology of social reality, both as objective expression of, and subjective resistance to, existing social facts. With this ontological foundation, we can move from the transactions of individual bodies to the level of collective transactions by groups of interacting bodies. It is this transition from the individual experience of unmet corporeal needs to the collective efforts of interacting bodies to address these needs that we find alternative standpoints for critical awareness and transcendence of system discourses, consumer goods, and institutional practices. These alternative standpoints assume many different forms, reflecting the diversity of the large number of communities and networks involved in the search for transcendent social realities. However, the thing that is common to all of these alternative social realities is their foundation in pragmatic, problem-solving strategies that challenge key system principles, a challenge that is ultimately rooted in the body's inherent resistance to social and cultural inscription. The common location of these emergent realities in social space that is not fully colonized by the system allows us to conceptualize this space as a type of "life-world" that stands in opposition to the dominant discourses and institutional practices of modern bureaucratic-capitalist society. The life-world concept, which is given a fully embodied meaning in the present interpretation, will occupy a prominent place in our further discussion of a transactional sociology for the real world. The promise of the transactional approach, particularly its potential for addressing some of the most daunting problems now faced by sociology, is the focus of the chapter that follows.

NOTES

1. Subjective agency is not to be confused with the different uses of subjectivity discussed in chapter 4.

2. Our conceptualization of the media of transaction contrasts with Frank's scheme. He defines the media of activity for the different body styles as follows: for the disciplined body, the medium is *regimentation*; for the mirroring body, the medium is *consumption*; for the dominating body, the medium is *force*; and for the communicative body, the medium is *recognition* (Frank 1995, 54).

3. In biomedical terms, the concept of "disease" refers to a particular form of morbid anatomy or tissue lesion, while "illness" is the patient's experience of a set of simultaneously occurring clinical manifestations of a disease condition (Murphy 1976).

4. Of course, it is important to exercise caution in generalizing about criminal behavior, considering the significant variations that exist in the character of criminal enterprises and the social types attracted to them.

5. We would speculate that potential victims of dominating bodies are least likely to be actually harmed when their body language is consistent with their verbalization (i.e., either consistently fearful or consistently fearless). Victims who give off nonverbal signs that are inconsistent with their verbal self-presentation may run the greatest risk of being harmed—the victim who talks tough but quivers with fear or one who claims to be terrified but is physically relaxed and controlled. To the dominating body, these kinds of contradictions signal contingency that must be destroyed.

◙   ◙   ◙

CHAPTER SEVEN

Transaction and a Sociological Method for Social Problems

Having discussed the transactional conception of relations such as subjectivity and objectivity, emotion and cognition, mind and body, we now direct attention to how the transactional approach can be employed in reframing the disciplinary goals of the sociological enterprise. The basic goals and analytical strategies of traditional sociological study rests firmly on the dualistic assumptions of rationalism. Therefore, a shift to the transactional ontology would necessitate a reformulation of sociology's purpose and method. In this chapter, we continue our dialogue about some new potential directions open to a transactionally oriented sociology.

There are many different ways to approach this task. Indeed, it will be critically important to consider a number of alternative avenues for constructing a transactional paradigm of sociological study in the future. However, in an effort to maintain continuity with the general themes of the preceding chapters, we will now consider the relevance of transaction to the sociological study of social problems. As noted earlier, the notion of human problem-solving figures prominently in the pragmatist philosophical system that inspired the transactional perspective. Consequently, focusing on social-problems research may be the most direct way to describe the distinctive character of the transactional method.

The social-problems focus is important for another reason. In recent years, a growing number of critics have described an emerging crisis of legitimacy for academic sociology (Lemert 1995; Sjoberg and Vaughan 1993; Turner 1989). While there are varying opinions about what ails the discipline and what should be done about it, many critics are concerned about the growing irrelevance of mainstream sociological research to civic discourse about social problems (Sjoberg and Vaughan 1993). In a time when the problems confronting us have never been more complex and the need for sophisticated, empirically based analyses of these problems has never been greater, the sociological voice is largely absent in the public debate on social problems. There are many reasons why this is so, as we presently discuss, but a fresh approach to the sociological study of social problems is clearly needed now. We believe that a transactional social-problems research model holds great promise as a paradigmatic alternative to the framework that guides most mainstream sociological research today.

Thus, in this chapter, we outline a transactional approach to the study of social problems and demonstrate how this approach addresses the crisis of legitimacy in academic sociology. As a first step, we identify some of the reasons why sociological theory and research presently has little influence on the public discussion of social problems. This analysis will inform our effort to articulate a social-problems research paradigm that can make a more substantive contribution to civic discourse.

SOCIAL-PROBLEMS RESEARCH AND CIVIC DISCOURSE[1]

Drawing from literature on a variety of topics, ranging from social commentary on political and intellectual life in the United States to systematic studies of media institutions and disciplinary critiques, we examine some of the cultural, organizational, economic, and technological factors that undermine sociology's influence in public-policy debates. We will also discuss the way in which the *content* of sociological theories about social problems contributes to the discipline's civic impotence. If recent changes in civic culture negatively influence the way in which the lay public receives sociological knowledge, how sociological narratives about social problems are theoretically constructed also contributes to sociology's marginal status in policy debates.

The literature reviewed here weaves together divergent strands of critical reflection on contemporary American society to reveal how forces currently transforming civic culture contribute to a view of sociological knowledge as either redundant or irrelevant to the public debate on social problems.

The Information Revolution and the Culture of Criticism

One of the most important influences on civic culture in the United States today are recent advances in information and communication technology. These technological changes have recently been addressed in general terms by a number of commentators (Abramson, Artherton, and Orren 1988; Bennett 1988; Elshtain 1995; Entman 1989; Lasch, 1995; Neuman 1991), but sociology's place in this new environment has not received much attention. The revolution in information-processing and media technology has produced an interesting paradox: While the emerging communications revolution has the potential to revitalize civic discourse, we are witnessing a trend toward an actual impoverishment of public debate on social problems.

On the one hand, the widespread availability of radio and television and a broad range of print media has created the potential for a mass audience for information related to civic affairs, a potential sometimes realized in the form of massive collective reactions to key social events. This potential may be further enhanced by the explosive growth of the market for personal computers in recent years and the expansion of the international network (the Internet) of electronic information exchange and dialogue.[2]

On the other hand, these technological innovations incorporate features that seem to encourage low-level participation in social-problems discourse and superficial political debate. In recent commentary on this problem, social critics such as Christopher Lasch (1995) focus on the destructive effects of televised political debates that emphasize personal style rather than the substance of arguments. Lasch also decries the emergence of "commercial persuasion" in which consumers of political ideas are subjected to advertising campaigns designed to manipulate personal needs and desires. Similarly, Jean Elshtain (1995) argues that innovations such as telepolling and interactive television are ushering in a political system based on instant plebiscite. Meaningful political debate is sacrificed as politicians strive to tap the public mood on specific subjects: "[T]here is no need for debate with one's fellow citizens on substantive questions. All that is required is a calculus of opinion" (1995, 29).

Thus analysts such as Lasch and Elshtain find the new information and communication technology subverting the institutional processes that have contributed historically to some degree of democratic exchange in civic culture. These technologies have created an environment in which sociological analyses of social problems have little chance for serious consideration. The distinguishing characteristics of sociological explanation—its emphasis on structural rather than individual forces and its orientation towards holistic, multivariate analyses—render it unsuitable for media formats designed to explain complex issues in terms of simple formulae. Successful political campaigns in this era of "instant plebiscite" increasingly rely on well-crafted appeals to the cultural biases of the electorate.[3] The structural logic of sociological inquiry does not resonate with the radical individualism of American culture, which means that sociological perspectives are not likely to win a following in today's media-dominated system.[4]

Radical individualism is not the only cultural principle expressed and promoted through media institutions that contributes to sociology's marginality in the public arena. Another recent trend more directly (but not exclusively) influenced by media institutions is a pattern best described as the "culture of criticism." Media preoccupation with individual "chiselers and cheats" and the failings of dominant social institutions has created a climate in which sociology's critical mission is viewed as redundant.

Research focusing on the ideological content of the news media has yielded a confusing picture of this institution's place in the political process, with some researchers emphasizing the "liberal bias" of media messages and others positing that news media contribute to the maintenance of ruling-class hegemony. However, the two camps agree that the media function as a critical voice, although they differ in interpreting the ultimate consequences of this critical focus. The present analysis incorporates elements of both the conservative and radical perspectives on the news media's ideological functions.

Neoconservative social commentators such as Moynihan (1973), Huntington (1975), and Crozier, Huntington, and Watanuki (1975) argue that the formal mandate of television and print news organizations to expose corruption within the public and private sectors has given rise to an "adversary culture" characterized by a growing public distrust of most major social institutions. While radicals do not necessarily disagree, they have been more concerned about the limited scope of media criticism. They point out that the critical mission of news organizations rarely extends beyond the identification of disconnected instances of corruption and scandal and thus falls short of a systematic examination of the structural basis of power and privilege in American society (Herman and Chomsky 1988; Parenti 1992; Tuchman 1974). Lack of empirical research on these issues makes it difficult to derive sound generalizations about the media's impact on civic culture, but the neoconservative and radical critiques paint a disturbing picture of a profoundly cynical public with little faith in existing institutions or tolerance for sophisticated social criticism. We believe that this is an accurate picture of the current state of civic culture in the United States (see also Wallerstein 1998).

The culture of criticism profoundly impacts the receptivity of lay audiences to sociological explanations of social life. Positivist sociological analyses, rooted in such theoretical perspectives as structural functionalism, exchange theory, rational choice theory, or in the atheoretical research of strict empiricists, are often dismissed by the public as either intellectual obfuscation of trivial issues or as idealized models of social life. Individuals and groups differentially situated to observe or experience certain types of oppression often regard positivist analyses of these domains as merely legitimating established power and privilege. Civic culture is not a fertile seedbed for social-problems perspectives based on positivist analyses. Public cynicism toward other social institutions seems to extend to mainstream social science as well.

Public-issue perspectives inspired by critically oriented sociology fare no better within the current culture of criticism. The key principles of critical sociology—the focus on taken-for-granted assumptions of hegemonic ideologies, questioning the basis of authority, and challenging entrenched power and privilege—are clearly redundant within a cultural environment awash with critical commentary of one kind or another. While critical commentary by the print and electronic media is not coherently organized or committed to sustained and detailed analysis, it nevertheless generates an information overload that diminishes the public's responsiveness to more sophisticated forms of critical analysis. Sociological perspectives on political and economic power or authority and truth claims are not seen by the public as novel viewpoints. Such perspectives are easily absorbed in the litany of criticism pouring from the public arena.

The changes in civic culture described here are important for understanding sociology's marginality in the social-problems debate, but other factors contributing to this outcome must be considered as well. At the same time that social, cultural, and technological changes have undermined the public's receptivity to sociological narratives, the production of such narratives has also been reshaped by important social changes. We will now focus attention on how social and organizational changes in the work environment of intellectuals, in general, and sociologists, in particular, have diminished the influence of sociological perspectives in the public debate on social problems.

The Bureaucratization of Intellectual and Sociological Inquiry

In a book dealing with the disappearance of the "public intellectual" in American civic culture, Russell Jacoby (1987) notes that the last generation of independent social critics—essayists, editorialists, book reviewers, and pamphleteers concerned with important social issues—failed to reproduce itself after the 1950s. Jacoby attributes the disappearance of a younger generation of free intellectuals to several interrelated social changes in American society. At the center of these changes was the movement of intellectuals into university bureaucracies:

> Younger intellectuals no longer need or want a larger public; they are almost exclusively professors. Campuses are their homes; colleagues their audiences; monographs and specialized journals their media. Unlike past intellectuals they situate themselves within fields and disciplines—for good reason. Their jobs, advancement, and salaries depend on the evaluation of specialists, and this dependence affects the issues broached and the language employed. (Jacoby 1987, 6)

Other changes have intersected with the expansion of universities to hasten the demise of the public intellectual. While younger intellectuals were pulled into university life by the attraction of steady salaries, they were also pushed in that direction by the gradual disappearance of an urban ecology and bohemian culture that served as the principal breeding ground for the free-lance writers and artists of an earlier age. As suburban tracts exploded and inner cities declined in the postwar period, "bohemian colonies" within the urban environment could no longer be sustained and their populations dispersed (Jacoby 1987, 28). The result was a loss of the interpersonal support networks and cultural institutions that nurture the development of public intellectuals.

Academic sociology has been one of the primary destinations of younger generations of intellectuals. Choosing the relative safety of academic organizations over the insecurities of free-lance work arrangements, recruits to sociology in the postwar period entered a profession undergoing fundamental changes in its mission and the character of its work, changes directly tied to the growing bureaucratization of academic institutions.

In a recent critique of contemporary American sociology, Sjoberg and Vaughan (1993) describe sociology's dramatic shift away from the earlier traditions of urban sociology pioneered by the Chicago School before the Second World War and the social and cultural criticism of sociologists like Daniel Bell, David Riesman, and C. Wright Mills in the

1950s and early 1960s. In the postwar period, a new type of research came to dominate the discipline as sociologists began to seek and receive state and corporate sponsorship for their research. Following the lead of colleagues in the natural sciences, sociologists began to promote a "big science" approach to research by organizing research groups engaged in highly technical analyses of large data sets. Tailoring their research to fit the expectations of powerful actors within the government, sociologists succeeded in winning large research grants administered through agencies like the National Science Foundation. The survey-research tradition advanced within the discipline as politicians came to appreciate the value of public-opinion polls for tracking public sentiment. Similarly, evaluation research received increasing financial support as advocates of the Great Society social programs of the 1960s looked for ways to judge the effectiveness of these government initiatives (Sjoberg and Vaughan 1993, 78).[5]

Jacoby's general treatment of contemporary intellectual culture, Sjoberg and Vaughan's description of the growth of bureaucratic sociology, and a number of similar analyses (Damrosch 1995; Klausner and Lidz 1986) reveal the broad structural changes in postwar U.S. society that shaped public demand for intellectual, sociologically informed perspectives on public issues. Changes in the urban and institutional environment eroded the culture of free intellectuals, and pushed new generations of intellectuals into the universities. Academic sociology became bureaucratized and firmly coupled with other large-scale organizations in the public and private sectors, and the main constituency for sociological research and publication narrowed to professional audiences increasingly differentiated into specialty and subspecialty groupings. The content of sociological production reflects the character of this audience, as work published in professional journals has become more methodologically or theoretically sophisticated and largely incomprehensible to nonspecialists (Smelser 1988; Vaughan 1993). In the contemporary academic environment, the possibilities for doing sociological research and writing that will appeal to lay audiences while, at the same time, win recognition from the profession are limited.

One obvious expression of this problem is the continuing debate over the role of applied research in sociology. Some argue that sociology must move more aggressively in the direction of applied or public-policy research in order to improve the discipline's standing (see Borgada and Cook 1988). Indeed, sociologists often play active roles in the development or evaluation of specific social-policy programs (Freeman et al. 1983; Freeman and Rossi 1984; Whyte 1986; 1991). But social commentary and policy analysis continue to be marginal enterprises in sociology, because these activities are not logically connected to the *central* disciplinary tasks of theory development and empirical validation. The dominant research models for academic sociology do not provide an epistemological justification for an active engagement in public discourse.

In addition to these institutional problems, opening civic debate to the sociological voice is further undermined by the discipline's intellectual approach to the study of social problems. Sociology's role in social-problems discourse is ironic: On the one hand, no other social science discipline is more formally committed to the study of social problems, with sociologists historically dominating the large and influential Society for the Study of Social Problems, playing leading roles in managing and contributing to the Society's prestigious journal *Social Problems*, teaching social-problems courses as a part of the formal curricula in sociology, and writing textbooks and supplementary readings for such courses. On the other hand, sociologists specializing in social-problems research do not often contribute to the public discussion of problems that afflict modern society or propose solutions to them. In order to fully understand this irony, we must look more carefully at the theoretical foundations of social-problems research.

The Stalemate in Social-Problems Theory

By all appearances, efforts during the last three or four decades to establish a general theoretical framework for social-problems research have led to a stalemate (see Best 1989; Hazelrigg 1985; 1986; Miller and Holstein 1993; Pfohl 1985; Rafter 1992; Schneider 1985; 1991; Troyer 1992; Woolgar and Pawluch 1985). Early research on social problems (pre-1970s) and some variants of contemporary research are rooted in the paradigmatic assumptions guiding the discipline of sociology as a whole. Social problems are seen as consequences of certain structural or social-system imperatives, related to the maintenance of privileging structures or the social system as a whole. Examination of social problems in such structural terms yields an "objective" analysis that contrasts with the subjective sensibilities of common-sense actors or the ideological constructions of interests groups. Hence, in this "objectivist" tradition, social problems are products of objective conditions tied to structural changes such as industrialization, bureaucratization, mechanization, and other modernization trends (Clinard 1974; Dynes 1964; Horton and Leslie 1974; Weinberg 1970).

In contrast, the social-constructionist approach (Blumer 1971; Spector and Kitsuse 1973; 1977) rejects the idea that social problems can always be treated as objectively real. Sensitive to the power of collective definition and public opinion, constructionists argue that objective conditions have very little to do with the cause or origin of social problems. Focusing on "the activities of individuals or groups making assertions of grievances and claims with respect to some putative conditions," constructionist emphasize "the process by which members of society define a putative condition as a social problem" (Spector and Kitsuse 1977, 75). More recent theoretical development in the social-problems field has involved, by and large, efforts to further elaborate the constructionist model. Hilgartner and Bosk's (1988) "public arenas model" incorporates elements of several distinct theoretical traditions, but it is still rooted in the central constructionist assumption that "social problems are projections of collective sentiments rather than simple mirrors of objective conditions in society" (1988, 53–54). The constructionist approach has come to clearly dominate the field in recent decades (Troyer 1992, 35).

While constructionism has been ascendant since the 1970s, its core presuppositions are now receiving critical attention. For instance, Woolgar and Pawluch's (1985) metaphor of "ontological gerrymandering" refers to a form of selective relativism that is a fundamental bulwark of the constructionist approach. Through ontological gerrymandering, constructionists

> make problematic the truth status of certain states of affairs selected for analysis and explanation, while backgrounding or minimizing the possibility that the same problems apply to assumptions upon which the analysis depends. By means of ontological gerrymandering, proponents of definitional explanation place a boundary between assumptions which are to be understood as (ostensibly) problematic and those which are not. (1985, 216)

Adherents of the constructionist perspective erect an ontological boundary between the objectivist claim that social conditions associated with a given social problem change across time, and the constructionist claim that putative conditions *do not* change (or change in a ways inconsistent with the perceived growth of the problem). Constructionists adopt a critical stance towards the first claim, but not the second. Without this selective relativism, the constructionist model collapses.

Woolgar and Pawluch's critique has stimulated an intense theoretical debate that has crystallized distinct camps within the constructionist tradition. The so-called "strict" constructionists accept Woolgar and Pawluch's criticism and endeavor to purge their analyses of any explicit or implicit assumptions about objective reality (Spector and Kitsuse 1987;

see also Troyer 1992). This version of constructionism, which has its roots
in phenomenological sociology, begins with the premise that all knowledge of the world is socially constructed, even the assertions of social
scientists that contradict those of claims makers. Consequently, strict
constructionists see no need to reconcile constructionism and objectivism in order to study the claims-making process. The focus of research
should be claims themselves, and not the validity of those claims.

An alternative to strict constructionism can be found in an approach
that Joel Best (1989) has called "contextual constructionism" (see Blumer 1971; Gusfield 1985; Rafter 1992). Best also accepts the Woolgar and
Pawluch criticism, but moves in the opposite direction from the strict
constructionists by arguing that selective relativism is simply unavoidable in constructionist analysis. Therefore, he opts for a "partial" constructionism that incorporates elements of objectivist analysis:

> [C]ontextual constructionist assume that they can know—with reason-
> able confidence—about social conditions. They acknowledge the
> socially constructed nature of [social scientific] information about
> social problems, but they assume that such information can be used to
> (imperfectly) describe the context within which claims-making occurs.
> (1989, 247)

Thus it appears that efforts by sociologists to advance social-problems theory have reached a stalemate. This impasse is defined by the
failure of either objectivist or constructionist analysis to adequately
account for the growth and decline of social problems while, at the same
time, neither approach can be dismissed out-of-hand. Consequently,
sociologists seeking to contribute their knowledge to public discourse
on social problems are hampered by the discipline's own critical reflection on the inadequacies of its knowledge-base in the field.

Consideration of these issues adds another crucial dimension to the
present account of sociology's marginal status in civic discourse on
social problems and policy. If the civic irrelevance of sociology is partly
due to the technological, cultural, professional, and organizational
forces described above, we must also acknowledge the part played by
the current impasse in social-problems theory. Sociology's civic disen-
gagement is a multifaceted problem that results from how sociological
knowledge is generated as well as how it is received within the social
and cultural environment of contemporary American society.

Toward a Transactional Model for Social-Problems Research

Having identified some of the reasons why the sociological perspective is not a more influential force in public-policy debate, we will now propose an alternative theoretical and methodological framework for social-problems research that can increase the relevance of sociological theory and research to civic discourse. In outlining the transactional approach, we draw on several distinct lines of theoretical development. First, we look to the critical theory of Jürgen Habermas (1973; 1984; 1987) for a metatheoretical approach that can be adapted to the transactional ontology and the embodied conception of human action developed in the earlier chapters of this volume. Second, despite our earlier criticisms of postmodernist social theory, we believe that postmodernism yields some important ideas about how to infuse social-problems research with the principles of democracy and community empowerment. And finally, the countersystem approach (Lyng 1988; 1990a; 2002; Sjoberg and Cain 1971) offers some concrete strategies for dealing with the bureaucratic and professional constraints that stand in the way of a transactional approach to social-problems research. We then use this material to introduce some tentative proposals for an alternative approach, proposals that will hopefully encourage a dialogue about sociology's role in the postmodern world.

In schematic form, the transactional approach incorporates the following principles:

1. Social theory must get beyond the impasse between objectivism and constructionism by offering a view of social problems as both socially constructed and objectively real. This can be accomplished by making the identification of *solutions* to problems an integral part of the critical analysis of modern society. Thus the research paradigm should offer a way to logically connect "deconstructive" and "reconstructive" analysis.

2. The identification of potential social reconstructions should not be guided by rational standards alone. Social reconstruction should also draw on *extrarational, embodied* sentiments and *conflicting life-forms* that reflect the body's inherent resistance to social determination.

3. The *bureaucratic constraints* on sociologists' ability to contribute to the public resolution of social problems must be transcended by identifying a constituency for research outputs

that includes, but also extends beyond, the traditional professional audience.

4. The research paradigm should provide a logical structure for linking these new goals with the more traditional disciplinary goals of empirical analyses and theoretical development.

We begin by exploring ways in which Habermas's critical framework can be adapted to the study of social problems through a transactional interpretation of some of his key concepts. This will eventually lead to a conceptual system that accords with the first principle of our transactional social-problems approach: the linking of deconstructive (critical) analysis and reconstructive (problem-solving) analysis.

Linking Deconstruction and Reconstruction: The Critical Theory of Jürgen Habermas

One of the most influential social theorists of the postwar period, Jürgen Habermas synthesized core concepts and themes from a number of theoretical traditions into a coherent system that has kept the critical-theory tradition alive and revived its emancipatory agenda. Habermas provides a useful metatheoretical framework for sociological analysis, which can serve as a point of departure for elaborating our transactional social-problems approach. Consequently, this chapter is devoted in part to reconceptualizing elements of Habermas's system along the lines of the transactional approach.

This work has already begun in some important respects. Indeed, our effort here has been inspired primarily by the increasing number of scholars who point to the promise of a greater cross-fertilization between Habermas's critical theory and pragmatism (Hinkle 1992; Joas 1992; Shalin 1992). This exploration continues the course charted by Habermas himself in the most sophisticated and comprehensive statement of his views, contained within his Theory of Communicative Action (TCA). Various theoretical traditions informed this impressive synthesis, but Habermas's use of pragmatist ideas in developing the "action-theoretic" dimension of TCA is an important part of his framework. However, while contemporary interpreters of pragmatism applaud Habermas's use of pragmatist ideas, they generally fault him for his lack of sensitivity to the ontological principles in which these ideas are rooted.

We endorse this critique, but now wish to take the next step by exploring the possibilities for reconfiguring Habermas's theoretical system. The key part of this reconfiguration involves a modification of

Habermas's notion of the "life-world" in order to take account of the embodied character of human transaction. As noted in the previous chapter, it is the *body*, not the "self" or any other abstracted aspect of the human agent, that acts. Starting from this premise, it follows that the action-theoretic problem at the heart of the life-world concept should address the embodied nature of such action. In other words, we should conceive of the life-world as a reality constituted by (to use Frank's terminology) "bodies coming to terms with one another." Thinking of the life-world in this way will have far-reaching consequences for the transactional approach to social problems.

We begin by outlining the key elements of universal pragmatics and TCA. Then, after reviewing the pragmatist critique of Habermas's work, we focus on the concepts of the "life-world" and "system" and suggest some ways to reconceptualize these ideas in light of insights derived from the earlier transactional analysis of emotions and the body. One of our primary concerns in this reconceptualization is to reveal how the embodied characteristics emphasized by the transactional perspective can be related to the search for solutions to social problems. This will demonstrate how resistance to system imperatives emerges within the life-world in the form of collective embodied responses to system colonization.

THE THEORY OF COMMUNICATIVE ACTION AND UNIVERSAL PRAGMATICS. If the transactional perspective rejects the dualistic oppositions of traditional social-problems theory, then we can look to TCA and its conceptual core, "universal pragmatics," as a starting point for an alternative social-problems approach. By linking deconstruction and reconstruction, Habermas offers a methodological strategy for social-problems research that is consistent with the notion of transaction. He calls for a form of social-scientific practice organized most fundamentally as a transformative enterprise (Habermas 1971). In the same way that human beings routinely transform reality as they act to solve everyday problems and, in the process, acquire knowledge about the workings of the material world, knowledge of the social order is best advanced through a method that gives priority to the reconstruction of society.

Habermas gives primary attention to establishing rational procedures for constructing conceptual models of alternative social arrangements. Pragmatist thought figures prominently in his notion of rationality, which explains, in part, the compatibility between recent interpretations of pragmatism and Habermas's system (see Shalin 1992). TCA is founded upon the pragmatist conception of reason as symbolically mediated interaction. As Mead (1967) asserted, reason arises when the individual takes into his or her own response the "attitude of the other"—hence, reason is a thoroughly social force. Habermas adds a missing structural dimension to this conception by emphasizing not only reason's movement through history towards self-consciousness and self-criticism but also its subversion by "systematically distorted" communications in a "money-bound," "media-steered" society that prevents the realization of reason's full critical potential (Habermas 1987, 256–82).

Objectivity here springs from reason, residing partly in the universal discursive standards that must guide the public discussion of alternative social arrangements. Such discussions take place within specially constituted "ideal speech situations" located in life-world institutions free from the contaminating influences of the political–economic system (Habermas 1987). In the ideal speech situation, public issues are addressed through rational argumentation, in contrast to the unreflexive process by which common-sense actors typically mediate issues of truth, justice, and authenticity. The only way to avoid the usual appeal to established custom in settling validity claims is to create a normative environment where "only reason should have force" (Habermas 1970, 7). This is the function of the ideal speech situation, an environment governed by procedural rules for achieving communicative rationality.[6]

In light of the first four chapters of the present volume, it would appear that Habermas is woefully naive in his overdistanced and disembodied approach to reason. However, this is not quite fair, as we will see in reviewing the formal critiques of TCA by contemporary pragmatists (see below). In any case, Habermas's approach to objectivity is not restricted to the rational mediation of validity claims. He also establishes explicit links between the social-construction process and objectivity by tying rational critique to the search for alternative structures. Ultimately, conflicting views of social issues can be objectively resolved only by transcending the existing order through the creation of a different hypothetical order. Hence, the principal goal of discourse within the ideal speech situation is to identify structural alternatives without subjective distortion:

> Rational reconstructions . . . deal with anonymous rule systems, which
> any subjects whatsoever can comply with, insofar as they have acquired
> the corresponding competence with respect to these rules. Recon-
> structions thus do not encompass subjectivity, within the horizon of
> which alone the experience of reflection is possible. (Habermas 1973,
> 22)

Habermas succeeds here in showing how the social-(re)construction process can be uncoupled from subjectivity. When social problems are defined from the perspective of an alternative institutional system, they emerge as socially constructed phenomena that are, nonetheless, objective in character. Objectivity in this sense derives from the "anonymous rule systems" associated with not-as-yet existing social systems that are used to define problems. This approach to social problems contrasts markedly with their social construction within an existing socioeconomic system, where resources are mobilized by various interests to construct ideologically based definitions of contentious issues.

Thus Habermas offers a potential solution to the impasse in social-problems theory. A theoretic approach that logically connects deconstructive and reconstructive analysis offers a way to transcend the theoretical incommensurability that currently plagues the field. The alternative perspective views putative social problems as always socially constructed and endorses the effort to better understand the process by which issues are defined as problems in the public arena. At the same time, however, this perspective also identifies a way to define social problems without ideological distortion. This is achieved by analyzing existing social structures and the problems they generate from the standpoint of the hypothetical model, which results in critical deconstruction tied to an explicit vision of an *alternative* to the existing order.

The deconstruction/reconstruction link takes on added significance when one considers the contemporary cultural context discussed earlier in this chapter. A sociological study of social problems that offers not only a critical analysis of the existing order but also a way of identifying potential *solutions* to problems (solutions that derive from hypothetical social models) could function as a unique voice within the current culture of criticism. Demonstrating systematic and complex logical connections between the critical analysis of current social conditions and the broad contours of alternative social structures could contribute a much-needed perspective to the discussion of public issues. Still, the model advanced here raises questions that must be addressed before we can fully articulate the alternative approach.

THE LIMITS OF DISEMBODIED REASON: THE PRAGMATIST CRITIQUE OF TCA. It is clear from the preceding discussion of Habermas's ideas that he is deeply committed to the modernist project and its focus on the liberating potential of reason and rational discourse. In this respect, it can be said that Habermas perhaps owes his greatest debt to Max Weber, who was less concerned in a critical sense about the role of reason in modern affairs than he was about the triumph of formal rationality over substantive rationality. Following Weber's logic, Habermas sees rationalized communicative action within the life-world as the antidote for the increasing influence of purposive-rational action emanating from the system. Although he is deft in his application of pragmatist thinking to this problem, it is precisely this use (or misuse) of the pragmatist tradition that concerns contemporary commentators the most.

As Dmitri Shalin (1992) reveals in his critical assessment of Habermas's general corpus and TCA in particular, contemporary pragmatists adopt a common stance in questioning the rationalist principles upon which Habermas bases his theoretical approach. Shalin neatly summarizes the pragmatist response to Habermas by creating a series of antinomies, which capture the fundamental differences between TCA and "pragmatic politics" (1992, 253–73).

He begins with the opposition between "disembodied reason," which occupies a central place in TCA, and the pragmatist notion of "embodied reasonableness." What is highlighted by this contrast is the importance that pragmatists place on "noncognitive forms of intelligence irreducible to verbal intellect," which are left out of TCA due to its privileging of consciousness and discursive practices. Reason, as it appears in TCA, "has no obvious relation to the human body and noncognitive processes (emotions, feelings, sentiments)." This is just the conception of pure reason that was destroyed by Damasio's (1994) clinical studies. These studies support the pragmatist view of communication as a process of "minding something together, carrying out a larger act in which participants are engaged bodily as well as mentally," which accounts for the pragmatist sensitivity to the nondiscursive element in culture. This focus reflects a deep appreciation for the insight, highlighted in the previous chapter, that just "as the body becomes 'encultured,' . . . so culture becomes embodied" (Alexander 1987, quoted in Shalin 1992, 255).

Next, in contrasting "determinant being" with "indeterminate reality," Shalin points to the limitations of TCA arising from its reliance on the categorical distinctions bequeathed by rationalism and its overdetermined view of reality. Opposing this view is the pluralism and perspectivism of the pragmatist tradition, which gives ontological priority to "objective uncertainty" in a universe existing in a perpetual state of becoming. Thus, while Habermas's rationalist ontology helps explain his faith in argumentation as a means for settling validity claims about a world of uncertainty, the pragmatist ontology suggests another consequence following from discursive techniques of validation: "Each time we pass judgment on the situation at hand—literally terminate indeterminacy—we bring out some of its potentialities and render obscure its other possible determinations" (1992, 258).

An important epistemological consequence of the pragmatist ontology is its demand for an alternative to "discursive validation" in rationalist inquiry. Pragmatism calls for an approach that achieves what Shalin refers to as "pragmatic certainty." This latter concept is critical to our effort to resuscitate "truth" as a meaningful idea for sociology, because it offers a way of addressing the limitations of discursive validation techniques while not abandoning the important distinction between truth and error. For pragmatists, "truth is no longer grasped . . . in the rationalist manner as *adequatio intellectus et rei* but instead is pragmatically conceived as a practically accomplished unity of knowledge and reality" (1992, 260). Moreover, to achieve pragmatic certainty in the unification of knowledge and reality one has to engage in "joint action," which can be described as "living and minding together where theoretical, normative, and aesthetic discourses merge into one, where humans feel, think, and transact at the same time, and where a different logic is called upon to help us master everyday contingencies" (1992, 260). Pragmatists find certainty in the ability of organized groups to make real situations conform to idealized plans through collective transformative actions (1992, 261).

In contrasting "rational consensus" and "reasonable dissent," Shalin addresses head-on Habermas's formula for constructing the kind of rational society that will ensure the effective resolution of social problems and humankind's emancipation. He inquires into the dangers of the consensus model of problem-solving embodied in Habermas's ideal speech situation and its orientation to policies based on purely theoretical calculations. What we find in pragmatism is an alternative approach, "one that accentuates the limits of theoretically grounded consensus and highlights the productive properties of dissent" (1992, 262). Thus pragmatists see conflict as no less important than consensus in the search for rational solutions to problems.

The pragmatist orientation towards dissent will be especially important for our effort to refashion the life-world concept, because we will assert that dissent, born of the body's resistance to cultural inscription, is an unavoidable consequence of life-world transactions. However, the type of dissenting posture emphasized by our conception of the life-world is not one based on discursive disagreement. Rather, it is dissent expressed through transactions between bodies and their social and physical environments in acts of production, consumption, and social interaction. Even with the shift in focus, these patterns of dissent have the same significance that Shalin attributes to "dissenting insights"—

they must be "safeguarded because they hint at the unrealized potentialities of being" (1992, 267).

The two remaining antinomies, "transcendental democracy" versus
"democratic transcendence" and "rational society" versus "sane community," refer primarily to the types of social and political arrangements
that reflect the competing principles of rationalism and pragmatism.
Thus, while both Habermas and contemporary pragmatists celebrate
democratic processes, the meaning of democracy for the two is not quite
the same. Consonant with TCA's general focus on discourse, the democratic ideal within this system is an institutional arrangement that ame-
liorates the distortions of communicative practices arising from market
and bureaucratic influences. The ideal speech situation is based on principles that ensure a consensual, democratic form of decision making
free of domination. Pragmatists, by contrast, see democracy as a system
more directly attuned to problem-solving in a world of great uncertainty
and unpredictability:

> If society is a semiordered chaos routinely generating unanticipated
> consequences, as pragmatism implies, then democracy is a historically
> specific mode of managing uncertainty. . . . Democratic systems thrive on
> uncertainty; they rely on market, competition, ad hocing, and muddling
> through as necessary, even if distortion-proned, mechanisms for han-
> dling a large number of incalculable variables. By the same token, dem-
> ocratic policies promote conflicting life-forms, open up public discourse
> for an ever-widening range of participants, and maximize the public's
> role in defining the terms in which indeterminacy can be legitimately ter-
> minated. (Shalin 1992, 266)

In this view, democracy is a political system that not only values open
political debate but also encourages multiple collective actions, many of
which are competing, in the search for solutions to complex social problems. Pragmatists accept that social reality and any problem it presents to
human beings are much too complex to be understood and adjudicated in
terms of any single perspective, no matter how much people may agree
about its validity. What pragmatists encourage most in the name of democracy is the value of the "conflicting life-forms" that every society generates
when transacting bodies resist cultural inscription and develop corporeal
potentialities through collective problem-solving. The body's capacity for
resistance and the conflicting life-forms produced by resistant bodies are
critical concerns of our alternative social-problems approach.

The clash between human qualities that are valued by rationalism—
cognition, discourse, logic, determinacy, consensus—and those qualities

it disdains or ignores—sentiment, common-sense, inconsistency, indeterminacy, conflict—not only informs the different interpretations of democracy embraced by Habermas and the pragmatists, but also their respective visions of a humane society. For Habermas, the only way to free public discourse of ideological distortions is to infuse communication with the principles of reason. This will purge the life-world of the communicative irrationalities generated by system imperatives and remove from discourse all contaminating influences associated with emotion, indeterminacy, parochialism, and the like.

In making the pragmatist case for the "sane community," Shalin notes that while

> Habermas wants to clear communications from inarticulate sentiments, private interests, logical inconsistencies, and similar distortions as inimical to reason, . . . [p]ragmatists find these essential to keeping one's sanity amidst the semichaotic order that surrounds us in everyday life. (1992, 270)

This suggests that an adequate conception of the life-world must leave room for emotion and transacting bodies. If one starts with this premise, it is possible to locate a domain of social life where values and norms are fully embodied: "values [are] inseparable from habit . . . [s]ocial norms have to find their way into mind's noncognitive recesses and become suffused with emotions, transformed into habits, translated into routine judgments" (1992, 271). In other words, values and norms are *objectified* by the body, while on another level they are also *resisted* by the body. Thus the dialectic between the body's objectifying and resisting response to social facts forms the central core of the life-world.

The capacity of transacting bodies within the life-world to generate creative alternatives to the system's colonizing forms derives from corporeal resistance. The life-world is rich with social adaptations to the problem complexes of everyday existence, adaptations that are ontologically connected to the objective uncertainty of the body—that is, its contingent and resisting character. As we will explain below, the recoupling of the life-world and system that Habermas advocates can happen only by fully exploiting the creative problem-solving capacities of contingent bodies involved in localized transactions with one another and their immediate environments:

> Above all, pragmatists call for personal efforts in one's immediate community. . . . [S]ocial reconstruction starts in one community, envelopes the city, moves to the state level, and then comes to the national legisla-

ture . . . suggest[ing] the kind of pragmatic, grass-root politics essential to democratic reconstruction. (1992, 273)

Having reviewed Shalin's pragmatist critique of Habermas, the stage is now set for the next step in our effort to outline a transactional social-problems approach. If the first principle guiding this effort is to establish a logical connection between deconstruction with reconstruction in social-problems analysis, the second principle is that the social-reconstruction process should make use of the full range of embodied capacities that human beings possess for collective problem-solving. We have seen that Habermas's focus on *rational* reconstruction is flawed, because it privileges cognition and rationality at the expense of embodied sentiments, emotions, and other nondiscursive ways of experiencing the world. Consequently, it will be necessary to modify Habermas's theoretical framework by infusing his approach more thoroughly with principles borrowed from pragmatist philosophy and its offspring, transactional sociology. As the preceding discussion suggests, the key to this modification is a rethinking of the concept of the life-world.

EMBODIED SOCIAL RECONSTRUCTION: THE PROMISE OF CONFLICTING LIFE-FORMS

As we have seen, the principal problem with Habermas's concept of the life-world is that it does not incorporate the broader range of capacities for reasoned action captured by the pragmatist notion of "living habit." As Eugene Halton (1995, 204) notes: "Habermas has conceived the life-world as a passive reservoir of knowledge with no capacities for reasonable activity . . . biology plays no part in his conception, he conceives life solely from the rationalist's viewpoint as 'tacit knowledge.'" By shifting the focus from knowledge to *experience* as the foundation of the life-world, a more encompassing concept can be constructed, one that now incorporates not only tacit knowledge but also "habits of belief providing common-sense prejudices, wisdom, traditions, and crafts" (1995, 205). While Habermas sees the life-world as storing the *interpretive* work of preceding generations, Halton views it as "the incorporation of prior experience in human traditions and practices" (1995, 205).

The Embodied Life-World: From Communicative Action to Corporeal Transaction

Following the work of Shalin, Halton, and other contemporary pragmatist critics of Habermas (Antonio and Kellner 1992; Joas 1992; Sciulli

1992), we think it imperative to make room in the life-world concept for the transacting bodies and the emergent products of these transactions. Therefore, we propose substituting the notion of "corporeal transaction" for Habermas's "communicative action" in the action-theoretical framework. This change would shift life-world analysis from an exclusive focus on patterns of symbolic interaction to include bodily transactions involved in production, consumption, and social interaction (via domination or communication). The transactional approach puts *embodied* actors at the center of the life-world by allowing us to see the body as both acting subject and resisting object—serving, in this way, as one important source of the conflicting life-forms that make up the life-world.

In proposing this broader conception of the life-world, it is important to retain the idea of the taken-for-granted character of the habitual patterns that constitute this domain. However, the scope of taken-for-granted experience is now much wider than just tacit knowledge. The unreflective habit that fills the life-world consists of corporeal wisdom passed across generations as bodies engage in productive, consumptive, and communicative transactions. This wisdom is fully embodied and not immediately available to critical consciousness and therefore remains, in Habermas's words, the "horizon-forming context" for processes of corporeal problem-solving.

As we argued in the previous chapter, the key problem for bodies is contingency. This problem is the focus of ongoing efforts to terminate the indeterminacy of human bodies and the rest of nature, on the one hand, through transactions undertaken by bodies engaged in production, consumption, and communicative alignment with one another, and on the other hand through the institutional mechanisms and technologies of a society moving towards higher levels of rational control and efficiency. In an extension of this analysis, we can now suggest that transactions of the former type belong to the *life-world*, while the institutional patterns of the latter type define the *system*.

Thus a crucial modification of the Habermasian scheme here is to see productive, consumptive, and communicative action as belonging to *both* the system and the life-world. In addition, it is now possible to analyze the differentiation of the life-world in terms of evolving corporeal transactions that produce localized solutions to indeterminacy, accompanied by a critical collective awareness of the problem-solving significance of these transactions. As we will show, possibilities for social reconstruction reside in the exploration of these localized and subcultural life-forms, and not in Habermas's misguided commitment to communicative rationality.

Embodied and Disembodied Production

From a transactional perspective, the life-world is a domain where human actors strive to come to terms with the inherent contingencies of their bodies partly through creative acts of embodied production. This approach to terminating indeterminacy fits most closely with the Marxian notion of "free labor" in which the undeveloped species potential of the body is expressed in the form of the organically based capacities and skills required to transform material substance into useful objects. Embodied, free labor is fully transactional—the body creates itself in the act of creating the object/product and corporeal contingency is managed in a self- and species-affirming fashion. In thinking about this kind of productive act, it is critically important to keep the life-world analytical focus: when we locate labor in this domain, we mean to highlight the part that it plays in allowing people to deal with the contingent nature of their bodies. This is *not* to deny the importance of that other key problem that human beings share with all other species: the need to ensure our material survival. However, the latter is properly conceptualized as a problem addressed within the system, which stands in some historically unique relationship with the life-world of transacting bodies. Seeing human productive acts (labor) as a focal activity of *both* the life-world *and* the system is central to the transactional view.

The importance of this dual analytical focus becomes especially clear when we consider the problem of the uncoupling of the life-world and the system. In the case of the simple, undifferentiated structure of tribal societies, in which system and life-world are coterminous, the productive activities involved in meeting one's survival needs are, by nature, highly embodied and holistic. As such, they provide a means for managing corporeal contingency and actualizing species capacities at the same time that they yield the resources required for survival. Hence, in these circumstances, the production functions of system and life-world are closely intertwined, which explains why survival and subsistence activities in tribal societies so often carry sacred and ritual significance: one's labor in fulfilling subsistence needs is also the means by which one attends to transcendental concerns inscribed in sacred practices.

With the development of bureaucratic, industrial society and the growing influence of the rationalization principle, the system and life-world become uncoupled and dialectically opposed. Now, labor devoted to acquiring the means of subsistence is shaped by purposive-rational calculation and becomes largely disembodied in character. This does not mean that productive activity in general can no longer address the problem of corporeal indeterminacy—only that labor structured by the *system* is not focused on producing solutions to this problem. Consequently, system differentiation and the attendant rationalization of labor creates a life-world imperative to maintain alternative forms of embodied labor.

In an extension of our analysis in the previous chapter, we can now see the *disciplined body* emerging as a consequence of system colonization of the life-world. Under the rationalization imperative of the system, manifested concretely as the promotion of economic and bureaucratic efficiency (Marx and Weber) and rational discourses for controlling and "improving" bodies and minds (Foucault), corporeal contingency is terminated in the form of disciplined regimens, which deeply inscribe bodies and minds. Part of what is imprinted in the body is one's location in the system's division of labor, reflected in the corporeal consequences of specialized occupational practices. Thus we find the labor practices of ditch diggers reflected in their hard muscles, stooped backs, and sun-damaged skin, as compared to the large posteriors, flaccid muscles, and pale skin of office workers who sit in front of computer screens all day. But the disciplinary regimens of the system cut even deeper into the body and mind than this. When workers of all types have their labor practices organized to maximize output, maintain quality standards, or please customers, their bodies (Braverman 1974), emotions (Hochschild 1983), and minds (Edwards 1979) are disciplined at a level that extends beyond the more immediately recognizable inscriptions produced by the division of labor. As noted above, this deeper-level inscription is a part of the taken-for-granted, "horizon-forming context" of corporeal experience.

Habermas's thesis about the increasing encroachment of the system on the life-world broadens our understanding of the other structural imperative highlighted by our earlier analysis of the disciplined body: the disciplining effects of the human sciences and related discourses. Although division of labor, managerial strategies, and related work regimens function as powerful colonizing forces in the life-world, embodied actors often resist these forces and come to view work as a necessary evil that does not merit a full commitment of body and soul. In contrast, the disciplining effects of Foucault's "panoptic system" are typically achieved with the active participation of the actors under surveillance in this system. Many people willingly submit their bodies and minds to therapeutic regimens prescribed by physicians, psychologists, and other members of the consulting professions. Their search for "health," "well-being," and related goals inspires them to actively embrace the "technologies of domination" that Foucault describes so brilliantly.

In short, increasing system differentiation in the domain of production and the colonization of the life-world by these forces of production have important consequences for the termination of corporeal contingency. The evolution of institutions and discourses for producing goods and services and desirable bodies and minds opens up the life-world to the disciplined body. However, as influential as this type of body usage and other colonizing types are in the contemporary life-world, they can never totally dominate corporeal transactions in this domain. As Habermas notes, the penetration of the life-world by the system "cannot be carried through without remainder" and thus the life-world is "never completely husked away" (1987, 311).

In looking for evidence of embodied production in the life-world, we are drawn to collectively organized productive transactions performed for the specific purpose of developing corporeal capacities beyond those associated with the disciplined body. To be sure, participation in these types of activities has steadily eroded in the postindustrial era, but these life-world transactions continue to be valued by many people. In the context of the rationalized economy of late capitalism, it is still possible to find marginalized occupational groups such as visual artists, musicians, craft workers, and the like who engage in embodied labor practices for the principal purpose of expressing the personal truths of their contingent bodies. Many more people look for opportunities to develop artistic or craft skills in their leisure time through participation in hobby groups, ranging from hot-rod assemblers to quilt makers. These groups often take on the characteristics of the craft guilds by developing institutionalized means of communication (newsletters, web sites, etc.) for sharing information and teaching skills to others. It is beyond the scope of our analysis to describe the full range of opportunities for leisure-time participation in embodied, craft-like activities, but suffice it to say that this represents a large and growing sector of modern social life.

What may be an even larger sector of life-world activities devoted to embodied production are the alternative institutional practices and discourses involved in directly constituting the body. The alternative ideas and practices to which we refer have emerged in large part in direct opposition to the rational discourses and technologies that define the panoptic system. Consider, for example, the large number of alternative health perspectives and practices that have attracted a wide following within Western societies in recent decades. These alternative medical paradigms typically incorporate concepts and therapeutic principles that specifically negate the scientific assumptions and concepts of the biomedical perspective and related approaches. For instance, Lyng's (1990a) case study of the holistic health movement reveals that most of the "modalities" subsumed under the holistic health banner involve medical ideas and practices that are antithetical in some specific way to established biomedical practice. Thus, in general terms, the notion of "holistic" practice challenges the "reductionist" orientation of established biomedical practice (i.e., the reduction of the illness to the level of tissue lesion). Similarly, the various mind-control techniques emphasized by holistic health advocates (meditation, dreamwork, visualization, biofeedback, etc.) contradict the biomedical principle of mind–body dualism (one expression of which is the institutionalized separation of "mental" and "physical" health in the biomedical paradigm). In one faction of the movement, the negation of biomedical principles has even reached the extreme of rejecting scientific-validation procedures as means of assessing the efficacy of treatment regimens. These examples are representative of a large number of holistic health ideas and practices that negate biomedical principles.

The holistic health movement is significant as a life-world pattern because it represents a type of embodied production that stands in direct contrast to the disembodied production practices of the system. In this case, the focus of productive transactions is the body itself, rather than the material objects produced by "free labor" as Marx conceived it. However, in seeking to realize the body's species potential by pursuing the holistic ideal of eclectic body practices (Lyng 1990a, 64), this form of production contradicts the disciplining thrust of human-science perspectives like the biomedical model. Thus with the emergence of holistic health and the many similar movements (including the craft movements of the leisure sector) as collective embodied responses to the corporeal inscriptions produced by the system's technologies of domination, we find confirmation for Habermas's claim that the life-world can never be completely husked away. As we argue below, these life-world patterns can be usefully explored by social scientists looking for solutions to social problems and avenues for social reconstruction.

Embodied and Disembodied Consumption

In addition to patterns of embodied labor, the life-world also incorporates embodied forms of consumption. As with production, the twin analytical focus defined by the system/life-world distinction is crucial for a full understanding of consumption. Thus, from the life-world perspective, the transactions involved in consumption are related to the key life-world problem of corporeal contingency while, from the system perspective, consumption is tied most directly to the problem of individual and collective survival. Once again, the contrast between undifferentiated tribal societies and complex modern societies is instructive. In tribal societies, consumption practices relating to the maintenance of survival are embodied insofar as individuals form intimate, corporeally based connections to the things they consume. Even the most basic form of consumption—the ingestion of food—often requires full engagement with the foodstuffs consumed, as reflected in the complex ritual practices associated with the preparation and eating of food in many tribal cultures.

The same can be said for other objects of consumption. Although production and consumption practices are not highly differentiated in tribal societies with no real equivalent of modern consumer culture, trading and bartering systems do result in an exchange of certain "consumer goods," such as the materials used for clothing and body adornment. The use of these materials illustrates the embodied nature of consumption in the tribal social context. In contrast to modern Western practices, these materials are not treated as temporary body coverings or decorative devices to be recycled by days of the week, social occasions, or moods. Rather, they are more or less permanent body accessories that cannot be easily discarded, because of emotional/spiritual considerations or because they are actually inscribed in the flesh (piercings, tattoos, etc.).

By contrast, in the modern case of an uncoupled life-world and the system, consumption practices differentiate into their embodied and disembodied forms, with the former evolving in the life-world and the latter developing under the influence of system rationality. As consumption becomes an imperative for the postmodern market economy and therefore a requisite for system maintenance, embodied actors become less and less engaged with the objects they consume. In the extreme case, consumption becomes entirely "conspicuous" in nature, with consumer goods serving only as signifiers of status and having little use-value for those who purchase them. The system imperative operating here is the goal of maximizing consumption by the purchasing public, which places a premium on individuals buying and discarding consumer goods for immediate replacement by "new and improved" forms. Planned obsolescence, ongoing product revisions, disposable goods, new product developments, and similar strategies ensure that consumer goods are discarded and replaced as quickly as possible. The radical expression of this principle is the "shop till you drop" ethic, in which the *experience* of purchasing consumer goods takes priority over the goods themselves. The shift in orientation from the value of the consumer objects to the value of the consumption experience is reflected most dramatically in the emergence of a therapeutic model of "shopping addiction." According to this model, shopping addiction is equivalent to addictions to psychoactive chemicals: the desire for the experience is uncontrolled and insatiable, while the objects that are the focus of one's shopping activities cease to be significant.

Under the influence of increasing system rationalization and the rise of the consumption imperative, possibilities for fully embodied transaction with the objects of consumption diminish. If the system requisite is to maximize consumption, then it becomes increasingly difficult for embodied actors to form deep and complex relations with the objects they consume. In a life-world cluttered with throw-away goods that hold people's attention for only brief periods, it is difficult to experience the kind of sustained transactions with consumer objects that would contribute to the development of unrealized human potential. Consequently, the hyperconsumerism of late capitalism has a deep impact on the life-world problem of terminating the body's indeterminacy. However, the inability to engage in these transactions does *not* mean that consumers fail to identify with the goods they purchase. Indeed, they form strong identifications with consumer goods, but use these goods only as prefabricated reflectors of institutionalized identities. One can assume identities as "cowboys," "bikers," "preppies," "hippies," or "punks" by merely wearing the appropriate clothing and acquiring the necessary accessories rather than actually embracing the lifestyle. The paradoxical character of this pattern is illustrated by corporate executives who trade their weekday business suits for Motorclothes (a Harley-Davidson trademark), removable tattoos, and turn-key Softtail Harleys in order to assume weekend "biker" identities (see Lyng and Bracey 1995).

Thus we can now see the *mirroring body* as the immediate consequence of life-world colonization by the system in the form of the consumption imperative of late capitalism. Consumer objects imprint the body, but corporeal contingency is terminated strictly in terms of the particular uses and superficial manufactured identities selected by the sellers of these goods. While the potential always exists for the formation of a deeply embodied connection to a consumer object, a potential that is sometimes realized, economic rationalization results in effective market strategies that undermine this possibility. Hence, the mirroring body is ephemeral—its form is constantly changing as customers cycle large quantities of consumer goods through their lives.

However deeply the life-world is penetrated by the system requisite for maximizing consumption, the body does not lose its capacity for resisting the corporeal inscriptions of the mirroring body. Thus, even in the context of late capitalism, the life-world continues to afford social actors opportunities for terminating corporeal contingency through alternative forms of embodied consumption. In the realm of life-world transactions, one manages the indeterminacy of the body by becoming holistically engaged with significant objects of consumption. As the focus of one's full body attention, a commodity form can serve as a means for organizing a set of cognitions, emotions and desires, and other body capacities around transcendental themes that order or terminate indeterminacy. Like embodied labor, this way of relating to material substance is fully transactional—the self-affirming qualities of the object are determined by the consumer's engagement with it as strongly as the characteristics of the object itself. In embodied consumption, the body creates itself transcendentally at the same time that it shapes the objects it consumes.

In this analysis, embodied consumption within the life-world contradicts the consumption imperative of the system. Since embodied consumption involves a full, multidimensional engagement with the object, a pattern of conspicuous consumption cannot suffice to make this happen. Being fully engaged with the objects that one purchases in the marketplace means that there is limited space in the life-world for such objects—people have room for only a few transactionally significant objects in their lives. Using consumer goods as signifiers of status also has little relevance to the life-world problem of corporeal indeterminacy. This problem can be addressed in consumer practice only through intensive engagement with the commodities—simple ownership is insufficient.

What is the evidence for embodied consumption in the life-world of contemporary Western society? As noted earlier, it is not our task here to catalogue the full range of alternative life forms relating to embodied transactions in each medium. However, it *is* useful to provide empirical illustrations of life-world alternatives to system colonization in support of our claim (following Habermas) that the colonization of the life-world "cannot be carried through without remainder." Thus when we look for ways in which people become deeply connected to objects of consumption through embodied transactions that express human potentials and corporeal truths, it may help to consider selected examples from radically different social locations.

At one end of the continuum, an exemplar of embodied consumption can be found in the appreciation of high art (see Marcuse 1978). The special significance of high art (including the visual, auditory, and performance categories) is that it serves essentially the same function in both the production and consumption mediums. Artists may look to their art as a way to realize personal human capacities and truths that cannot be experienced through existing cultural forms, but serious consumers of this art have come to expect the same thing from observing it. Indeed, to engage in a deeply embodied appreciation of art is equivalent to "consuming" it—taking it into one's body and soul where it calls forth ideas, sentiments, and capacities not previously expressed. As art historians have taught us, the greatest artworks are those productions that engender in the observer new ways of seeing or new ways of being in the world. Thus the aesthetic experience is found in the corporeal transaction between the observer/consumer and the art piece—the observer's body is constituted by the art while its aesthetic content arises through the act of observing it (Dewey [1934] 1958).

While the practice of appreciating high art may represent a form of embodied consumption enjoyed by relatively few people in contemporary society, we find similar kinds of embodied consumption taking place in very different social locations within the life-world. To demonstrate that the forms of embodied consumption can vary significantly while the substance of this transactional process remains the same, we could consider the life-world phenomenon of "product cults" as another example of embodied actors forming complex connections to objects of consumption. The depth of these connections varies from one product cult to the next, but cults associated with the sport of motorcycling represents an archetype of the kind of embodied relations we have in mind.

An examination of any of the major periodicals devoted to sport motorcycling in the United States today provides evidence of the fully embodied connections that many "bikers" have with their machines. This is found, in part, in the extreme form of brand loyalty exhibited in letters-to-the-editor sections and in articles describing personal motorcycle adventures. Testimonials to the unique feel and look of Triumphs, Nortons, Ducatis, Moto Guzzis, BMWs, Harley-Davidsons, and a wide range of other brands regularly appear in the pages of motorcycle magazines, reflecting the deep devotion of many riders to an intense involvement with their motorcycles (in contrast to the "weekend bikers" described above). In addition to the time spent riding, committed bikers invest many hours maintaining and customizing their motorcycles, sharing their experiences with other owners of their brands, and, in something akin to the observer's gaze in experiencing high art, studying the visual aesthetics of their bikes. In the purest expression of this form of embodied consumption, the "outlaw" bikers of the 1960s and 1970s often dispensed with all possessions except for their Harley-Davidson–based "chopped hogs" so that they could dedicate complete attention to exploring the aesthetic and experiential possibilities residing in their motorcycles (Lyng and Bracey 1995; Thompson 1966).

As difficult as it may be for some readers to logically connect the art patron's appreciation of high art and a biker's devotion to his or her chopped hog, both are forms of embodied consumption that conflict with bodies imprinted by a never-ending cascade of product uses and manufactured identities created by corporate institutions. Art patrons and bikers may appear to have little in common, but they do share a capacity for corporeal resistance to the colonizing influence of the mirroring body. The resistance represented by these forms of embodied consumption, and other forms not mentioned here, constituted another life-world domain of alternative structures that can be explored in the search for new possibilities for social reconstruction and solutions to social problems.

Embodied and Disembodied Communication

Finally, we must consider how embodied communication relates to the life-world issue of corporeal contingency. Dealing with embodied communication is where we can see most clearly how the focus on corporeal transaction leads us away from Habermas's key theoretical problem in analyzing the life-world. While he sees communicative action as the basis of social order in the life-world, our focus is how communicative transactions are involved in embodied actors coming to terms with corporeal contingencies in themselves and others. As we have seen, it is possible to manage the indeterminacy of the body in transactions with the *material* world through production and consumption practices. But it is also important to relate this problem to the distinctive human capacity for organizing and ordering indeterminate reality through the social construction of *meaning*.

This process was of particular concern to the classical pragmatists of the early twentieth century, with George Herbert Mead providing what many would regard as the definitive treatment of the problem. As noted in previous chapters, Mead's distinction between the "I" and the "me" refers specifically to the dynamic between a contingent body capable of spontaneous, unpredictable behavior and a social mind that gives meaningful form to this behavior. In conceptualizing the "two phases of the act" in terms of the "I" and the "me," Mead was mindful of the dialectic between spontaneity and constraint, chaos and order in human experience (Blake 1976). One of the critical insights of his analysis is that the unpredictable element in human behavior is the focus of ongoing efforts by co-present actors to intersubjectively formulate its meaning. As the term "formulate" suggests, the primary goal of communicative exchange between actors is to give "form" to behavior that would otherwise be formless in a meaningful sense. Thus face-to-face communication is one way to extinguish corporeal contingency.

It is by no means coincidental that Mead and his pragmatist colleagues chose to focus on face-to-face interaction in analyzing the dynamic between form and formlessness in human experience. This focus reveals an understanding of the special significance of embodied communication in human experience, an understanding that was lost to some of Mead's later interpreters who emphasized symbolic interaction at the expense of corporeal processes. Mead perhaps had only an intuitive sense of the importance of corporeal contingency as a key human problem and the significance of *embodied* communication for this problem, but the life-world concept allows us to elaborate his ideas in this new direction. As the domain in which embodied actors struggle with corporeal contingency, the life-world is constituted in part by patterns of face-to-face, embodied communicative transactions among co-present individuals.

In discussing the nature of embodied communication in the previous chapter, we referred to mounting evidence from the neurosciences and other fields that the social construction of meaning involves much more than just linguistic exchange. As Goffman suggested in his early work and the neurosciences are demonstrating with sophisticated empirical studies, meaning is transmitted through embodied communicative exchanges that are often precognitive in nature and too fast for the actor's awareness (Turner 1999). Indeed, the accumulating neuroscientific evidence is merely confirming what pragmatists have long understood as the central fact about the social construction of meaning: "Human communication is a sign-process involving the varied human capacities and touching the deepest *extrarational* sources of intelligence built into and grown out of the human body" (Halton 1995, 195 [emphasis in original]). However, the extrarational-communication capacities referred to here come into full play only within the webs of embodied interactions that sustain the life-world. These corporeal capacities are largely absent from communicative action within the system.

The uncoupling of the system and life-world is revealed, in part, by the starkly different communication patterns that characterized each domain. Indeed, because of the signal importance of communicative sign-processes in the evolution of the human species, this capacity is a particularly useful marker for examining the historical differentiation of the system out of the life-world. Much of the growth of human civilization can be understood in terms of the development of various forms of disembodied communication. With the evolution of written languages, it became possible for bodies to communicate outside of face-to-face contexts and share meaning across significant distances of space and time (Habermas 1987, 184). The development of this communication technology created unprecedented possibilities for disseminating information and organizing large collectivities around common belief systems—the Bible's role in the evolution of the theocratic societies of the Middle Ages is a case in point. Written language was a crucial prerequisite for the emergence of social *systems* per se, but by the same token, system differentiation created the residual space of the life-world, where communication remained embodied and profoundly shaped by the experience of corporeal contingency.

Under the growing influence of written language, communication became bifurcated into two fundamentally different forms. While face-to-face communication is reciprocal in nature, with two or more individuals negotiating the meaning of one another's embodied actions (with a mix of spontaneous and predictable elements), meaning constructed by written language is largely unidirectional. With the development of sophisticated communication technologies that increasingly drive post-industrial societies, disembodied communication has become even more prevalent. By the twentieth century, embodied actors separated in time and space can share voice communication in addition to written language. The emergence of the telephone and other technologies of electronic voice communication, the technologies of visual images, and now in the twenty-first century, computer-based communication technology capable of linking the entire earth and creating "virtual realities" has further expanded the sphere of disembodied communication.

Focusing on the growth of disembodied communication under the influence of system rationalization adds an important dimension to Habermas's analysis of the systemic distortion of discourse. He emphasizes delinguistified media in the form of money and power as forces that deform communication in the life-world and undermine language as a means of coordinating action. However, money and power also put the disembodied, one-way communication of the print and electronic media under the managerial control of a relatively small number of social agents. These agents use their control over the means of disembodied communication principally to disseminate relatively narrow, ideologically based views of reality that ignore or attempt to obscure the indeterminacy of nature and the body.

This emphasis is not inconsistent with Habermas's critical analysis of the communicative distortions imposed by the system, but it shifts the focus away from the problem of "delinguistification" of communication to the issue of its "disembodiment." Reflecting once again the contrast between Habermas's linguistic bias and the transactional focus on the embodied nature of human action, the present analysis sees the impoverishment of communication arising from the steady encroachment on the fully embodied transactions of face-to-face communication by the system requisite for disembodied communication. What is lost in the media-steered communications that displace face-to-face communication in the life-world is the full range of corporeal signs exchanged between individuals engaged in interaction. We have argued at some length that the meaning emerging out of interaction derives not only from the exchange of linguistic symbols but also from corporeal signs. Meaning is "given" through language as well as "given off" by the body. However, the most important feature of face-to-face communication is the corporeal condition that is reflected in contradictions between the "given" and the "given off"—the body's contingent nature. As we have seen, the possibility for the *creative* construction of meaning ultimately depends on transactions between face-to-face actors seeking new ways of symbolically terminating corporeal indeterminacy. Dictated by the needs of the system rather than the life-world problem of corporeal indeterminacy, disembodied communications do not draw on the body's creative reservoir of contingency and therefore assume a rigidified, impoverished, and fragmented character.

The *dominating body* can now be seen as the product of the colonization process in the medium of interaction. Placing the dominating body within the Habermasian framework allows us to relate this type of body usage to disembodied communication, which, as a colonizing force in the life-world, imprints bodies in the same way that the other system imperatives we discussed do. Approaching the dominating body in this way adds an important dimension to Frank's analysis, because we can now understand the role that totalizing discourses play in constituting this body style. Communications emanating from the system are disembodied and therefore insulated from the contingent character of nature and the body. Indeed, contingency is denied because it challenges the validity of

rigid discourses that attempt to reduce complex phenomena to simple for-
mulations. This is why the dominating body fears contingency in the other
and seeks to force the other to succumb to its determinant symbolic universe. In the most extreme case, the corporeal indeterminacy of the other
so threatens the dominating body's rigidified symbolic terminations that
the "final solution" for this problem is to destroy the other.

Thus Frank's decision to focus on the German Freikorps as an empirical illustration of the dominating body is analytically important, even
though he did not emphasize the connection between this body style and
the emerging Nazi symbolic universe embraced by members of the
Freikorps. The Freikorps's dominating practices emerged in a life-world
context in which Nazi propaganda emanating from the system was
increasingly at odds with the contingencies of face-to-face interaction.
Consequently, the only way that this dissonance could be removed as a
threat to the Nazi's symbolic universe was to annihilate the source of the
challenging contingency. This dynamic is exquisitely captured in the
movie *Schindler's List* when we see a Nazi concentration camp com-
mandant struggling to come to terms with his contingent sexual desire
for a young Jewish woman interned in the camp. He deals with the dissonance of his strong attractions to someone who is viewed as subhu-
man in his Nazi consciousness by brutalizing and very nearly murdering
her. Through the paradoxical process described in the previous chapter,
this dominating body draws on his own corporeal contingency for the
violent capacity to annihilate the contingent other and, in doing so,
denies his own unpredictable responses to an embodied other more
complex than his worldview will allow.

While the case of the German Freikorps provides a powerful illustration of the connection between disembodied communication and the
dominating body, less dramatic examples abound in the contemporary
world system. Ideological frameworks covering the entire political spec-
trum from left to right are routinely imposed on the life-worlds of
embodied actors in most contemporary nation-states. In the United
States today, disembodied communications pouring from the system
promote a wide range of discourses, extending from ideologies involved
in electoral and "identity" politics to fundamentalist religious orientations and entertainment culture (Postman 1985). Each of these discourse systems inscribes dominating bodies when they inspire actors to
deny the existence of indeterminacy and assume a one-dimensional
stance towards the world. Armed with a totalizing symbol system, the
dominating body approaches face-to-face interaction with the goal of
imposing its own subjectivity on the other—making the other submit to

his or her truth—as opposed to seeking an intersubjective understanding of emergent indeterminacy.

Finally, we come to the problem of corporeal resistance to colonization by the system's communication imperative. To reiterate an earlier point raised in discussing the production and consumption mediums, regardless of how deformed the life-world is by system colonization, it is never completely dissolved. Vestiges of embodied communication can still be found in the life-world in the form of face-to-face exchanges that draw on corporeal contingency as a wellspring for the creative construction of meaning. While ephemeral forms of embodied communications are widely dispersed throughout the life-world in face-to-face exchanges between neighbors, co-workers, family members, and leisure-group participants, institutionalized forms are more difficult to identify. However, it *is* possible to point to the embodied communications of various institutionalized groups organized for the specific purpose of fostering mutual understanding. Participants in certain "self-help" groups, "encounter" groups, and "dialogue" groups often share a commitment to search for new ways to achieve meaningful collective experience and mutual understanding. Caution must be exercised in making this claim, because some of these groups, particularly certain self-help organizations, are less interested in the creative construction of meaning than they are in imposing an established interpretive scheme on their members. (The quasi-religious orientation of the group, Alcoholics Anonymous is a case in point.) However, it does appear that many of these groups are explicitly committed to the goal of creating a space for open dialogue about the complex problems and experiences shared by their members.

The environment for open dialogue fostered by these groups seems to accord in some respects with Habermas's notion of the ideal speech situation, but the way in which they differ from this construct underscores the importance of embodied communication to our analysis. In contrast to Habermas's concern that the procedural rules for achieving communicative rationality be followed in ideal speech situations, the groups we identify here give primary emphasis to the embodied expressions of meaning—emotions, sentiments, bodily displays involved in role-playing, and the like—the very things that Habermas wants to eliminate as sources of communicative distortion. It is not insignificant that all of these groups strive for intersubjectivity through face-to-face communication. The reliance on embodied exchanges is crucial for elaborating meaning structures that tap into unexpressed human capacities and sentiments—new symbolic terminations of corporeal contingency. This differs significantly from the use of rational procedures in ideal speech situations, which does not depend at all on embodied communication. Indeed, ideal speech exchanges could be conducted just as easily over the Internet as they could in face-to-face contexts. As another form of disembodied communication, Habermas's version of free speech is not *fundamentally* different from communication emerging from the system.

What we see in the institutionalized forms of embodied communication within the life-world are, once again, intriguing possibilities for social reconstruction and solutions to social problems. Earlier in this chapter, we referred to Shalin's (1992, 273) call for a "pragmatic politics" that begins with "personal efforts in one's immediate community." It is possible now to be even more specific about the starting point for social reconstruction. In order to take full advantage of the creative potential that resides in a community of embodied actors collectively seeking to discover and realize human potential, reconstruction can begin with those groups engaged in embodied communication. Embodied communicative practices, intertwined with practices involving embodied production and consumption, are the basis of life forms that offer the greatest potential for solving human problems.

Recoupling the Life-World and System

By way of summarizing this section, we will now direct attention to one of the principal implications of our modified approach to the life-world. By substituting *corporeal transaction* for Habermas's communicative action as the conceptual complement to the life-world, we have been able to develop a much broader conception of the possibilities that exist for social reconstruction. Within the Habermasian framework, social reconstruction requires the creation of institutional arrangements that ensure the possibility of free and open communication. The rationalization of the system and life-world is a doubled-edge sword, producing (through rationalization of purposive action) steering media that lead to communicative distortions but also creating (through rationalization of communicative action) the possibility for reasoned discourse that can lead to unconstrained agreement. The starting point for social reconstruction is to establish a reasoned consensus about the *truth* of the matters at hand, which can be achieved by following the procedural rules of the ideal speech situation. Hence, the pursuit of rationally achieved understanding has the short-term consequence of allowing communicative actors to seek normative and factual consensus about appropriate solutions to social problems, which, in turn, contributes to the long-term social-reconstruction goal of recoupling the life-world and system.

Missing in this emancipatory program is any clear indication of where the alternative social arrangements for social problem-solving are to be found. As important as it may be to achieve normative and factual consensus about social problems, the more challenging task is to identify creative alternatives. Habermas (1987, 391–96) does acknowledge the important role played by protest movements in postliberal societies, but he sees such movements as a form of resistance to colonization rather than offering solutions to problems. In his nominalistic framework, members of protest groups can best contribute to progressive change by joining with others in reasoned discourse and striving for consensus. Dissenting from what the majority sees as justifiable and valid by proposing radical alternatives to prevailing arrangements has no place in this model.

Whereas TCA is focused primarily on the *process* by which social reconstruction is ultimately achieved—that is, the process of democratic consensus building, the transactional approach is more concerned with the substantive *content* of reconstructed forms. As we have seen, the penetration of the life-world by disembodied production, consumption, and communication practices terminate corporeal contingency in the form of the disciplining, mirroring, and dominating bodies, respectively. But these inscriptions are always resisted by embodied selves at some level, because corporeal contingency can never be completely extinguished. Thus even as system imperatives imprint bodies and minds in these powerful ways, the central problem of life-world never disappears. As "unfinished animals" (Nieztche), embodied human beings must constantly search for new ways to come to terms with corporeal contingency within themselves and in others. This, of course, is the source of the socially constructed life forms that are sustained through embodied transactions of production, consumption, and communication—creative life forms that have the greatest potential as models of alternative institutional arrangements for addressing difficult social problems.

What remains as a critical problem for our modified version of TCA is the issue of reestablishing the dialectic between the life-world and system, the recoupling of these two dimensions of social reality. If forms of embodied production, consumption, and communication that emerge and thrive within the life-world are to be used as models for social-reconstruction purposes, then how will these life forms be introduced into the system? And what role does the *system* play in sustaining the dialectic between itself and the life-world? In other words, by what means can the relationship between these two dimensions become mutually enriching and enhancing? In answering these questions, we will also address the

key problem introduced at the beginning of this chapter, which seems to
have all but disappeared in our lengthy discussion of system and life-
world: the task of identifying a new role for sociology in dealing with
social problems. These are the issues to which we now turn.

BREAKING DOWN BUREAUCRATIC CONSTRAINTS

In proposing a transactional social-problems framework, we have argued for a method that borrows from the Critical Theory tradition by
linking analytical deconstruction with synthetic reconstruction in social-
problems research. In light of sociology's difficulties documented at the
beginning of this chapter, we believe that the theoretical link between
critical and synthetic forms of analysis can empower sociologists by
arming them with an important resource for dealing with the culture of
criticism. The proposed approach not only provides a way to objectively
define social problems, but also ties this to the articulation of potential
solutions to problems.

Following the discussion of pragmatist ontology and the embodied
nature of human transaction in earlier chapters, we have also suggested
a way to modify Habermas's critical theory framework to explore how
indeterminacy, emotions and sentiments, nondiscursive ways of knowing, and extrarational corporeal capacities are involved in human problem-solving. What emerged from this modification of the TCA framework
is an approach to reconstruction that helps in identifying alternative
social arrangements used as standpoints from which to define social
problems and fashion solutions. The conflicting life-forms that emerge in
the life-world as expressions of corporeally based *resistance* to system
colonization offer the greatest potential as creative solutions to social
problems and emancipatory social reconstructions.

However, at this point, we seem to face a significant contradiction.
The ultimate goal of this chapter is to articulate an alternative social-
problems approach for the field of *sociology*. And yet, the discussion has
led us to the conclusion that the analysis of social problems should
begin with life-world institutions far removed from the institutional
domain of sociological practice. Indeed, sociology and institutions of
scientific knowledge-production in general are parts of the very system
that most threatens the life-world. In Habermasian terms, as we have
seen, science and sociology are products of the rationalization of knowledge that has developed in parallel with the other rationalizing trends
within the system. The most important of these parallel trends for sociology is the increasing bureaucratization of system institutions, includ-

ing the institutional arrangements of contemporary sociological practice, as described at the beginning of this chapter. As a fully rationalized
and bureaucratized practice, academic sociology is far away from problem-solving transactions that take place in the life-world.

This problem is at the heart of a broader critique of sociology recently advanced by advocates of a "postmodernist" approach to social
research. We will remember that Steven Seidman (1991) criticizes the
rationalist assumptions undergirding most forms of sociological theory
and research and the discipline's foundational program. Like Habermas,
postmodernists make social reconstruction a central goal of the theoretical enterprise. But unlike Habermas, their approach to the social-
reconstruction process is inclusive. Habermas's call for strict adherence
to rational standards among all parties involved in the discussion of
social reconstruction is seen by postmodernists as exclusionary (see
Halton 1992). In contrast, the postmodernist strategy abandons the rationalist project and instead explores ways to legitimize multiple, nonprofessional narratives oriented to social groups engaged in social and
moral discourse about contemporary social life.

Although the principal purpose of this strategy is to "expand the
number of parties who may participate more or less as equals in a debate
about society" (Seidman 1991, 135), it can also vitalize sociological discourse. Sociologists who collaborate with groups tied to life-world institutions can explore the creative problem-solving strategies these groups
develop in response to system colonization. At the same time, con-
stituencies for sociological knowledge can be developed outside the
bureaucratic and professional structures within which most sociologists
presently work. Expanding sociology's audience and connections to
groups outside of established bureaucracies would serve to counterbal-
ance the powerful forces currently contributing to the increasing
bureaucratization of academic work. Thus while there is much in the
postmodernist project we cannot endorse,[7] the program does suggest
some important additions to social-problems research. We can now conceive of an approach to the study of social problems that would orient
sociologists to a social-reconstruction agenda while also empowering
nonprofessional audiences outside of academic bureaucracies.

This proposal has important implications for the issue of bridging the
gap between the life-world institutions that generate new problem-solving adaptations and the system institutions devoted to academic or policy analysis of social problems. If embodied transactions of the life-world
offer the greatest hope for creative problem-solving, then researchers
should seek to establish collaborative relations with groups organized to

promote these practices. Collaboration between sociologists and nonaca-
demic groups already occurs in some areas of social-problems research,
but these collaborations typically involve projects focused on narrowly
defined issues of interest to professional policy makers. In several lines
of recent scholarship, however, a new form of collaborative research is
beginning to take shape. This approach explores ways in which academic
sociologists can connect with grass-roots organizations or social-movement groups. Variously termed "participatory research" (Cancian and
Armstead 1992; Gaventa 1988; Maguire 1987; Tandon 1981; 1988), "collaborative research" (Delgado 1989; Nyden et al. 1997), or "participatory
action research" (Whyte 1991), this body of literature offers some prom-
ising ideas about how to link social-problems researchers to groups outside of academic or professional policy circles.

The participatory action research (PAR) model has been adopted by
researchers involved in a wide variety of community-oriented projects
and is, by no means, uniquely appropriate for sociological research on
the life-world patterns emphasized in this volume. However, we see the
PAR model as a useful tool for linking social-problems researchers to
groups engaged in the kinds of embodied transactions that offer possibilities for reconstructing system institutions. As an illustration of the
kind of collaboration we have in mind, we could refer to Lyng's (1990a)
case study of the holistic health movement. Although this study was not
formally organized as a PAR project, it incorporated many of the core
principles of this method by organizing a research agenda based on the
collaboration between movement participants (at both the local and
national level) and the social researcher. Using social-scientific data-col-
lection methods (interviews, document analysis, etc.), the researcher
constructed a systematic model of the health practices and concepts
advocated by the movement. Although a large number of specific
"modalities" are subsumed under the banner of holistic health, the
research produced a general model of health practice that clearly
revealed its status as a form of embodied production (see above). Using
this life-world pattern as a base, the researcher then infused the model
with sociological concepts and research findings to create a "countersystem" model, described below, that could be employed as a critical
standpoint for analyzing the existing health care system. The collabora-
tively produced countersystem served both as a reference point for
defining social problems within the biomedically based health care system and as source of potential *solutions* to these problems.

These additions to our alternative social-problems framework inspired by postmodernist thought and action research address some

important concerns about transactional sociology, but they also raise some new concerns. If sociologists embrace the proposals put forth here, will they be forced to abandon the traditional goals of sociological study? Is the social-reconstruction component inconsistent with the traditional disciplinary commitment to producing basic theory about society? Does the call for research and writing directed to nonprofessional audiences exclude continuing efforts to disseminate research findings among professional, academic audiences? In answering these questions, we will add one more important dimension to the theoretical model.

LINKING THEORY AND PRAXIS:
THE COUNTERSYSTEM METHOD

The questions posed here force us to return to the transactional principles that served as the starting point for the present chapter. We have noted the pragmatist commitment to breaking down the troubling dualisms bequeathed by rationalism, a goal shared by postmodern theory. This focus is reflected in the transactional conception of the subject/object relation discussed earlier. But the most significant transactional challenge to dualistic thought can be found in the perspective's approach to issues of validity and explanation. A succinct expression of this approach is the pragmatist assertion that truth is "a practically accomplished unity of knowledge and reality" (Shalin 1992, 266). This statement is full of implications for various matters addressed in this chapter, but we will restrict the discussion at this point to one key problem. In response to the questions posed above, we focus on what the pragmatist definition of truth implies about the relationship between "basic" and "applied" research in sociology.[8]

One of the most enduring features of the division of labor in postwar American sociology is the clear separation between the various activities devoted to developing and verifying of theoretical models—"basic research," and efforts to apply this knowledge to the resolution of practical problems—"applied research." This separation has been made possible in part by the development of verification procedures that are disconnected from the application of sociological knowledge to real-world problem-solving. But such a separation was anathema to the early pragmatists who argued that the verification of ideas can be achieved only through transaction in the world of indeterminacy. Valid ideas are those that lead to efficacious action in the external environment. And when ideas directing action lead to unexpected results, the validity of these ideas must be questioned and a reformulation is in order. Hence, in the pragmatist framework, separating basic research from the activities associated with the application of research findings cannot be justified—valid knowledge, as we have argued, is produced through the use of systematic procedures for implementing ideas in a practical context.[9]

Pragmatism provides a strong theoretical rationale for connecting basic and applied research, theory and praxis; but as noted above, the highly abstract character of pragmatist thought makes it difficult to derive concrete methodological strategies from this system. Thus the pragmatist framework offers no guidance for determining the level at which ideas must be implemented in order to achieve pragmatic reality testing and also contribute to structural changes in the social order. It is also unclear how ideas and conceptual systems used in pragmatic problem-solving are precisely related to the analysis of existing social conditions. These issues can be addressed by identifying a method of analysis that establishes a more detailed logic and procedure for linking basic and applied research. The method of countersystem analysis (Lyng 1988; 1990a; 2002; Sjoberg 1997; Sjoberg and Cain 1971; Vaughan 1993) constitutes such an approach.

The countersystem method pulls together the various strands of theoretical thought discussed in this chapter by logically connecting deconstruction and reconstruction as components of a continuous research process. In this framework, the reconstructive dimension serves multiple purposes. First, the construction of alternative social arrangements (reconstructing existing conditions) is oriented to the goals that typically guide pragmatically oriented researchers, running the gamut from critical and postmodern theorists to applied researchers. This part of the research agenda is dedicated to identifying solutions to social problems, but it accomplishes this task in a novel way. In order to avoid defining problems and their potential solutions in an ideologically determined way, a model of alternative social arrangements (a "countersystem") is constructed and used as a reference point for identifying social problems within the existing system. This strategy draws on Habermas's insight about the use of hypothetical models to ensure the objectivity of one's analysis of the existing social order. Defining social problems from the standpoint of a hypothetical system—that is, identifying the ways in which existing conditions diverge from ideal arrangements—mitigates against the influence of the prevailing interest structure in determining what constitutes a social problem. The countersystem also serves as a general template for constructing solutions to the problems identified. In confronting the broad range of alternatives for dealing with a problem, priority can be given to approaches that contribute to social change in the direction of the countersystem ideal.

Conducting applied research in this way creates the need for a strong analytical component insofar as social problems are defined through comparative, structural analysis. This is the place where the applied program logically connects to a program of basic research, and it is here that we find a second major purpose of the reconstructive dimension. The construction of alternative social models can also fulfill an important function in the development of basic theory. By serving as a systematic contrast to the existing social system, the countersystem can be used as a reference point from which to critically analyze the current system. A (re)constructed social model serves as an essential resource for a deconstructive analysis of prevailing structural imperatives—hence, reconstruction and deconstruction are linked as inseparable parts of the research process.

The countersystem logic, "analysis through contrast," allows researchers to deal with an inevitable problem they face as fully socialized members of the very same sociocultural systems they seek to critically analyze. What works against a thoroughgoing critique of one's own culture are the many taken-for-granted assumptions underlying the analyst's worldview. This problem has been recognized in several different intellectual domains in recent decades. It was brought to the attention of sociologists when Alvin Gouldner (1970) discussed the pervasive influence of "domain assumptions" in mainstream sociological research. Philosopher of science Paul Feyerabend (1978) demonstrated its relevance to *all* scientific disciplines by framing the issue in general epistemological terms. Feyerabend challenges the positivist distinction between abstract theory and the world of empirical "facts," arguing that scientists' perceptions of empirical patterns are structured by overlapping conceptual systems that arise in earlier historical times and become institutionalized within the existing culture. Consequently, standard procedures of empirical verification in science serve only to validate theoretical explanations that accord with institutionalized ideological and cosmological systems of the dominant culture. Feyerabend's solution to this problem employs a countersystem strategy:

> How can we analyze the terms in which we habitually express our most simple and straightforward observations, and reveal their presuppositions? . . . The answer is clear: we cannot discover it from the *inside*. We need an *external* standard of criticism, we need a set of alternative assumptions or, as these assumptions will be quite general, constituting, as it were, an entire alternative world. (1978, 31–32)

Feyerabend is all-inclusive in designating alternative models that can be used for counterinductive purposes, reflecting his broad interest in sci-

entific theorizing as a whole. He sees all conceptual systems as potentially useful "external standards of criticism," whether they are invented
from whole cloth or imported from outside of science, "from religion,
from mythology, from the ideas of incompetents, or the ramblings of
madmen" (1978, 68). As a modification of Feyerabend's approach, the
countersystem method requires that the contrasting standard of criticism be based on models of alternative social arrangements—preferably
alternatives deriving from the embodied transactions of the life-world.
In this framework, social reconstructions serve as the contrasting reference points for critical analysis.

While countersystem analysis may seem to be an unusual way to generate theoretical insights, there are notable cases in which the logic of
counterinduction has been successfully employed, either implicitly or
explicitly, as a method of theory development in the social sciences.
Perhaps the most obvious use of the countersystem strategy can be
found in the long tradition of anthropological study that relies on the
comparisons between tribal cultures and contemporary Western culture
to call attention to the unrecognized peculiarities of Western cultural
practices (see especially Harris 1974; 1977). Elsewhere, comparative reasoning has yielded enduring insights within a number of diverse theoretical traditions, ranging from Talcott Parsons's (1951; 1964) analysis of
medical practice to Marx's (1964a) study of capitalist economic relations.
For instance, Parsons's (1951, 428–79) point of departure in his seminal
study of the medical institutional complex is the simple question: Why
can't modern medical practice (and, by extension, other professional
services) be organized according to the same free-market principles that
govern the provision of goods and services in all other sectors of modern
capitalist economies? Parsons's comment that his "problem could not be
stated this way without (the) comparative perspective" (1964, 334) is a
clear acknowledgment that his analysis is ultimately driven by the contrast between the ideal market and the professional model.

The classical Marxian framework provides an even better illustration
of this method. While Parsons chose to contrast two existing institutional subsystems, Marx's countersystem for analyzing the structure of
capitalist society was, in the true sense of the term, a hypothetical system. In the period that he completed his most important work, the com-
munist model was an analytical construct, not an actual system of
socioeconomic relations that existed anywhere in the world. But it is
safe to say that many of Marx's most important insights about the nature
of capitalism derived from contrasting this system against the commu-
nist alternative. A case in point is Marx's (1964a) use of the "labor theory

of value" to analyze the structural basis of worker exploitation under capitalism—a clear instance of using an alternative social model to redefine a core cultural concept that then brings forth previously taken-for-granted features of the existing system.

In addition to offering a clear-cut logic for linking basic analysis and research devoted to pragmatic problem-solving, the countersystem method also incorporates concrete strategies for dealing with other theoretical issues discussed above. Thus we can reconsider the postmodernist call for a fully democratic model of civic discourse and the dilemma this creates. If sociologists avoid making special claims of authority in the analysis of social issues, how can they find an audience for their views in the intensely competitive political environment that exists in the United States today? It appears that any effort to enhance sociology's authority in civic discourse would also serve to undermine democracy in the civic arena.

While it may not be possible to completely transcend this problem, it can be ameliorated through the use of another countersystem tactic. Following Seidman's postmodernist lead, countersystem analysts are encouraged to look outside of traditional academic and policy-making circles for alternative social models. One way to accomplish this goal is to adopt the collaborative model described in the previous section. Stronger ties between academic sociologists and loosely organized groups or social movements promoting embodied production, consumption, or communication practices could be the basis of useful reciprocal relationships. Life-world groups introduce researchers to innovative ideas and perspectives that can be used to elaborate countersystems, while movement groups gain access to the analytical and empirical research skills of sociologists to refine and expand their own perspectives. The collaboration would ultimately contribute to the advancement of basic research by providing resources to develop countersystems used for analytical purposes, as well as efforts to resolve actual problems through the application of sociological knowledge by organized community groups.

It is important to remain aware of the degree to which countersystems will inevitably depart from the original life-world practices that inspire them. In constructing a countersystem based on a movement perspective, analysts must make certain that the model is rigorous, grounded in appropriate empirical research and framed in terms of key structural issues. As a consequence of this process, the resulting countersystem may differ substantially from the model promoted by the movement and, in this sense, it meets Habermas's standard of a truly hypothetical system. Of course, this result must be seen as a double-edged sword in that the very same qualities required to maintain objectivity in the analysis of social problems may also serve to alienate the partisan groups with which sociologists collaborate. Thus researchers adopting the countersystem approach must successfully negotiate the dialectical tension between partisanship and analytical objectivity. In the true sense of the dialectic, these opposing demands are absolutely necessary to one another: objectivity is achieve through the elaboration of partisan viewpoints in the direction of hypothetical models, while partisan agendas are most effectively promoted when they receive support from objective analyses of social problems.

Sociologists who successfully negotiate this tension can contribute to a pragmatic, collectively organized campaign to promote social reconstruction while also advancing democratic goals. By exploring life-world institutions within the local environment, researchers support the social-change efforts of the people most directly affected by social problems, but who are typically left out of the policy-making process. This allows for the development of social-problems definitions and policy alternatives that reflect local community or regional traditions. At the same time, however, the structural and global orientation of social-problems researchers should help to infuse local perspectives with a macro-level dimension, focusing attention on the role of broad structural forces (patriarchy, racism, bureaucracy, capital, etc.) in generating problems, thereby contributing to more broad-based efforts to deal with structurally rooted social problems. We have in mind here the organization of social-movement coalitions at the national and transnational level or "social-movement industries" (McCarthy and Zald 1977). Thus what this strategy offers in the way of a unique paradigm for policy development is a life-world inspired "bottom-up" approach.

Once the initial countersystem has been constructed in this fashion, the researcher moves to the analytical phase of the research process. Armed with a model that springs from corporeal *resistance* to the inscriptions imposed by system colonization, which therefore *negates* the existing system, one can engage in counterinductive reasoning to produce theoretical insights and empirical evidence that challenge the assumptive order of the system under examination, as described above. With the completion of the analytical phase, the research cycle is repeated: the countersystem can now be refined and elaborated on the basis of knowledge acquired in the study of existing structural arrangements. Hence, the countersystem method involves a reiterative process in which alternative policy models are critical tools for analyzing the existing system, and this analysis, in turn, becomes the foundation for reformulating the model.

This chapter has been devoted to exploring the promise that the transactional perspective holds for giving sociologists a more constructive role to play in the public discussion and resolution of social problems. After describing the barriers that have emerged in the postwar period to sociology's participation in the social-problems debate, we proposed an alternative transactional approach to the study of social issues. This approach draws on the core transactional principles outlined in earlier chapters and the broader pragmatist framework from which they were derived. Indeed, the pragmatist conception of truth is what ultimately led us to focus on social-problems research. This conception holds that truth is found in the unification of knowledge and reality achieved through the collective problem-solving efforts of embodied actors. If sociology is to take seriously the search for truth—and we believe that it should—then it must find a way to contribute its knowledge-base to the collective resolution of social problems. Here, truth is embedded in objectivity as "effectiveness" and our fifth level of action—praxis.

The transactional approach to social-problems research is distinguished by its emphasis on social reconstruction, embodied life forms, democratic participation, and the countersystem method. In articulating these principles, we relied heavily on Habermas's critical theory perspective, although we have modified his framework by making the notion of corporeal transaction the conceptual linchpin of the model. This modification made it possible to introduce the body and its extrarational capacities into the life-world where, previously, there was only the detached mind and tacit knowledge. With our broader conceptualization of an embodied life-world, we can now see this dimension of social reality as a domain where actors not only engage in face-to-face interaction with other human beings, but also in corporeal transactions with things either produced or consumed. Viewed from a transactional perspective, the life-world is a more complex reality than Habermas allows and a rich source of often-conflicting life-forms.

This modification of TCA has important implications for the sociological study of social problems. By broadening the focus of the colonization process to include the social inscription of bodies (in the form of the disciplined, mirroring, and dominating bodies), it has been possible to identify the objective foundations of human *resistance* to colonization and the

source of potential *solutions* to the problems created by system rationalization. As we have argued, resistance to system rationalization and colonization of the life-world ultimately derives from the inherent indeterminacy of the body: Although the body is inscribed by the production,
consumption, and communication imperatives of the system, corporeal
contingency can never be fully extinguished. Hence, embodied actors
must continue to struggle with this basic life-world problem and search
for new ways to terminate the indeterminacy of the body and impersonal
reality. The socially constructed products of this search can function as
grist for social reconstructions, which ultimately serve as objective standpoints for the identification and resolution of social problems.

Adoption of the countersystem method and collaborative research
arrangements with life-world groups are critical links in the process of
translating embodied life forms into models for system reconstruction.
At the same time, participation by sociologists in this process also represents the most effective way to advance the knowledge-base of the discipline and move sociological knowledge closer to the validity standard
of "pragmatic certainty." In applying our knowledge to the resolution of
real-world problems, we will confront evidence of the efficacy or resistance that reality offers to collective actions guided by that knowledge.

Thus the real promise we find in the transactional perspective is a
way for sociology to contribute to the recoupling of the life-world and
system. A product of system rationalization, sociology can nonetheless
empower life-world groups and enrich life-world institutions by expanding the theoretical and empirical base of life-world perspectives. By
serving the crucial function of translating life-world practices into countersystem models for analysis and reconstruction of system institutions,
sociology can make it possible for the life-world to humanize the system—life-world perspectives and practices expand sociological knowledge and open up the system to critical analysis and reorganization.
Drawing on the power of a fully embodied praxis, transactional sociology thus helps to reestablish the dialectical tension between the life-
world and system as well as our theories and the real world.

NOTES

1. The following section is taken from Stephen Lyng, "Social Problems and
Civic Discourse," *Humanity and Society* 21, no. 2 (May 1997): 162–81.
2. At present, only a small percentage of the U.S. population has access to
the Internet, but the dramatic growth rate of new subscribers suggests that a sizable proportion of the population is likely to use the Internet in coming years.
3. An important refinement of this strategy involves the use of "focus groups"

by political campaigns to identify issues that elicit strong emotional responses from potential voters.

4. As every teacher of sociology knows, to succeed in moving common-sense actors in our culture from individualistic interpretations of social life to structural viewpoints requires that one make maximum use of *instructional* resources and strategies. The direction of technological and stylistic developments within the electronic and print media generally undermine rather than enhance the instructional potential of this information-distribution system.

5. Sjoberg and Vaughan are primarily concerned with the dominance of the natural science model within sociology, which they believe is fostered by the bureaucratization of the academy and, in their view, ultimately serves the interests of other powerful bureaucratic structures in the public and private spheres (1993, 98). Of greater significance to the present analysis, however, is the way in which the dominant forms of sociological research (including but not restricted to positivism) and the bureaucratization process have worked in concert to diminish sociology's relevance to public-policy discourse. Beyond the specific interests that may be served by the natural science model, it is clear that the disciplinary agenda dictated by this model has little value for the advancement of civic discourse: With its "emphasis on techniques and methods, shorn of broader sociological theory and ideas," sociology "cannot address the overriding social and moral issues that confront humankind" (1993, 86).

But the inability to contribute to civic discourse is not unique to those embracing the natural science model in sociology. Sjoberg and Vaughan may overstate their case when they attribute these limitations exclusively to the natural science model. The more fundamental problem has to do with the general practice among sociologists, irrespective of the research tradition they follow, of directing their scholarship to relatively narrow professional audiences. A case in point is the work within the increasingly popular "postmodernist" tradition. Although postmodernists are highly critical of all forms of rationalist social science, the alternative forms of scholarship they advocate are often more impenetrable to general readers (within both professional and nonprofessional audiences) than the most technically advanced forms of positivist research.

6. See Shalin (1992) for one interpretation of these rules.

7. For critical commentary on the postmodernist project for sociology, see Farberman (1991), Lemert (1995), Antonio (1991), and Shalin (1993).

8. The following section is taken from Stephen Lyng, "Gideon Sjoberg and the Countersystem Method," *Symbolic Interaction* (2002, in press).

9. This principle is reflected most clearly in Mead's distinction between "information" and "knowledge." "Information" refers to a level of consciousness tied to symbolic interaction between actors: each person's gesture calls out in that person the same response it calls out in the other, a process organized cognitively through the use of significant symbols. "Knowledge" is produced by using conceptualizations to solve problems that prevent us from acting effectively in the world: "The test of success of the process of knowledge, that is, the test of truth, is found in the discovery or construction of such objects as will mediate our conflicting and checked activities and allow conduct to proceed" (Mead 1959, 68).

CHAPTER EIGHT

🔲   🔲   🔲

Conclusion

In these pages we have followed Halton (Rochberg-Halton) (1986; 1995) and Shalin (1993) among others in their opposition to the extreme relativism and nominalism of our age. These extremes have made it difficult for many of us to think about the real world and sociology's relation to it. We have identified some elements of academic discursive practices that maintain what we see as a costly return to dualism. Here, the hyperreal has recently been privileged over the real, the verbal over the nonverbal, and subjectivity over objectivity. Objectivity, the real, and truth are words many people feel reluctant to use. The latter, we agree, has been difficult to keep afloat and even at that its head is barely out of the water. The metamethod of transaction and relationalism has been used to make our argument against a one-sided subjectivism and a mindframe that has no acceptable vocabulary for the real and the objective. We have shown that thought for thought's sake, unattached to our manipulative relations with an impartial world beyond our admittedly constant interpretations, leads not only to a distancing from the real world, but proves insufficient for the decision-making necessary for effective action. Chapter 2 has shown how we can verbalize the nonverbal realities of immediacy and actuality and why we should do so. The world beyond words proves much larger than the extrasensory symbols that we so proudly see as encompassing everything worthwhile. In chapter 4 the subjective and the objective are shown to be inseparable. If we choose to think of the subjective, we need to admit the objective. Not to do so is refusing to own up to our actual

covert thinking. Having thoroughly explored these issues and their implications for sociological theory, research, and practice, we now turn to
the most challenging problem of truth.

If something is real, some version of truth should be close by. In chapter 4, like many sociologists, we rejected the popular belief that the
objective refers to a real world independent of the means by which we
render it sensible. We showed how this "dictionary" understanding of
the objective along with its cousins, the real and the true, lead quickly
into muddied waters. Here, in what is recognized as a dangerous hypothetization, the idea of an objective world ignores our knowing apparatus, while "the real" hangs aloof in the reified, self-actional realm. The
pragmatic version of the real as process and flux was also contrasted to
the static view in chapter 1. Dualism separates knowing from the known
by ignoring the simple fact that our senses are transducers. Leaving out
the part played by our brains and perceptors in changing stimuli into
something our bodies can make sensible is a clear mistake, earning the
title of "stimulus error." A similar error is committed in the popular
notion of a fixed, independent reality and the notion of truth this implies:
*Like sound and color, we mistakenly place truth as an attribute
belonging solely to the independent, real world.*

Rorty makes an important distinction between the claim that the
world is "out there" and the claim that the truth is out there. He is not
rejecting truth in this context. He is rejecting truth as an attribute
belonging to the external world. For him, where there are no human sen-
tences there is no truth. Admitting this degree of social construction
does not imply a self-actional subjectivist retreat into believing that
there is no world beyond our making. We are the ones who make *linguistic sense* out of the world impartial to us (Anderson 1995).

This makes our challenge clear. Truth must retain a human, discursive face. At the same time, it must not be corroded by the arbitrariness
of the symbolic—arbitrary from nature's point of view, if not so arbitrary
from the perspective of social convention. The argument against truth as
an attribute of fixed reality seen as a thing in itself is also implicit in
"intersubjective objectivity." Here, we point to the difficulties this type
of objectivity raises for a viable notion of truth. We need to avoid the
purely consensus model of intersubjectivity that dilutes truth into as
many variations as there are discursive-thought communities.

Truth within Intersubjectivity: Another Dead End

The recognition that the idea of one objective world common to all of us must be a theoretical inference is so important for truth that it must be reviewed. Such a notion, as common and necessary as it is, cannot be built up from empirical experience and perception. Insofar as some significant use of our senses defines empiricism, the qualia of these senses vary from one person to another and this subjective reality cannot be ignored. Variation, we argued, characterizes the empirical world of appearance. Though we cannot deny obvious commonalties, objects as a whole can be experienced very differently among people. Luckily for us, there is a fairly wide discrepancy in who looks personally attractive in spite of powerful forces to standardize "good looks."

Nonetheless, the intersubjective need for commonality flies in the face of the embodied person's different experiences with what we theoretically infer is the same object. A consistent empiricism would end up with the preposterous belief that since two people see a tree differently, there must be two trees. Even disagreement only seems real when it is presumed to be over the same subject matter. Talking past each other means that we are not talking to each other at all. In chapter 4 we pointed to the irony of referring to this necessary, but very abstract commonality as the one true reality when it doggedly leaves out perceptual differences and the realities of lived experience. A coherent usage of objectivity, reality, and truth cannot exclusively privilege the empirical and also exclusively privilege the conceptual over each other simultaneously. In disregarding these contradictions, the common world is seen as the objective world and granted concreteness. Objectivity here is separated from action and makes irrelevant the sense of objectivity as effectiveness.

In chapter 7 we extended this critique to a more sophisticated formula for achieving intersubjectivity—Habermas's consensus model of truth. In reorienting Habermas's conceptual system to the notion of an embodied life-world, we are forced to reject the idea that truth claims can be redeemed by a search for rational consensus. As we have seen, Habermas calls for an adjudication of validity claims by communicative actors taking yes/no positions on criticizable propositions and striving for consensus through discursive means. But it is not clear that this is always possible in practical terms. As Shalin (1992, 260) states: "[t]he pragmatist logic . . . stipulates that reality does not always lend itself squarely to yes/no judgments and allows practical knowers to say 'perhaps,' 'it depends,' 'who knows,' and to use other indeterminate truth values that help us handle situational indeterminacy." Even when conflicts can be unambiguously resolved through theoretical means, the resulting intersubjective agreements that underlie discursive validation can obscure rather than illuminate truth. Often, overlooked truths can only be discovered by means of a process that makes room for reasoned dissent. History certainly attests to the real dangers of institutions ranging from state systems to academic disciplines that quash dissent in the name of certain consensual truths.

The quandaries resulting from the pathways described above do not allow our definition of truth to benefit from the type of fidelity implicit in transaction and the fit between organism and environment.

TRUTH AND FIDELITY IN EMBODIMENT

We have argued that sensation and motor activity from which concepts develop are an outcome of a relationship between human activity and the "patience" of the world to our intentions. A certain kind of truth may well make sense within this transaction. Such a relationship seems to exist in the transactional "slab" implied by the term "patience" and was elaborated in Mead's "objective reality of perspectives." If intersubjective objectivity is seen as purely ideation, it leaves out our transactional embeddedness in the world and thus a viable notion of truth. In this section we sketch Lakoff and Johnson's (1999) treatment of such embeddedness and how they define truth and reality in its context. For them, we are coupled to the world transactionally in a way quite consistent with the priority placed on motor actions by the Chicago pragmatists. For many, it may seem contradictory that symbolic interaction, so given to the constructed and the interpretive, could also be so rooted in the *realities* emerging from Mead's manipulative stage of the act, but according to the two authors above, even higher-level concepts are formed by metaphors derived from sensorimotor experience.

Our suggestion that a viable definition of objectivity and reality is possible and necessary derives from these neglected aspects of Meadian theory and from neuroscience. Both support Whitehead's (1958, 237) statement that "the sense of effectiveness is the sense of reality." As with its cousins, a transactional notion of truth exists on the level of "successful action." In contrast to the world of symbols, we are meaningfully in touch with the grounded answering back to our actions. We will remember White's (1963, 69) observation:

> The knowledge that we gain of the environment is a knowledge of the
> probable consequences of action. It is a knowledge of the potentialities

for action, of what one can surely do, probably do, probably cannot do, and surely cannot do with objects and situations that arise. . . . Reality leaves its record, then, in the form of action possibilities.

This accords with our earlier call for the pursuit of "pragmatic certainty" in settling truth claims. While discursive validation techniques play an important role in adjudicating conceptual conflicts, they must be part of a larger human *practice* in order to bring actors any closer to a valid understanding of their worlds. The focus on pragmatic certainty forces us to always make formal logic subservient to a logic in use, in which we attempt a unity of knowledge and reality in collective transformative action. As we argued in chapter 7, it is pragmatic certainty that common-sense actors seek when they devise collective solutions to lifeworld problems. In our view, social scientists should take advantage of the truths that emerge from these creative terminations of situational indeterminacies. We argued that this goal can be achieved through a form of action research based on the countersystem method.

We must also recognize that embodied truth cannot discount the action of our sensory transducers. In spite of the damage it does to any mirror theory of perception, the notion of transducers suggests a clearly *determinant* transactional "fit" with the objective world. We selectively attend such a world, but it is not initiated by us. It does not heed our symbols, but it does respond to efficacious physical action. In Lakoff and Johnson's view, many of our concepts have evolved to optimally fit our bodily experiences of entities and differences in the natural environment confronted in manipulative action.

We have seen that on this level our concepts do appear to mirror our worlds, and truth as well as objectivity seem unproblematic. Philosophers arguing for correspondence epistemologies use basic-level concepts for examples. These, we will remember, key on shapes of particulars like a chair rather than furniture, which includes so many different shapes that it defies such simple imagery. We also use similar motor actions for category members of basic-level concepts, which means that they allow for our most stable kinds of knowledge. Hammers reliably force nails through wood, and scissors if sharp reliably cut and if dull reliably tear. Relational truth finds a home here.

Scientific instruments extend the range of basic-level concepts to create even more stable knowledge. In contrast, spatial-relations concepts perform the critical function of making sense out of space. Nearness and farness are, however, extrasensory. As we have said, a tree may be seen as having a front and a back, but being round, this determination depends on some landmark—namely us. Truth here will change as our perspective does. Nonetheless, we all share similar embodied basic-level and spatial-relations experiences, resulting in a very wide range of shared behavioral truths within the equally wide range of linguistic variations. The constructed part of social constructionism is linguistic. This gives variety. The sensorimotor manipulative act confronts another world that might not heed our words but gives stability and is cross-cultural. Social constructionists frequently forget this.

Less behavioristic treatments of truth contain important lessons. For example, Lakoff and Johnson make a point that wreaks havoc with the correspondence theory of truth and any absolutist approach. According to them, truths must change with at least three levels of embodiment: First is the embodiment concerning the neural level.[1] The second level is phenomenological, or the perceptual level of lived experience and subjective quale. The third level concerns the relatively new appreciation for the unconscious demonstrated effectively in the early experiments by Gazzaniga (1985) on "split brain" patients. Here, we acquire a world of metaphors that guide our conscious thought. The problem for correspondence theory is that truth claims at one level contradict truth claims at other levels. For example, on the phenomenological level of lived experience grass is usually green. It is true that it looks that way to us perceptively. However, from the perspective of neuroscience, seeing color as "in" objects is the "stimulus error" and thus untrue.

The neural level clearly contradicts the phenomenal level, yet it would be hard to deny either truth. If we take Rorty's and Lakoff and Johnson's plausible position that any truth must be humanly conceptualized and understandable, the neural and phenomenal levels provide different modes of understanding in which both truths are coherent and there is no contradiction. However, this *does* mean that there is no absolute, one, objective truth. Rather than weakening truth, this should strengthen it. Absolute truth, as the postmodernists recognized, is a power play. For pragmatists it is a denial of reality as contingency and process. For persons concerned with the state of humanity, it is one of our most severe threats, since in its name believers and their dominating bodies justify their slaughter of nonbelievers. This is not a truth that we should miss.

In the final analysis, however, the level of embodiment that matters most in calling forth the emergent truths of nature and human existence are the corporeal transactions of communicating bodies engaged in collective problem-solving. New collective terminations of contingency are always possible as communicating bodies experiment with various ideas about the ways of the world. New truths can be found in the unfolding of these alternative collective terminations, revealed to us as new ways to achieve a "unity of knowledge and reality" (Shalin 1992, 260). Once again, this understanding of how collective transactions transform reality undermines all claims to absolute truth. Like the reality to which it speaks, truth is emergent that can never be nailed down once and for all.

To summarize and come to a more substantive conclusion, we can repeat that truth must be human and, in part, discursive. Truth does not lie in the world independent of human discussion. Truth statements cannot be absolute. They must be conceived within what we know about our means of knowing that is within a relational, transactional framework. This perspective avoids privileging either the subjective or the objective. It must also take account of our senses as transducers and the serious limitation this places on what we can know about the world beyond us. Other animals are able to sense things that we cannot, and within the human species there are examples of traumatized patients hearing shapes and smelling colors. We are hardly equipped to know what is "out there" (Christian 1977). This is one reason why final truth will always allude us. What is true for truth obtains for proof. Methodologically, most of us know the technical reasons why proof is never final. Since proof means final, there is no proof. It can be totally convincing, but this is not proof. Unfortunately, proof rolls off the tongue much easier than "a preponderance of evidence." Like truth, it is never finished and is frequently abused. However, truth and proof can, indeed, be ideals that we move toward. Following Lakoff and Johnson as well as the pragmatists, the most useful conception of truth is that most firmly lodged in our interpretations from effective action in an objective world that sets its own terms on what we can and cannot do, both as individuals and as collectivities.

This is congruent with the perspective on sociological truth presented in chapter 7. In arguing for a transactional approach to the study of social problems, we have been guided by the pragmatist principle that the validity of our concepts must be judged in terms of the efficacy of the problem-solving actions they direct. By seeking solutions to social problems through the development of life-world–inspired countersystems, which serve practical and analytical tasks simultaneously, it is possible to gauge the effectiveness of our reconstruction efforts and, in turn, the validity of the ideas that guide these efforts. This can never be a neat-and-tidy process, nor will be the establishment of truth. Problems will inevitably arise in reaching agreement about whether solutions to problems are actually effective or, if they are deemed effective, determining *why* they are effective. However, as difficult as these problems are, struggling with them is justified by what is gained through the reality-testing process. Using this process as the basis for judging the validity of our ideas puts us on much firmer ground than any of the abstract validity standards employed by academic sociologists today. The truth-value of sociological knowledge that is put to work in the real world can be assessed much more objectively than anything we can determine about this knowledge based merely on tests of significance or the amount of explained variance.

The relevance of our transactional, countersystem perspective for truth can also be found in its potential for critical analysis. Habermas attempts to differentiate between distorted communications and undistorted ones—undistorted in this case meaning communications that conform to the principles of reason. But the establishment of undistorted communication carries within it the unacceptable assumption of a Kantian, purely logical establishment of truth free from emotional/cultural bias. There is no question here that clear and willful distortion abounds among many forms of communication. But if all communication is emotionally and culturally shaped, we cannot constructively conclude that *all* are lies and distortion. Room must be left for that large part of human thought that is *selectively guided* by values and their predispositions. Such generic selectivity is hardly a lie or epistemic deficiency. It is important to establish a domain of truth that transcends the contrast between distorted and rational communication.

Moreover, if an ironclad consensus is impossible when emotion sets the agenda for our thought, we have to accept this loss. We live, after all, in a pluralistic society that is antithetical to any static form of eternal agreement and self-actual truth. We must accept a dynamic world that knows no such peace. Habermas's ideal speech community is rational in the idealistic sense of providing truths leading to emancipation. Once again, the danger is that we assume emancipation as a final state, a done deal with fixed, abstract truths to match.

Habermas notwithstanding, the issue is not to distinguish between distorted communications by establishing undistorted truth in the name of emancipation. Rather, we must identify ways in which taken-for-granted assumptions preclude the elaboration of *possible* truths. Our version of truth places it outside of the confines of pure reason, as it must if emotion sets the agenda for thought in the first place. As we have seen, the analytical power of countersystem analysis lies in its potential to expose the taken-for-granted presuppositions, values, and emotions underlying collectively constructed perceptions. These taken-for-granted elements often function as the most daunting impediments to social reconstruction, because they are assigned by the dualistic consciousness to an objective self-actual reality. Hence, domain assumptions establish incontrovertible "facts" that support some terminations but not others (Feyerabend 1978). Values are so deeply embodied that they seem to belong to an objective order that transcends any particular individual or group. "Social norms . . . find their way into mind's noncognitive recesses and become suffused with emotions, transformed into habits, translated into routine judgments" (Shalin 1992, 271). Communicative rationality cannot penetrate this taken-for-granted dimension of human sentiment and perception. Consequently, it cannot reveal the substrate of embodied social constraints that works against some reconstruction possibilities even after all distorted communications have been removed from the field of discourse.

Through the logic of counterinduction, the countersystem method offers a way to deconstruct the existing social order, identifying the forces that maintain present structures and extinguish other possible arrangements. It is a method for exploring emergent, pragmatic truths, in the sense of new possibilities for unifying knowledge and reality, while also infusing this process with a deep and critical understanding of present social institutions. In this sense, our transactional approach subscribes to a diachronic form of truth, in which our knowledge of the present takes account of its relations to the past and its unfolding into a future that human actors help to create in a self-conscious and purposive way. This does not rid truth of its substantial character, since not all imagined futures are possible. Again, the truth of any vision of a possible future can only be found in its effectiveness in terminating objective uncertainty.

REALITY IN DIFFERENT CLOTHING

Reality as presented here is that which resists our push—a favorite "sound bite" of pragmatism. Of course, this applies to the tangible world where every object takes up its own particular space and time. We have applied this metaphor to impartial, socially constructed systems like laws, grammars, geometric systems, and taboos. These intangibles do not take up space because they are extrasensory, but they resist our "push" in the sense that they are either enforced by those so empowered, or in the more benign sense that we cannot be effective socially if we ignore them.

The more positive notion of enablement implicit in such rules is sometimes overlooked. Because these intangible social realities also answer back to our manipulations (and to our violations when laws are enforced), they have an objectivity of their own sort that can act on us regardless of our own will. As is often observed, the fact that something is socially constructed does not mean it has no reality. The ego-alien reality of emotion is a clear case in point. This is a reality that stems from the phenomenological perspective of lived experience. Like transactional truth, reality has its own solid place within this level. This is the world that is real to us. If our transducers are such that we actually experience beer as the best-tasting thing in the world, beer is the best-tasting thing to us. There is no reason to deny that this is true. Our understandings, as Lakoff and Johnson would argue, fit in to this level. To deprive our personal experience of reality-to-us is an arbitrary privileging of the tyranny of abstraction. These sensory and social constructions define our social environment as surely as the impartiality of the tangible world defines our "natural environment."

As we have consistently argued, the tangible environment has its own reality over and beyond our constant definitions and interpretations. It does not answer to our words, but only to our nonverbal motor actions as guided as they may be by words and thoughts. Our position, consistent with Layoff and Johnson's, is that we even understand our symbolic worlds in large part through our experiences with manipulative efforts in the physical world. The suggestion that upper-level concepts derive from the neurological circuitry of sensory motor activity is intriguing from a social psychological point of view that avoids extreme relativism.

Next, we will turn to the implications of embodiment and our rootedness in the realities of manipulative motor actions for a more accurate social psychology that understands the importance of such a real world and real-world application.

THE NONVERBAL AND SOCIAL PSYCHOLOGICAL THEORY

In concluding this volume it is also important to address the implications of our argument for social psychological theory. We have argued that social interaction and transactional thought proceed much too quickly for self-conscious deliberations. We join Katz (1999) in arguing that linguistic symbols play only a part in the construction of human meaning, much of which is corporeal and independent of conscious reflection. To elaborate our discussion in chapter 2 about Sugar Ray Robinson, any class athlete moves before he knows it and, indeed, as films show, moves *without* knowing it. This is not to deny the importance of a *kind* of thought. A professor on a "real roll" in class may be thinking of, or better concentrating on, what she wants to say and the qualifications necessary, but the words that come out of her mouth are there before she knows it. This is observed easily enough in ordinary conversation. As Sudnow (1979) argues, the hands of the piano player have a corporal language of their own that by necessity is faster than any reflective cognition. Tears well up in our eyes and throats grow thick in a patently ego-alien way quite typically without our reflective understanding. Certainly, the corporeality of our emotions has within it a meaning structure of its own. For example, Averill and Nunley (1992) discuss the "constitutive" rules of emotion wherein it makes sense to be awed by the relative expanse of the stars or the ocean, but taking pride in them makes such little sense that no one does so. Pride implies that the object is yours in some way, however vague. Much of our argument has been that self-conscious, verbalized cognition is insufficient to explain human meaning and lived experience. In short, regardless of how we must always interpret our worlds, words alone with no transactional subjects beyond them cannot be the end-all of our semiotic enterprise.

Katz (1999) also insists that social psychology must get out of the box of deliberate, self-conscious thinking and into nonverbal processes. His approach has not been as epistemological as ours, but is certainly congruent with the preceding pages. He has demonstrated in depth that our body has a nonverbal, corporeal semiotic of its own, exemplified in emotional gesture. Blumer and Goffman are criticized for giving preemptory focus on deliberate self-consciousness and leading us away from attention to the preobjective. Katz (1999, 358) is talking explicitly about the nonverbal semiotics of the body and its importance to self-theory. He makes clear, however, that lived emotions are indeed reflective. But they borrow from the "corporeally enlivened, sensually captured aspects of the nonreflective practices that we have been engaging." To Katz, Blumer's emphasis on the process of constructing lines of behavior on the basis of one's anticipated response of others places deliberate conscious thought center-stage when most of the time we are too engaged for such pondering.

It is possible to read Goffman in the same light. While he explicitly concentrated on the "face" we present to others, this was done only on methodological grounds. But the implication is that anything else involving selfhood is not important enough for his attention, since he offered nothing on the person in later works to balance the model. Since Goffman was so very influential, his work may hold another clue to our tendency to gloss the reality of the person. At the end of his influential *Presentation of Self in Everyday Life*, Goffman slips out of his self-imposed limits and writes his only lines about the person behind the mask. No doubt it was late at night and his heart was on his sleeve. There he writes of "a solitary player with a harried concern for his production." The player is "wearing an unsocialized look of one engaged in a difficult, treacherous task" (1959, 236–37). With this in mind—that Goffman himself may have epitomize the alienated Western man and that his words rang intuitively true to a large number of readers—let us remember his classic portrayal of Preedy at the beach. Note that Preedy's perception is not on the actual beach or the ocean that he gazed across in such a knowing manner. His perception is exclusively on himself, or more precisely, the images that he imagines others have of him. Such a view is deficient on two grounds: First, in spite of the partial but important truth that is in this model, it exclusively emphasizes *deliberate* self-consciousness and manipulation. Even in his notion of impressions given off as corporeal and spontaneous, they become tools of deliberate deception. The preobjective corporeality of lived experience is ignored in exclusive attention to the "looking-glass self" that even Cooley (1964) rejected as insufficient for self-theory (Franks and Gecas 1992, 52).

There is another implication of Goffman's imagery of the person: Preedy is more a reflection of our whole culture than he is an example of generic self-processes. This reflection would be consistent with those writers concerned with our rampant subjectivization and "culture of narcissism." The metaphors so deficient in our long-embraced individualistic epistemology have become descriptors of our inner lives. We actually experience ourselves as being self-contained. Goffman's portrayal of the duplicitous self is tied to the context of our peculiar super-individualized culture and social conditions. These conditions, as many argue, are so subjectivized that, as Coles (1980, 137) observes, "for psychology the self is the only and main form of reality."

THE LOSS OF THE OBJECTIVE CHARACTER OF THE WORLD IN A SUBJECTIVIZED AGE

The stress on objectivity and a transactional view of the real world presented in this book goes against the strong cultural tide of what writers have referred to as the "subjectivization" of our times. Included in the subjective turn of our culture is our strong emphasis on analysis that takes its abstract positions in a mind-formed world far removed from the earthy immediacy of lived experience. The analytic mentality, so reflexive and concentrated on one's own productions, fosters this turn to the subjective according to the leading cultural geographer Yi-Fu Tuan (1982). There is an important parallel between Tuan's and Sennett's (1977) tracing of the slow historical switch from valuing the public realm to an exclusive value on the private. Here, the important component of the self is popularly viewed as "authentic inner feelings." The intentional or relational quality of emotion is lost in this self-actional portrayal. Tuan argues that the resulting self-absorption leads to the loss of the felt objective character of the world. Ironically, we are preoccupied with ourselves while intellectually so many deny self's existence. Perhaps textualism, which is so strongly analytic and subjective, was encouraged by this cultural turn. The same would apply to the anxious self-absorption of Goffman's Preedy at the beach where the problems of our age are reflected in our theories.

Indeed, we may be moving from a model of persons as "doers" to a model of persons as "feelers" ignoring transactional features altogether (Franks and Heffernan 1998). According to Tuan, we become prisoners of our own ineluctable subjectivity. Sennett starts his *The Fall of Public Man* with this observation about our inward turn from the world:

> The most common form in which narcissism makes itself known to the person is by a process of inversion: If only I could feel more, or if only I could really feel, then I could relate to others or have real relations with them. But in each moment of encounter I never seem to feel enough. The obvious content of this inversion is a self-accusation, but buried beneath it is a feeling that the world is failing me. (1977, 9)

Sennett then continues with the forces reinforcing the fruitless search for an identity composed of materials from within. Again, he is just one of the writers concerned with the pathology of this misreading of emotion and the lack of a fully transactional lifestyle where the objective world is felt to be as real as the self. Our self-absorption becomes our personal ontology and sickness. We hope this book will help balance this turn away from the objective quality of the world outside of our own doings.

NOTE

1. This involves the physical actions of neurons, yet much of what we take as true on this level is stated in metaphoric terms like circuitry, which abstracts away from ion channels and supporting glial cells.

References

Abramson, Jeffrey B., F. Christopher Artherton, and Gary R. Orren. 1988. *The Electronic Commonwealth: The Impact of New Media Technologies on Democratic Politics*. New York: Basic Books.

Alexander, Thomas M. 1987. *John Dewey's Theory of Art, Experience, and Nature: The Horizons of Feeling*. Albany: State University of New York Press.

Anderson, Walter T. 1995. *The Truth about the Truth: Deconfusing and Reconstructing the Postmodern World*. New York: Putnam.

Antonio, Robert J. "Postmodern Storytelling Versus Pragmatic Truth-seeking: The Discursive Bases of Social Theory." *Sociological Theory* 9, no. 2 (1991): 154–63.

Antonio, Robert, and Douglas Kellner. "Communication, Modernity, and Democracy in Habermas and Dewey." *Symbolic Interaction* 15, no. 3 (1992): 277–97.

Arendt, Hannah. 1958. *The Human Condition*. Chicago: University of Chicago Press.

Austin, J. L. 1975. *How to Do Things with Words*. Cambridge, MA: Harvard University Press.

Averill, James, and Elma Nunley. 1992. *Voyages of the Heart*. New York: Free Press.

Bandura, Albert. 1986. *Social Foundations of Thought and Action: A Social Cognitive Theory*. Englewood Cliffs, NJ: Prentice-Hall.

Baudrillard, Jean. 1983. "The Ecstasy of Communication," in *The Anti-Aesthetic: Essays on Postmodern Culture*, ed. Hal Foster. Port Townsend, WA: Bay Press, 126–34.

———. 1988. *America.* London: Verso.

Baumeister, R. 1986. *Identity: Cultural Change and the Struggle for Self.* New York: Oxford University Press.

Becker, Ernest. 1964. *The Revolution in Psychiatry: The New Understanding of Man.* New York: Free Press.

Bennett, W. Lance. 1988. *News: The Politics of Illusion.* White Plains, NY: Longman.

Berger, Peter, and Thomas Luckmann. 1967. *The Social Construction of Reality: A Treatise in the Sociology of Knowledge.* New York: Anchor Books.

Berlin, B., and P. Kay. 1969. *Basic Color Terms: Their Universality and Evolution.* Berkeley: University of California Press.

Best, Joel. 1989. "Afterword: Extending the Constructionist Perspective. A Conclusion and an Introduction," in *Images of Issues: Typifying Contemporary Social Problems,* ed. Joel Best. New York: Aldine de Gruyter, 243–54.

Best, Steven, and Douglas Kellner. 1991. *Postmodern Theory: Critical Interrogations.* New York: Guilford Press.

Blake, J. A. "Self and Society in Mead and Marx." *Cornell Journal of Social Relations* 11, no. 2 (1976): 129–38.

Blumer, Herbert. "Social Problems as Collective Behavior." *Social Problems* 18 (1971): 298–306.

Borgada, Edgar F., and Karen S. Cook., eds. 1988. *The Future of Sociology.* Beverly Hills, CA: Sage.

Bourdieu, Pierre. 1984. *Distinction: A Social Critique of the Judgement of Taste.* Cambridge, MA: Harvard University Press.

Braverman, Harry. 1974. *Labor and Monopoly Capital: The Degradation of Work in the Twentieth Century.* New York: Monthly Review Press.

Bronowski, J. 1958. *The Common Sense of Science.* New York: Vintage Books.

Brothers, Leslie. 1997. *Friday's Footprint.* New York: Oxford University Press, 1997.

Burke, Kenneth. 1968. *Language as Symbolic Action: Essays on Life, Literature, and Method.* Berkeley: University of California Press, 1968.

Butler, Judith. 1997. *Executive Speech: A Politics of the Performative.* New York: Rouledge.

Calhoun, Cheshire. "Subjectivity and Emotions." *Philosophical Forum* 20, no. 3 (1989): 195–210.

Callinicos, Alex. "Postmodernism, Post-Structuralism, Post-Marxism?" *Theory, Culture, and Society* 2, no. 3 (1985): 85–102.

———. 1990. *Against Postmodernism.* New York: St. Martin's Press.

Cancian, Francesca M., and Cathleen Armstead. 1992. "Participatory Research," in *Encyclopedia of Sociology,* ed. Edgar Borgatta and Marie Borgatta. New York: Macmillan.

Cassirer, Ernst. 1944. *An Essay on Man.* New Haven, CT: Yale University Press.

———. 1953. *Substance and Function and Einstein's Theory of Relativity.* Chicago: Dover Publications.

Christian, James. 1977. *Philosophy*, 2d ed. New York: Holt, Rinehart and Winston.
Clinard, Marshall B. 1974. *The Sociology of Deviant Behavior.* New York: Holt, Rinehart and Winston.
Coles, Robert. "Civility and Psychology." *Daedalus* 109, no. 3 (1980): 133–41.
Cooley, Charles H. 1964. *Human Nature and the Social Order.* New York: Schocken Books.
Cornelius, Randolph R. 1996. *The Science of Emotion: Research and Tradition in the Psychology of Emotion.* Englewood Cliffs, NJ: Prentice-Hall.
Coulter, Jeff. 1979. *The Social Construction of Mind.* Totowa, NJ: Rowman & Littlefield.
Crawford, Robert. 1984. "A Cultural Account of "Health": Control, Release, and the Social Body," in *Issues in the Political Economy of Health Care*, ed. John B. McKinlay. New York: Tavistock.
Crozier, Michel, Samuel Huntington, and Joji Watanuki. 1975. *The Crisis of Democracy.* New York: NYU Press.
Damasio, Antonio. 1994. *Descartes' Error: Emotion, Reason, and the Human Brain.* New York: Avon Books.
———. 1999. *The Feeling of What Happens: Body and Emotion in the Making of Consciousness.* New York: Harcourt, Brace.
Damrosch, David. 1995. *We Scholars: Changing the Culture of the University.* Cambridge, MA: Harvard University Press.
Delgado, Louis. "CBOs and the Public Policy Initiative: Funding a Collaborative Model." *National Civic Review* 78, no. 3 (1989): 197–201.
Dennett, Daniel. 1996. *Kinds of Minds: Toward an Understanding of Consciousness.* New York: Basic Books.
Denzin, Norman. 1992. *Symbolic Interactionism and Cultural Studies: The Politics of Interpretation.* Cambridge: Blackwell.
Derrida, Jacques. 1970. "Structure, Sign, and Play in the Discourse of the Human Sciences," in *The Language of Criticism and the Sciences of Man.* Baltimore: Johns Hopkins University Press, 249.
De Sousa, R. 1987. *The Rationality of Emotions.* Boston: MIT Press.
Deutscher, Irwin, Fred P. Pestello, and Francis H. Pestello. 1993. *Sentiments and Acts.* New York: Aldine de Gruyter.
Dewey, John. "The Theory of Emotion." *Psychological Review* no. 1 (November 1894): 553–69.
———. "The Theory of Emotion." *Psychological Review* no. 2 (January 1895): 13–32.
———. 1910. *How We Think.* New York: Heath.
———. 1920. *Reconstruction in Philosophy.* New York: Henry Holt.
———. [1925] 1958. *Experience and Nature.* New York: Dover Publications.
———. [1934] 1958. *Art as Experience.* New York: Capricorn Books.
———. 1946. *The Problems of Men.* New York: Philosophical Library.
Dewey, John, and Authur F. Bentley. 1949. *Knowing and the Known.* Boston: Beacon Press.

Duncan, Hugh Dalziel. 1968. *Symbols in Society.* New York: Oxford University Press.

Dynes, Russell R. 1964. *Social Problems: Dissensus and Deviation in Industrial Society.* New York: Oxford University Press.

Edwards, Richard. 1979. *Contested Terrain: The Transformation of the Workplace in the Twentieth Century.* New York: Basic Books.

Elias, N. 1978. *The Civilizing Process,* vol. 1: *The History of Manners.* New York: Pantheon.

Elshtain, Jean B. 1995. *Democracy on Trial.* New York: Basic Books.

Emirbayer, Mustafa. "Manifesto for a Relational Sociology." *American Journal of Sociology* 103, no. 2 (September 1997): 281–317.

Emirbayer, Mustafa, and Ann Mische. "What Is Agency?" *American Journal of Sociology* 103, no. 4 (January 1998): 962–1023.

Entman, Robert M. 1989. *Democracy Without Citizens: Media and the Decay of American Politics.* New York: Oxford University Press.

Evans, Robert G. 1994. "Introduction," in *Why Are Some People Healthy and Others Not? The Determinants of Health of Populations,* ed. Robert G. Evans, Morris L. Barer, and Theodore R. Marmor. New York: Aldine de Gruyter, 3–26.

Evans, Robert G., Morris L. Barer, and Theodore R. Marmor, eds. 1994. *Why Are Some People Healthy and Others Not? The Determinants of Health of Populations.* New York: Aldine de Gruyter.

Farberman, Harvey A. "Symbolic Interaction and Postmodernism: Close Encounter of a Dubious Kind." *Symbolic Interaction* 14, no. 4 (1991): 471–88.

Featherstone, Mike. 1995. "The Body in Consumer Culture," in *The Body: Social Process and Cultural Theory,* ed. Mike Featherstone, Mike Hepworth, and Bryan S. Turner. London: Sage Publications, 170–96.

Featherstone, Mike, Mike Hepworth, and Bryan S. Turner, eds. 1995. *The Body: Social Process and Cultural Theory.* London: Sage Publications.

Feyerabend, Paul. 1978. *Against Method: Outline of an Anarchistic Theory of Knowledge.* London: Verso.

Fine, Gary Allan, and Sherryl Kleinman. "Interpreting the Classic: Can There Be a 'True' Meaning of Mead?" *Symbolic Interaction* 9 (1986): 129–46.

Forte, James A. 2001. *Theories of Practice: Symbolic Interactionist Translations.* Lanham, MD: University Press of America.

Foucault, Michel. 1978. *The History of Sexuality,* vol. 1. New York: Pantheon.

———. 1979. *Discipline and Punish: The Birth of the Prison.* New York: Vintage Books.

———. 1980. *Power and Knowledge: Selected Interviews and Other Writings, 1972–1977,* ed. Colin Gordon. New York: Pantheon.

Fowles, J. 1982. *Television Viewers versus Media Snobs.* New York: Stein and Day.

Fox, Nicholas J. 1994. *Postmodernism, Sociology, and Health.* Toronto: University of Toronto Press.

Frank, Arthur W. 1995. "For a Sociology of the Body: An Analytical Review," in *The Body: Social Process and Cultural Theory*, ed. Mike Featherstone, Mike Hepworth, and Bryan S. Turner. London: Sage Publications, 36–102.

Franks, David D. 1985. "Role-Taking, Social Power and Imperceptiveness," in *Studies in Symbolic Interaction*, ed. Norman Denzin. Greenwich, CT: JAI Press, 229–59.

———. "Alternatives to Collins's Use of Emotion in the Theory of Ritualistic Chains." *Symbolic Interaction* 12 (1989): 97–101.

———. "Individualism and Mead's Self Process." *Newsletter of the Society for the Study of Symbolic Interaction* 17, no. 3 (1990): 13–14.

———. "Mead and Dewey's Theory of Emotion." *Journal of Mental Imagery* 15 (1991): 119–38.

———. 1999. "Some Convergences and Divergences between Neuroscience and Symbolic Interaction," in *Mind, Brain, and Society: Toward a Neurosociology of Emotion*, ed. David D. Franks and Thomas S. Smith. Stamford, CT: JAI Press, 157–82.

———. 2001. "The Sociology of Emotions," in *International Encyclopedia of the Social and Behavioral Sciences*, ed. Neil J. Smelser and Paul Baltes. New York: Pergamon.

Franks, David D., and Viktor Gecas, eds. 1992. *Social Perspectives on Emotion: A Research Annual*. Greenwich, CT: JAI Press.

Franks, David D., and Susan Heffernan. 1998. "The Pursuit of Happiness: Constructions from a Social Psychology of Emotions," in *Emotions and Pathology*, ed. William F. Flack, Jr. and James Laird. New York: Oxford University Press, 145–57.

Franks, David D., and Carol Keller. "Thoughts on the Postmodern Rejection of Truth." *Michigan Sociology Review* 10 (1997): 32–50.

Franks, David D., and Francis Seeberger. "On the Person Beyond the Word: Mead's Theory of Universals and a Shift of Focus in Symbolic Interaction." *Symbolic Interaction* 3 (Spring) 1980: 41–58.

Freeman, Howard, Russell Dynes, Peter Rossi, and William F. Whyte. 1983. *Applied Sociology*. San Francisco: Jossey-Bass.

Freeman, Howard, and Peter Rossi. "Furthering the Applied Side of Sociology." *American Sociological Review* 49 (1984): 571–80.

Garfinkel, Harold. 1967. *Studies in Ethnomethodology*. Englewood Cliffs, NJ: Prentice-Hall.

Gaventa, John. "Participatory Research in North America." *Convergence* 21 (1988): 19–29.

Gazzaniga, Michael S. 1985. *The Social Brain: Discovering the Networks of the Mind*. New York: Basic Books.

———. 1998. *The Mind's Past*. Berkeley: University of California Press.

Geertz, Clifford. 1979. "From the Natives' Point of View: On the Nature of Anthropological Understanding," in *Interpretive Social Science*, ed. P. Rabinow and W. M. Sullivan. Berkeley: University of California Press, 225–41.

Gergen, Kenneth J. 1991. *The Saturated Self: Dilemmas of Identity in Contemporary Life.* New York: Basic Books.

Gerth, Hans H., and C. Wright Mills, eds. 1958. *From Max Weber: Essays in Sociology.* New York: Oxford University Press.

Giddens, Anthony. 1984. *The Constitution of Society: Outline of the Theory of Structuration.* Berkeley: University of California Press.

Gitlin, Todd. 1980. *The Whole World Is Watching: The Mass Media in the Making and Unmaking of the New Left.* Berkeley: University of California Press.

Glynn, E. 1956. "Television and the American Character: A Psychiatrist Looks at Television," in *Television's Impact on American Culture*, ed. W. Elliot. East Lansing: Michigan State University Press, 177–82.

Goff, Tom W. 1980. *Marx and Mead: Contributions to a Sociology of Knowledge.* London: Routledge and Kegan Paul.

Goffman, Erving. 1959. *Presentation of Self in Everyday Life.* Garden City, NY: Anchor.

Gouldner, Alvin W. 1970. *The Coming Crisis of Western Sociology.* New York: Basic Books.

Gramsci, A. 1971. *Selections from the Prison Notebooks.* London: Lawrence and Wishart.

Greenwald, Anthony G. "The Totalitarian Ego: Fabrication and Revision of Personal History." *American Psychologist* 35, no. 7 (1980): 608–18.

Gusfield, Joseph R. "Theories and Hobgoblins." *SSSP Newsletter* 17 (Fall 1985): 16–18.

———, ed. 1998. *Kenneth Burke: On Symbols and Society.* Chicago: University of Chicago Press.

Habermas, Jürgen. [1962] 1989. *The Structural Transformation of the Public Sphere: An Inquiry into a Category of Bourgeois Society.* Cambridge, MA: MIT Press.

———. 1970. *Toward a Rational Society.* Boston: Beacon Press.

———. 1971. *Knowledge and the Human Interest.* Boston: Beacon Press.

———. 1973. *Theory and Practice.* Boston: Beacon Press.

———. 1984. *The Theory of Communicative Action*, vol. 1: *Reason and the Realization of Society.* Boston: Beacon Press.

———. 1987. *The Theory of Communicative Action*, vol. 2: *Life-World and System: A Critique of Functionalist Reason.* Boston: Beacon Press.

Halton, Eugene. "Habermas and Rorty: Between Scylla and Charybdis." *Symbolic Interaction* 15 (1992): 333–58.

———. 1995. *Bereft of Reason.* Chicago: University of Chicago Press.

Harré, Rom, ed. 1986. *The Social Construction of Emotion.* New York: Basil Blackwell.

Harris, Marvin. 1974. *Cows, Pigs, Wars, and Witches.* New York: Vintage Books.

———. 1977. *Cannibals and Kings: The Origins of Cultures.* New York: Vintage Books.

Harth, Erich. 1993. *The Creative Loop: How the Brain Makes a Mind.* Reading, MA: Addison-Wesley.

Hazelrigg, Lawrence E. "Were It Not for Words." *Social Problems* 32 (1985): 234–37.

———. "Is There a Choice between 'Constructionism' and 'Objectivism'?" *Social Problems* 33 (1986): S1–S13.

Hebdige, Dick. 1979. *Subculture: The Meaning of Style.* London: Methuen.

Herman, Edward, and Noam Chomsky. 1988. *Manufacturing Consent: The Political Economy of Mass Media.* New York: Pantheon.

Hilgartner, Stephen, and Charles L. Bosk. "The Rise and Fall of Social Problems: A Public Arenas Model." *American Journal of Sociology* 94, no.1 (1988): 53–78.

Hinkle, Gisela. "Habermas, Mead, and Rationality." *Symbolic Interaction* 15, no. 3 (Fall 1992): 315–31.

Hochschild, Arlie. 1983. *The Managed Heart: Commercialization of Human Feeling.* Berkeley: University of California Press.

Horkheimer, M., and Adorno, T. W. 1972. "The Culture Industry: Enlightenment as Mass Deception," in *The Dialectics of Enlightenment,* ed. M. Horkheimer and T. W. Adorno. New York: Seebury Press, 120–67.

Horton, Paul B., and Gerald R. Leslie. 1974. *The Sociology of Social Problems.* Englewood Cliffs, NJ: Prentice-Hall.

Huntington, Samuel. 1975. "The Democratic Distemper," in *The Crisis of Democracy,* ed. Michel Crozier, Samuel Huntington, and Joji Watanuki. New York: NYU Press, 102–13.

Jacoby, Russell. "Narcissim and the Crisis of Capitalism." *Telos* 44 (1980): 58–65.

———. 1987. *The Last Intellectuals: American Culture in the Age of Academe.* New York: Basic Books.

James, William. [1925] 1953. *The Philosophy of William James.* New York: Random House.

Joas, Hans. 1985. *G. H. Mead: A Contemporary Reexamination of His Thought,* trans. Raymond Meyer. Cambridge, MA: MIT Press.

———. "An Underestimated Alternative: America and the Limits of 'Critical Theory.'" *Symbolic Interaction* 15, no. 3 (Fall 1992): 261–75.

———. 1993. *Pragmatism and Social Theory.* Chicago: University of Chicago Press.

———. 1997. *The Creativity of Action,* trans. Jeremy Gaines and Paul Keast. Chicago: University of Chicago Press.

Karasek, Robert, and Tores Theorell. 1990. *Healthy Work: Stress, Productivity, and the Reconstruction of Working Life.* New York: Basic Books.

Katz, Jack. 1988. *The Seductions of Crime: Moral and Sensual Attractions of Doing Evil.* New York: Basic Books.

———. 1999. *How Emotions Work.* Chicago: University of Chicago Press.

Klapp, O. E. 1986. *Overload and Boredom: Essays on the Quality of Life in the Information Age.* Westport, CT: Greenwood Press.

Klausner, Samuel Z., and Victor M. Lidz. 1986. "Nationalization and the Social Sciences," in *The Nationalization of the Social Sciences*, ed. Samuel Z. Klausner and Victor M. Litz. Philadelphia: University of Pennsylvania Press, 267–86.

Kleinman, Arthur. 1988. *The Illness Narratives: Suffering, Healing, and the Human Condition*. New York: Basic Books.

Laing, R. D. 1960. *The Divided Self: A Study of Sanity and Madness*. Chicago: University of Chicago Press.

Lakoff, George, and Mark Johnson. 1999. *Philosophy in the Flesh: The Embodied Mind and its Challenge to Western Society*. New York: Basic Books.

Lasch, Christopher. 1995. *The Revolt of the Elites and the Betrayal of Democracy*. New York: W. W. Norton.

LeDoux, Joseph. 1996. *The Emotional Brain: The Mysterious Underpinnings of Emotional Life*. New York: Simon & Schuster.

Lemert, Charles. 1995. *Sociology after the Crisis*. Boulder, CO: Westview Press.

Lewis, J. David. "The Classic American Pragmatists as Forerunners to Symbolic Interaction." *Sociological Quarterly* 17 (Summer 1976): 347–59.

———. "A Social Behaviorist Interpretation of the Meadian 'I.'" *American Journal of Sociology* 85, no. 2 (1979): 261–87.

Lindesmith, Alfred R., Anslem Strauss, and Norman K. Denzin. 1991. *Social Psychology*. Englewood Cliffs, NJ: Prentice-Hall.

Lorenz, Konrad. 1977. *Behind the Mirror*. New York: Harcourt Brace Jovanovich.

Lyng, Stephen. "Holism and Reductionism within Applied Behavioral Science." *Journal of Applied Behavioral Science* 24, no. 1 (1988): 101–17.

———. 1990a. *Holistic Health and Biomedical Medicine: A Countersystem Analysis*. Albany: State University of New York Press.

———. "Edgework: A Social Psychological Analysis of Voluntary Risk Taking." *American Journal of Sociology* 95, no. 4 (January 1990b): 851–86.

———. "Social Problems and Civic Discourse." *Humanity and Society* 21, no. 2 (May 1997): 162–81.

———. "Gideon Sjoberg and the Countersystem Method." *Symbolic Interaction* 25 (2002, in press).

Lyng, Stephen, and Mitchell L. Bracey, Jr. 1995. "Squaring the One Percent: Biker Style and the Selling of Cultural Resistance," in *Cultural Criminology*, ed. Jeff Ferrell and Clinton R. Sanders. Boston: Northeastern University Press, 235–76.

Lyotard, Jean-François. 1971. *Discourse, Figure*. Paris: Klincksiec.

———. "For a Pseudo-Theory." *Yale French Studies* 52 (1975): 115–27.

Maguire, Patricia. 1987. *Doing Participatory Research: A Feminist Approach*. Amherst: Center for International Education, School of Education, University of Massachusetts.

Maines, David R. 1995. "Some Comments on Postmodernism: The So-Called New Interpretive Turn." Paper presented at the annual meeting of the Midwest Sociological Society, Chicago.

Manis, Jerome, and Benard N. Meltzer, eds. 1978. *Symbolic Interaction: A Reader in Social Psychology*. Boston: Allyn and Bacon.

Marcuse, Herbert. 1964. *One-Dimensional Man.* Boston: Beacon Press.

———. 1978. *The Aesthetic Dimension: Toward a Critique of Marxist Aesthetics.* Boston: Beacon Press.

Marmot, M. G. 1986. "Social Inequalities in Mortality: The Social Environment," in *Class and Health: Research and Longitudinal Data*, ed. R. G. Wilkinson. London: Tavistock, 21–33.

Marmot, M. G., M. Kogevinas, and M. A. Elston. "Social/Economic Status and Disease." *Annual Review of Public Health* 8 (1987): 111–35.

Marx, Karl. 1964a. *Capital: A Critical Analysis of Capitalist Production*, vol. 1. Moscow: Foreign Languages Publishing House.

———. 1964b. *Early Writings*, ed. T. B. Bottomore. Toronto: McGraw-Hill.

Mauss, Armand L. 1975. *Social Problems as Social Movements.* New York: Lippincott.

McCarthy, Doyle. 1979. "Toward a Sociology of the Physical World: George Herbert Mead on Physical Objects." A revision of a paper presented at the American Sociological Association Meetings. Fordham University.

———. 1996. *Knowledge as Culture: The New Sociology of Knowledge.* New York: Routledge.

McCarthy, John D., and Mayer N. Zald. "Resource Mobilization and Social Movements: A Partial Theory." *American Journal of Sociology* 82, no. 6 (1977): 1213–41.

Mead, George H. "A Behavioristic Account of the Significant Symbol." *Journal of Philosophy* 19 (January–December 1922).

———. [1932] 1959. *The Philosophy of the Present.* La Salle, IL: Open Court.

———. [1934] 1967. *Mind, Self, and Society*, ed. Charles W. Morris. Chicago: University of Chicago Press.

———. [1938] 1972. *The Philosophy of the Act.* Chicago: University of Chicago Press.

Merleau-Ponty, Maurice. 1962. *Phenomenology of Perception*, trans. C. Smith. Atlantic Highlands, NJ: Humanities Press.

Mervis, C., and E. Rosch. "Categorization of Natural Objects." *Annual Review of Psychology* 32 (1981): 89–115.

Miller, David. 1982. *The Individual and the Social Self: Unpublished Work of George Herbert Mead.* Chicago: University of Chicago Press.

Miller, Gale, and James A. Holstein. 1993. *Constructionist Controversies: Issues in Social Problems Theory.* New York: Aldine de Gruyter.

Morgan, John, and J. Averill. 1992. "True Feelings, the Self, and Authenticity: A Psychosocial Perspective," in *Social Perspectives on Emotion*, vol. 1, ed. David D. Franks and Viktor Gecas. Greenwich CT: JAI Press, 95–126.

Moynihan, Daniel P. 1973. *Coping: On the Practice of Government.* New York: Vintage Books.

Murphy, Edmond A. 1976. *The Logic of Medicine.* Baltimore: Johns Hopkins University Press.

Neuman, W. Russell. 1991. *The Future of the Mass Audience.* New York: Cambridge University Press.

Northrop, F. S. C. 1948. *The Logic of the Sciences and Humanities*. New York: Macmillan.

Nyden, Philip, Anne Figert, Mark Shibley, and Darryl Burrows. 1997. *Building Community: Social Science in Action*. Thousand Oaks, CA: Pine Forge Press.

Oatley, K., and P. N. Johnson-Laird. "Towards a Cognitive Theory of Emotions." *Cognition and Emotion* 1 (1987): 29–50.

O'Brien, Mary. 1989. *Reproducing the World*. London: Westview Press.

Ollman, Bertell. 1971. *Alienation: Marx's Conception of Man in Capitalist Society*. Cambridge: Cambridge University Press.

O'Neill, John. 1973. "On Simmel's 'Sociological Apriorities,'" in *Phenomenological Sociology*, ed. John Psathas. New York: Wiley, 91–108.

Ostrow, James M. 1990. *Social Sensitivity: A Study of Habit and Experience*. Albany: State University of New York Press.

Parenti, Michael. 1992. *Inventing Reality: The Politics of the News Media*. New York: St. Martin's Press.

Parsons, Talcott. 1951. *The Social System*, chap. 10: "Social Structure and Dynamic Process: The Case of Modern Medical Practice." New York: Free Press.

———. 1964. *Social Structure and Personality*, chap. 12: "Some Theoretical Considerations Bearing on the Field of Medical Sociology." New York: Free Press.

Perinbanayagam, Robert S. 1985. *Signifying Acts*. Carbondale: Southern Illinois University Press.

———. 2000. *The Presence of Self*. Boulder, CO: Rowman & Littlefield.

Pfohl, Stephen. "Toward a Sociological Deconstruction of Social Problems." *Social Problems* 32 (1985): 228–32.

Polanyi, Michael. 1962. *Personal Knowledge: Towards a Post-Critical Philosophy*. Chicago: University of Chicago Press.

Population Reference Bureau. 2000. *World Population Data Sheet*.

Poster, Mark. 1988. "Introduction," in *Jean Baudrillard: Selected Writings*, ed. Mark Poster. Stanford, CA: Stanford University Press.

Postman, Neil. 1985. *Amusing Ourselves to Death: Public Discourse in the Age of Show Business*. New York: Viking Press.

Rafter, Nicole H. "Some Consequences of Strict Constructionism." *Social Problems* 39 (1992): 38–39.

Rime, Bernard, and Loris Schiaratura. 1991. "Gesture and Speech," in *Fundamentals of Nonverbal Behavior*, ed. Robert S. Feldman and Bernard Rime. Cambridge: Cambridge University Press, 239–81.

Rochberg-Halton, Eugene. 1986. *Meaning and Modernity: Social Theory and the Pragmatic Attitude*. Chicago: University of Chicago Press.

———. "Why Pragmatism Now?" *Sociological Theory* 5 (Fall 1987): 194–200.

Roos, Noralou P., and Leslie L. Roos. 1994. "Small Area Variations, Practice Style, and Quality of Care," in *Why Are Some People Healthy and Others Not? The Determinants of Health of Populations*, ed. Robert G. Evans, Morris L. Barer, and Theodore R. Marmor. New York: Aldine de Gruyter, 231–52.

Rorty, Richard. 1982. *Contingency, Irony, and Solidarity.* New York: Cambridge University Press.

———. 1985. "Habermas and Lyotard on Postmodernity," in *Habermas and Modernity*, ed. Richard J. Bernstein. Cambridge, MA: MIT Press, 161–75.

Rosaldo, M. Z. 1984. "Toward an Anthology of Self and Feeling," in *Culture Theory: Essays on Mind, Self, and Emotion*, ed. R. Scweder and R. A. Levine. Cambridge: Cambridge University Press, 137–57.

Sampson, Edward. "Cognitive Psychology as Ideology." *American Psychologist* 36 (1981): 730–43.

———. "The Decentralization of Identity: Toward a Revised Concept of Personal and Social Order." *American Psychologist* 40, no. 11 (November 1985): 1203–11.

Sarbin, Theodore R. 1986. "Emotion and Act: Roles and Rhetoric," in *The Social Construction of Emotion*, ed. Rom Harré. New York: Basil Blackwell.

Saussure, Ferdinand de. 1966. *Course in General Linguistics.* New York: Mc-Graw-Hill.

Scheff, Thomas J. 1979. *Catharsis in Healing, Ritual, and Drama.* Berkeley: University of California Press.

———. 1990. *Microsociology: Discourse, Emotion and Social Structure.* Chicago: University of Chicago Press.

Schneider, Joseph W. "Defining the Definitional Perspective on Social Problems." *Social Problems* 32 (1985): 232–34.

———. "Troubles with Textual Authority in Sociology." *Symbolic Interaction* 14, no. 3 (1991): 295–319.

Sciulli, David. "Habermas, Critical Theory, and the Relativistic Predicament." *Symbolic Interaction* 15, no. 3 (1992): 299–313.

Scweder, R., and A. Levine, eds. 1984. *Culture Theory: Essays on Mind, Self, and Emotion.* Cambridge: Cambridge University Press.

Seeberger, Francis F. 1992. "Blind Sight and Brute Feeling: The Divorce of Cognition from Emotion," in *Social Perspectives on Emotion: A Research Annual*, ed. David D. Franks and Viktor Gecas. Greenwich, CT: JAI Press, 47–58.

Seidman, Steven. "The End of Sociological Theory: The Postmodern Hope." *Sociological Theory* 9, no. 2 (1991): 131–46.

Sennett, Robert. 1977. *The Fall of Public Man: On the Social Psychology of Capitalism.* New York: Vintage Books.

Shalin, Dmitri N. "Critical Theory and the Pragmatist Challenge." *American Journal of Sociology* 98, no. 2 (1992): 237–79.

———. "Modernity, Postmodernity, and Pragmatist Inquiry." *Symbolic Interaction* 16, no. 4 (1993): 303–32.

Shott, S. "Emotion and Social Life: A Symbolic Interactionist Analysis." *American Journal of Sociology* 84 (1979): 1317–34.

Sjoberg, Gideon. 1997. "Reflective Methodology: The Foundations of Social Inquiry," in *A Methodology for Social Research*, by Gideon Sjoberg and Roger Nett. Prospect Heights, IL: Waveland Press, xiii–lvi.

Sjoberg, Gideon, and Leonard Cain. 1971. "Negative Values, Countersystem Models, and the Analysis of Social Systems," in *Institutions and Social Exchange: The Sociologies of Talcott Parsons and George H. Homans*, ed. H. Turk and R. Simpson. Indianapolis: Bobbs-Merrill, 212–29.

Sjoberg, Gideon, and Ted R. Vaughan. 1993. "The Bureaucratization of Sociology: Its Impact on Theory and Research," in *A Critique of Contemporary American Sociology*, ed. Ted R. Vaughan, Gideon Sjoberg, and Larry T. Reynolds. Dix Hills, NY: General Hall.

Smelser, Neil J., ed. 1988. *Handbook of Sociology*. Newbury Park, CA: Sage Publications.

Smith, M. Brewester. 1968. "Competence and Socialization," in *Socialization and Society*, ed. J. Clausen. Boston: Little, Brown, 271–320.

Spector, Malcolm, and John I. Kitsuse. "Social Problems: A Reformulation." *Social Problems* 21 (1973): 145–59.

———. [1977] 1987. *Constructing Social Problems*. Menlo Park, CA: Cummings.

Stone, Gregory, and Harvey A. Farberman. 1970. *Social Psychology Through Symbolic Interaction*. Ginn-Blaisdell.

Strauss, Anselm L. 1959. *Mirrors and Masks: The Search for Identity*. New York: Free Press of Glencoe.

Sudnow, David. 1979. *Talk's Body: A Mediation between Two Keyboards*. New York: Knopf.

Swanson, Guy E. 1989. "On the Motives and Motivation of Selves," in *The Sociology of Emotions: Original Essays and Research Papers*, ed. David D. Franks and Doyle McCarthy. Greenwich, CT: JAI Press, 3–32.

Tandon, Rajesh. "Participatory Research in the Empowerment of People." *Convergence* 14 (1981): 20–29.

———. "Social Transformation and Participatory Research." *Convergence* 21 (1988): 5–18.

Tavris, Carol. 1989. *Anger: The Misunderstood Emotion*. New York: Touchstone/ Simon & Schuster.

Theweleit, Klaus. [1977] 1987. *Male Fantasies*, vol. 1: *Women, Floods, Bodies, History*. Minneapolis: University of Minnesota Press.

Thompson, Hunter S. 1966. *Hell's Angels: The Strange and Terrible Saga of the Outlaw Motorcycle Gangs*. New York: Ballantine Books.

Tibbetts, Paul. "Mead's Theory of the Act and Perception: Some Empirical Confirmation." *Personalist* 55, no. 2 (Winter 1974): 115–38.

Troyer, Ronald J. "Some Consequences of Contexual Constructionism." *Social Problems* 39, no. 1 (1992): 35–37.

Tuan, Yi-Fu. 1982. *Segmented Worlds and Self*. Minneapolis: University of Minnesota Press.

Tuchman, Gaye. 1974. *The TV Establishment*. Englewood Cliffs, NJ: Prentice-Hall.

Turner, Bryan S. 1984. *The Body and Society*. Oxford: Blackwell.

———. 1995. "Recent Developments in the Theory of the Body," in *The Body: Social Process and Cultural Theory*, ed. Mike Featherstone, Mike Hepworth, and Bryan S. Turner. London: Sage Publications, 1–35.

Turner, Jonathan H. "The Disintegration of American Sociology." *Sociological Perspectives* 32, no. 4 (1989): 419–33.

———. 1999. "The Neurology of Emotion: Implications for Sociological Theories of Interpersonal Behavior," in *Mind, Brain, and Society: Toward a Neurosociology of Emotion*, ed. David D. Franks and Thomas S. Smith. Stamford, CT: JAI Press, 41–80.

———. 2000. *On the Origins of Human Emotions: A Sociological Inquiry into the Evolution of Human Affect*. Stanford, CA: Stanford University Press.

Turner, Ralph H. 1962. "Role Taking Process Versus Conformity," in *Human Behavior and Social Processes*, ed. A. M. Rose. Boston: Houghton-Mifflin, 20–40.

———. 1968. "The Self-Conception in Social Interaction," in *The Self in Social Interaction*, ed. Chad Gordon and Kenneth Gergen. New York: Wiley, 93–106.

Vaughan, Ted R. 1993. "The Crisis in Contemporary American Sociology: A Critique of the Discipline's Dominant Paradigm," in A *Critique of Contemporary American Sociology*, ed. Ted R. Vaughan, Gideon Sjoberg, and Larry T. Reynolds. Dix Hills, NY: General Hall, 10–53.

Veblen, Thorstein. [1934] 1992. *The Theory of the Leisure Class*. New Brunswick, NJ: Transaction Publishers.

Wallerstein, Immanuel. 1998. *Utopistics*. New York: New Press.

Weinberg, S. Kirson. 1970. *Social Problems in Modern Urban Society*. Englewood Cliffs, NJ: Prentice-Hall.

Weinstein, Jay. "A (Further) Comment on the Differences between Applied and Academic Sociology." *Contemporary Sociology* 29, no. 2 (March 2000): 344–347.

Wentworth, William, and J. Ryan. 1992. "Balancing Body, Mind, and Culture," in *Social Perspectives on Emotion*, vol. 1, ed. David D. Franks and Viktor Gecas. Greenwich, CT: JAI Press, 61–95.

Westen, Drew. 1985. *Self and Society: Narcissism, Collectivism and the Development of Morals*. Cambridge: Cambridge University Press.

Wheelwright, Philip. 1960. *The Presocratics*. Indianapolis: Bobbs-Merrill.

White, Leslie A. 1949. *The Science of Culture: A Study of Man and Civilization*. New York: Grove Press.

White, Robert W. 1963. *Ego and Reality in Psychoanalytic Theory*. New York: International Universities Press.

———. "The Experience of Efficacy in Schizophrenia." *Psychiatry* 28 (1965): 199–211.

Whitehead, Alfred North. 1958. *Essays in Science and Philosophy*. New York: Philosophical Library.

Whorf, Benjamin. 1964. "Science and Linguistics," in *Language, Thought, and Reality*, ed. John B. Carrol. Cambridge, MA: MIT Press, 207–19.

Whyte, William F. "The Uses of Social Science Research." *American Sociological Review* 51 (1986): 555–63.

———. 1991. *Social Theory for Action: How Individuals and Organizations Learn to Change*. London: Sage Publications.

Wild, John. "Contemporary Phenomenology and the Problem of Existence." *Philosophy and Phenomenological Research* 20 (1959–1960): 166–80.

Wood, Linda A. 1986. "Loneliness," in *The Social Construction of Emotion*, ed. Rom Harré. New York: Basil Blackwell, 184–208.

Woolgar, Steve, and Dorothy Pawluch. "Ontological Gerrymandering: The Anatomy of Social Problems Explanations." *Social Problems* 32, no. 3 (1985): 215–27.

Wrong, Dennis H. "The Oversocialized Conception of Man in Modern Sociology." *American Sociological Review* 26, no. 2 (April 1961): 183–93.

Zietlin, Irving M. 1973. *Rethinking Sociology*. New York: Meredith Corp.

Index

About the Authors

STEPHEN LYNG is currently an associate professor of sociology at Virginia Commonwealth University, where he has taught since 1987. He received his Ph.D. in sociology from the University of Texas at Austin in 1982. He has held positions at Union College and Florida Atlantic University and has served as director of graduate studies in sociology at Virginia Commonwealth University from 1992 to 2001. He has published research on the sociology of risk, medical sociology, work and leisure, and social movements in professional journals and edited books. He is the author of the book *Holistic Health and Biomedical Medicine: A Countersystem Analysis* (1990), and is currently completing an edited book titled *Edgework: The Sociology of Risk*. He lives with his wife and two children in Mechanicsville, Virginia.

DAVID D. FRANKS is professor emeritus of sociology at Virginia Commonwealth University. He received his Ph.D. from the University of Minnesota in 1970 and taught at the University of Denver from 1968 to 1977. He has been a member of the Society for the Study of Symbolic Interaction from its inception and was twice its vice president. In 1978, he came to Virginia Commonwealth University as chair of the Department of Sociology and Anthropology and acting coordinator of a joint Ph.D. program in social policy and social work. In 1985, he was on the steering committee for the new subsection on emotions and, among other writings in the social psychology of emotions, he edited a series titled *Social Perspectives on Emotion*. Presently, he is chair of the American Sociological Association's subsection on Emotions.